BOSTON LOOKS SEAWARD

The Story of the Port

1630-1940

BOSTON
LOOKS SEAWARD

The Story of the Port

1630-1940

Compiled by

WORKERS OF THE WRITERS' PROGRAM
OF THE WORK PROJECTS ADMINISTRATION
IN THE STATE OF MASSACHUSETTS

*With a Foreword and Epilogue
by William M. Fowler, Jr.*

NORTHEASTERN UNIVERSITY PRESS

Boston

Sponsored by the Boston Port Authority
and first published in 1941

Reprinted 1985 by Northeastern University Press
Foreword and Epilogue © 1985 by William M. Fowler, Jr.

Library of Congress Cataloging in Publication Data
Main entry under title:
Boston looks seaward.
Reprint. Originally published: Boston: B. Humphries,
1941.
Includes index.
1. Boston (Mass.)—Harbor—History. 2. Boston
(Mass.)—History. I. Writers' Program (Mass.)
HE554.B6B59 1985   387.1'09744'61   84-29600
ISBN 0-930350-71-5 (pbk: alk. paper)

Printed and bound by The Alpine Press, Stoughton, Massachusetts.
The paper is Warren's Old Style, an acid-free sheet.

Manufactured in the United States of America
90 89 88 87 86 85   5 4 3 2 1

FOREWORD

FROM ITS BIRTH in the summer of 1935 until its demise in the midst of World War II, the Federal Writers Project invited brickbats and bouquets. One of the eclectic schemes of Franklin Roosevelt's New Deal, the F.W.P. was a program of unprecedented federal largesse that funded unemployed writers to do what they did best—write. All together they produced thousands of manuscripts ranging from radio scripts and agricultural bulletins to pamphlets and books. Topics ran the gamut from the particular (a history of the Reading, Pennsylvania, volunteer fire department) to the general (an illustrated book on American wildlife). But whatever their focus, their subject was America and its people.

Among the best books were those in the American Guide Series. These were more than just American Baedekers, for they reflected not only on what America was in the 1930s but on how it got there and indeed what it might be in the generations to come. They were upbeat and optimistic—no small accomplishment for men and women writing amidst the worst economic crisis in the republic's history. And they were chock-full of the curiosities of local lore.

Boston Looks Seaward is a member of the American Guide Series and has all of the innocent charm of its genre. But the book has something else as well, for here is the best history of the port of Boston: the story of a town that nestles between the granite face of Cape Ann and the beckoning finger of Cape Cod and has been home to seafaring folk for nearly four centuries.

It is the tale of puritans and pirates, of merchant princes and smugglers, of tea and opium, of clipper ships and packets. Clearly, the anonymous authors knew and loved their subject. They wrote at a time when the remnants of the harbor's glorious past were still to be seen. Some are still there and with a good imagination the sensitive reader can hear the rhythmic pinging of caulker's mallets in Donald McKay's yard and the snapping of loose canvas as a Liverpool packet hauls into a dock, or smell the fish being carted along T wharf. It's all there for those wise enough to take this book, march down to the waterfront, take up a spot with a view to the east—and read.

WILLIAM M. FOWLER, JR.

PREFACE

ALONG THE COAST of Massachusetts the maritime tradition is more than a phrase or a romantic legend. A regional habit of looking to the sea, born in the necessities of past generations, persists despite urban influences, the encroachment of the machine, the trend of the nineteenth century to the West, and all the various factors that have helped to lessen the relative importance of the merchant fleet in our national economy.

For those who live in Boston, once the carrying center of the Nation and still among its greatest ports, the study of maritime history has both academic and immediate interest: it is a challenge to present efforts toward obtaining for this port the recognition, the just concessions under governmental regulation, the expansion of services, which would enable it to develop to the full its magnificent potentialities.

The Massachusetts WPA Writers' Project conceived the notion that it could make a contribution, not only to the Port of Boston, but to the city and the Commonwealth, perhaps even to the country in a time of national emergency, by telling the story of the Port from the time when the first shallop skimmed the harbor waters to the strenuous days when destroyers are building along the shores. It would, we thought, be especially helpful to interpret to the general public in non-technical terms the economic and legalistic problems now confronting champions of the Port.

We first broached our idea to the Honorable John F. Fitzgerald, known for his achievements on behalf of the Port during his terms as Mayor of Boston and, more recently, as an active member of the Boston Port Authority. With his encouragement we offered our services to the Boston Port Authority, who agreed to sponsor this book as one of their numerous activities on behalf of Port development. Our wholehearted thanks are due especially to Mr. Richard Parkhurst, Vice-Chairman, who has given 11 years to his work for the Port and achieved substantial results in this voluntary public service; his meticulous analysis of our manuscript has assured its authenticity.

7

The Writers' Project has come to know that we may confidently rely upon co-operation from both the public and the private agencies with whom our work brings us in contact. Custom, however, has not staled our lively sense of gratitude to those who are generous with their time and thought in our behalf. We wish to acknowledge the assistance given us by the Librarians of the Massachusetts Historical Society and the Bostonian Society and the staff of the Boston Public Library; by the Maritime Division of the Boston Chamber of Commerce; the Boston Marine Society; the Boston office staff of the United States Bureau of Fisheries; the District office staff of the United States Army Corps of Engineers; the Massachusetts Fisheries Association; the State Street Trust Company; and the Shipbuilding Division of the Bethlehem Steel Company at Fore River. We are grateful, too, for the information provided by the agents and operators of shipping services, the operators of waterfront property, the representatives of maritime and longshoremen's unions, the staffs of Federal, State, and city agencies associated with marine activities, and many other individuals and representatives of business firms, so numerous that we must thank them collectively rather than by name.

Although the Writers' Project technique is one of collaboration among many workers, it is just and pleasurable to recognize major contributions to the growth of a book. *Boston Looks Seaward* has been, from the first tentative prospectus to the reading of page proof, under the immediate direction of Mr. Melvin D. Peach, Supervisor. During the later stages of the work, Mr. Roger Thomas has served as chief of the Project editorial staff. The corps of writers and research workers included Mr. Arthur Addelson (who until his resignation acted as editorial assistant to the supervisor), Mr. Warren M. Bean, Mr. Felix Doherty, Mr. David Englund, Mr. Frank Irwin, Mr. Francis McCarthy, Mr. William Raymond, Mr. Victor Rinestein, Mr. Arthur J. Saltman, Mr. Russell Seaver, and Mr. Edward Vial. Mr. Earle Bishop checked all final copy for factual accuracy; Mr. Edmund Hawes, Project photographer, is responsible for illustrations not otherwise credited; and Mr. Herbert Pierce, our cartographer, drew the maps of the Port. Our thanks are due the Massachusetts WPA Art Project for their courtesy in permitting us to use as endpapers Mr. Stanley Scott's blockprint of Boston Harbor.

Those who produced this book and those who contributed

to it are hoping for an intangible reward: increased awareness in Boston and New England, and even beyond those boundaries, of the distinguished record of the Port of Boston and of the vigorous part it will continue to play, given public support, in the maritime enterprises of the United States.

MURIEL E. HAWKS
State Supervisor

CONTENTS

ILLUSTRATIONS

MAPS

CHAPTER I

EXPLORERS, FISHERMEN, TRADERS

Early Explorers

THE MARITIME history of Boston began in the fifteenth century, when fishermen from the Basque region of Spain, from Portugal, from Normandie and Brittany were venturing to the Grand Banks. True, Norsemen may have visited the region as early as the year 1000, and no one can deny with certainty the legend of Thorvald's burial upon the coast where he had prophesied that he should "dwell forever." But the visits of the Vikings were individual adventures, while in those of the fishing vessels lay the promise that men would return in greater numbers as the years passed. Seafarers who sailed into Massachusetts Bay in search of fish or to escape strong northeast gales found a 40-mile expanse of water between Cape Ann's granite headland and the sandy tip of Cape Cod. Off the great bay opened sheltered coves and natural harbors teeming with cod and haddock. Of these harbors the largest and most protected was the island-studded indentation later known as Boston Bay.

More significant than fishermen's tall tales, left without chapter and verse, was England's claim, based on the recorded voyage of John Cabot in 1497, to the whole continent of North America. For this claim, and the European economic and social situation, determined that developments about the Bay of Boston should become increasingly English, rather than Spanish, French, or Dutch. The navigator, Bartholomew Gosnold, and a few of his party, who skirted the coast in 1602, were the first Englishmen known to have landed on the soil of Massachusetts. Gosnold's naming of Cape Cod because of the abundance of cod he found in the Bay was more noteworthy than was any actual exploration of the harbor by the Frenchman DeMont, or the Dutch navigator, Adrian Block, a few years later. Another enterprising Englishman, Captain John Smith, has left us a map and a description of his explorations in 1614, which indicate that he at least entered the outer harbor of Boston. He viewed Massachusetts as "the Paradise of all those parts," admitting at the same time that the French had been trading for 6 weeks in the Boston Bay locality and had "left nothing."

The outstanding features of Boston Bay early became familiar to the Pilgrims while sailing from Plymouth to visit their neighbors in Salem. One of the Plymouth excursionists, Isaac Allerton, named after himself the bluff known as Point Allerton, in the present town of Hull. Even before the founding of Salem, on September 29, 1621, a shallop from Plymouth had carried Captain Miles Standish, with 10 white men and 3 Indians, through the autumn haze to the first authenticated exploring of the inner harbor of Boston. Because of the somber visitation of pestilence that had ravaged the powerful tribe of Massachusetts, the expedition found few Indian inhabitants and could do little toward establishing immediate trade. The islands of Boston Bay, which John Smith had seen inhabited and tilled, presented to Miles Standish only abandoned traces of human life. At Medford were discovered a few women and one man, he showing himself "shaking and trembling for feare."

The Indians whom Standish did encounter in the Boston Bay region were not averse to trade in furs, however, and, a few months after his September trip, a fishing station was set up at Natascot (Hull), near the southeastern limits of Boston Harbor. Nor was the Bay region as depopulated as Standish's experience might imply. For many years the harbor had been familiar to fishermen and traders of all the maritime nations, and their visits may have caused the Indians to withdraw a little from the shore. Long before the first permanent settlement in 1623, a fleet of not less than 50 vessels was cruising yearly along the Massachusetts' coast.

The first permanent settlement around Boston harbor was made at Wessagusset (in present Weymouth) by Robert Gorges in September 1623. The Gorges Grant provided for complete political, religious, and criminal jurisdiction over 10 miles of coast from Nahant to Charlestown, and over territory extending 30 miles inland. Robert Gorges wished to establish an episcopacy on these shores, his plan calling for the complete colonization of New England. As a strategic measure toward accomplishing this somewhat grandiose project, the Wessagusset settlement was planted outside the tract awarded him. Although Robert Gorges found himself unequal even to the responsibility for the administration of the original grant, so far below his ambitions, his early departure for England did not affect the continuance of Wessagusset as a community.

Settlers on the Harbor

From this early South Shore settlement may be traced a series of developments of lasting importance to the area around Boston, where the Charles and the Mystic Rivers meet the waters of the Bay. About 1625 three men—Samuel Maverick, a trader, William Blackstone, a Church of England clergyman, and Thomas Walford, a blacksmith—settled in the upper Bay region and became the first permanent white inhabitants in or near the present Boston. Blackstone had come with Gorges; Maverick and Walford were in close sympathy with the aims of the Gorges plan of colonization. Blackstone, melancholic lover of solitude, built his cabin on the west slope of Beacon Hill, the sole white resident on Shawmut Peninsula. Walford, with his wife and children, moved to Charlestown, where he constructed a thatched hut enclosed with a stockade. Maverick's fortified house at Winnissimet (Chelsea) was ideally placed for trade. From its well-chosen situation, better communication could be maintained with the roving fishermen and with the coastal settlements than could be had from Wessagusset. The Indians brought furs by canoe to Winnissimet from the headwaters, where their villages were numerous. Fish served as barter for furs. At Maverick's house on one occasion, gayety and gain mingled even with gospel exhortations from a visiting Church of England clergyman. The Reverend Francis Bright, Maverick's guest in 1629-30, after a moving warning against covetousness and the sin of Sunday trade, upon delivering the benediction lost no time in bargaining successfully for the rich beaver coat worn by an Indian in the congregation.

The North Shore colony at Salem, founded late in 1626 by remnants of the Dorchester Company, soon made consequential moves about Boston Bay. It had been the intention of the New England Company, when John Endecott was appointed governor of the Salem region in 1628, to make that town the center of affairs in New England. But Matthew Cradock, Governor of the Company in London, directed that maritime activities be pushed beyond Salem, and, on his instructions, there was established, shortly before Winthrop's coming in 1630, a shipyard at Medford on the Mystic. Also attracted to the superior maritime and living conditions to the south, the Sprague brothers and a number of companions from Salem were granted permission, in the summer of 1629, to settle in Charlestown.

Winthrop's seekers after a new heaven and a new earth, numbering some 900 souls, began one of the largest migrations in the history of England's colonial ventures. John Winthrop found Salem not to his liking as a capital, and Charlestown unlivable because of the brackish water which sickened his whole company. At the invitation of the Episcopal Blackstone, the Puritan Governor crossed the Charles in the autumn of 1630 and settled on Shawmut Peninsula. To the eyes of Anne Pollard, the young girl who was the first to leap ashore when the migrants landed from their boats on the shores of the present North End, the Peninsula seemed a place "very uneven, abounding in small hollows and swamps, covered with blueberries and other bushes." Such was her recollection in old age of a child's vivid impression.

The Boston of that day resembled a chain of islands. The abrupt mass of Copp's Hill on the north was separated slightly from the rest of Shawmut Peninsula by a marsh extending between two coves. At the high-water mark, "Mill Pond," on the northern side of the Peninsula, became a channel up to the marshes. Winthrop saw the waters of the "Great Cove" sweeping inland, covering the area near which Faneuil Hall was later erected. Occasional high tides, flowing across the narrow "Neck" of the Peninsula, detached it from the mainland. Out in the harbor eastward was Noddle's Island (East Boston), to which Samuel Maverick was to move after having established himself in the coasting trade.

A talented young Englishman, William Wood, graphically described the Bay region in 1633:

This Bay is both safe, spacious, and deep, free from such cockling seas as run upon the coast of Ireland and in the channels of England. There be no stiff running currents, or rocks, shelves, bars, quicksands . . . the surrounding shore being high, and showing many white cliffs, in a most pleasant prospect, with divers places of low land, out of which divers rivers vent themselves into the ocean. . . . It is a safe and pleasant harbour within, having but one common and safe entrance, and that not very broad, there scarce being room for three ships to come in, board and board, at a time; but being once within, there is room for the anchorage of five hundred ships.

To New Ports

Though the first settlers intended to become farmers, many found the hardscrabble, upland pastures hardly worth the clearing, and the building of stone walls fruitless labor. Some turned for their livelihood to the sea, where the shoals and offshore banks teemed with great schools of fish. Establishing themselves in settlements along the coast, they used the sea as the recognized highway from village to village, since land travel over the rude forest trails was difficult and hazardous. To meet the immediate need for small craft, shallops were built of rough-hewn timbers. Within a few months the shallops were being used in opening up trade with the Indians of the Kennebec River.

Commerce increased rapidly among the settlements along the Bay. The hundred bushels of corn Samuel Maverick's pinnace brought back from the Cape Cod Indians in the autumn of 1630 were a modest forerunner of the rich maritime exchanges which before long made Boston the chief trading port of the Atlantic coast. To open up new trade routes, John Oldham was sent 3 years later on a land expedition to the Connecticut River country. He brought back hemp, beaver skins, and black lead; and gave sanguine accounts based on what the Indians told him of the lavish productiveness of the region.

The Indian and local trade were soon followed by more distant coastal commerce. In May 1631, an 18-ton pinnace brought corn and tobacco from the southern settlements. Early the following year a Virginia bark, having unloaded at Salem, stopped for a month in Boston harbor. Mr. Maverick's pinnace then accompanied it on its homeward voyage to establish new trade relations between Boston and Virginia. Only 2 years later, 10,000 bushels of corn entered the harbor from the southern colony, in return for which many barrels of fish were shipped south. Boston trade with the Dutch colonies of Manhattan and Long Island was also well under way. By 1634, the Dutch of these regions were providing the Boston people with sugar, brass pieces, beaver skins, and considerable numbers of sheep, in exchange for liquor and linen cloth.

Many interesting episodes accompanied the opening up of the coastal trade. Commerce with Maryland had various complications to overcome. The opposition of the Boston Calvinists to the Catholic faith of the Marylanders was an initial barrier. Letters from the Governor of Maryland, reenforced by one from the Governor of Virginia, served to smooth the way, and the arrival of a Maryland pinnace in 1634, bringing corn for fish, made exchange a simple matter. A Captain Young of Maryland also wrote, offering to bring cattle. But when, in 1642, a Mr. Neale brought two pinnaces under commission from Governor Calvert to buy mares and sheep in Massachusetts, he could offer only bills of exchange, payable by Lord Baltimore in London. We scarcely need John Winthrop's laconic comment to know that "no man would deal with him." The refusal of the Swedish and Dutch governors of the Delaware River region to allow traffic with the Indians in 1644 sent a Boston ship home empty. The following year another Boston ship, about to return from the same territories, laden with skins and other commodities, was attacked and plundered by Indians.

The trade relations of Boston merchants with the French colonies in Canada form an entertaining chapter of their own. The impressions of the French themselves of the commercial and maritime prestige of Boston are shown in their naive conception of Massachusetts as "the colony of Boston." In their zeal for trade relations with Acadia, the Boston merchants and the Colonial government pursued the hazardous policy of attempting to disentangle the conflicting claims of the two Frenchmen, D'Aulnay and La Tour, each of whom asserted himself to be the rightful governor of Acadia. From documents presented in Boston by La Tour's agents, it seemed clear that he, rather than D'Aulnay, was in the favor of the French King. In return for promised trade concessions, the General Court and town authorities allowed La Tour in 1643 to hire whatever ships he could and enlist as many men as were willing to accompany him in his military operations against D'Aulnay. The expedition was not successful, and 2 years later D'Aulnay was able to present proof of his rightful standing as Governor. He then destroyed La Tour's base at St. John's. But La Tour, though discredited officially, found himself still personally popular in Boston. He had many friends here who outfitted him for a trading voyage. Sailing from the Port of Boston, this gentleman of France dumped the Boston members of his ship's company on shore at Cape Sable in dead of winter, and turned pirate.

The Frenchman was not the first pirate to prey upon Boston

shipping, for Dixey Bull has the distinction of being the pioneer in that line for Boston and New England. He came from England in 1631 and, a year later, was known as a respectable trader in the beaver traffic of Penobscot Bay. When a group of roving Frenchmen came upon him and made off with his shallop and stock of coats, rugs, blankets, and even his biscuits, the outraged Bull decided an honest trader's lot was a hard one. He gathered a crew of adventurers and searched widely but vainly for his French attackers. Disappointed and still angry, he revenged himself by plundering colonial vessels along the coast and forcing a few of their crew to join his company. After several such escapades Dixey Bull steeled to the business. He is reported to have written a circular letter to all governors in the region advising them that he and his companions intended no further harm to their citizens; that they were going southward; and that efforts to capture them would be useless, as they were determined to sink before allowing themselves to be taken. Nevertheless, an expedition of four or five pinnaces, commanded by Samuel Maverick of Noddle's Island, was sent against Dixey Bull in 1632. The orders were to find and bring home for trial the first pirate of the town. After combing the seas for 2 months, the expedition returned without having found a trace of Bull. Accounts of his subsequent career vary. One version is that he reached England safely, the other that he went over to "the enemy" (the French).

The Shipbuilders

The founder of Boston died in 1649. John Winthrop had seen a town hewn out of a wilderness in less than 20 years. A vigorous and profitable commerce with ports beyond the horizon had already begun to transform the sprawling cluster of sticks and clapboards into a "city-like towne" of brick-tile, stone, and slate. An anonymous Englishman about this time described Charlestown as consisting

of about a hundred and fifty dwelling houses, many of them beautified with pleasant Gardens and Orchards: near the water-side is a large Market-place, forth of which issue two faire streets, and in it stands a large and a well built Church, over against the Island neare the Sea side stands Dorchester, a Frontire-town, water'd with two small rivers, built in form of a Serpent turning its head Northward, it consists of one hundred and forty dwelling houses with Orchards and gardens full of fruit trees . . . Boston the Center and Metropolis of the rest, built in form of a heart, and fortified with two hills on the frontice part thereof, the one having great store of Artillerie mounted thereon, the other having a strong batterie built of whole Timber and filled with Earth, at the descent of the Hill, lies a large Cave or bay, on which the cheife part of this towne is built, over topped with a third Hill, all three like over-topping Towers keeping a constant watch to fore-see the approach of forraign dangers, the cheifest part of this . . . town, is crouded upon the Seabanks, and wharfed out with a great industry and cost, the edifiese large and beautifull, whose continuall inlargement presageth some sump-tuous City.

Winthrop had guided his people as they caught fish, built ships, and became shrewd traders. A pioneer of shipbuilding in Massachusetts, he has often been referred to as the father of the American Merchant Marine. Before Boston was a year old, he had ordered the building of a vessel near his Medford estate, and on July 4, 1631, the *Blessing of the Bay* was launched on the Mystic, the first sizable ship constructed in Massachusetts. Built mainly of locust, of between 30 and 40 tons burden, the vessel was bark-rigged and cost between £145 and £165. The practical reason for her building was the Gov-ernor's distrust of England's sending over necessary supplies for the storehouses of the Colony. On August 9, a group gath-ered near Winthrop's home, and offered prayers for the pros-perity and safe return of the vessel as she started on her maiden voyage to trade with the Dutch on Long Island. The *Blessing of the Bay* was later reconditioned for pursuit of pirates, and has been called the first war vessel in the country.

Smaller boats, however, had been built before the *Blessing of the Bay* by fishermen themselves during the spare time of winter. They were fashioned from timber gathered in the common woods. The material was shaped and fitted piece-meal, and the cash outlay usually involved little more than rope and canvas. With the builder at the helm and his sons as the crew, vessels of this type went on fishing voyages to "the Banks," and a decade or two later were sailing to the West Indies.

Medford became the center for Boston's shipbuilding. The Mystic River had no rocks or shoals and gave easy passage to an empty vessel of 25 tons. Its winding course made possible many shipyards within a narrow radius, and in each yard from one to three ships rose upon the stocks. A year after the *Blessing of the Bay* had been completed, a 100-ton ship was launched from Matthew Cradock's yard. In 1633 Cradock's agent laid the keels for one vessel of 200 tons. The *Rebecca* of unknown tonnage was also built that year.

Private enterprise and governmental encouragement worked

in active cooperation to make Boston a maritime center. Laws were enacted to exempt ship carpenters, millers, and fishermen from military training. An act of the General Court in 1639 added provisions which freed from taxes and duties for 7 years any ship or other property used in the fisheries. By 1641 shipbuilding was important enough to warrant stringent regulations by the General Court, designed to assure the proper construction of all vessels. One such act read:

> Whereas the country is now in hand with the building of ships, which is a business of great importance for the common good, and therefore suitable care is to be taken that it will be well performed, according to the commendable course of England and other places: it is therefore ordered that when any ship is to be built within this jurisdiction it shall be lawful for the owner to appoint and put in some able man to survey the work and workmen from time to time, as is usual in England, and the same so appointed shall have such liberty and power as belongs to his office.

Three years later, the General Court urged the formation of the shipbuilders into a company, for the better ordering of the industry and the maintenance of standards conducive to the public good. Shipbuilding became a community undertaking. The artisans who fashioned the planks, the merchants who supplied the material, the seamen who sailed the vessel, all became part owners, and so directly concerned in every voyage. The seamen were mainly former fishermen who, instead of fishing off "the Banks", carried dried and salted fish to Europe, the Barbados, and Bermuda, in exchange for the products of these foreign lands.

Because an English law prevented shipowners and shipmasters from leaving the mother country, Nehemiah Bourne, son of the shipwright Robert Bourne of London, had to obtain special permission to come to Boston. After working as a shipwright in Dorchester, Bourne established his own yard in the North End, where he built the *Trial*, of 160 tons burden in 1641. The maiden trip of this first vessel built in Boston took her to the Azores and the West Indies.

Another famous shipyard, just north of Copp's Hill, belonged to Benjamin Gillan & Company. Some of the ships it turned out were of remarkable size, among them the *Welcome*, of 300 tons, built by Valentine Hill in the early forties. In beauty and size the 400-ton *Seafort*, built by Captain Thomas Hawkins and launched in 1644, probably surpassed any vessel previously constructed in the Colony. But her glory was brief, for within a few months the ship was wrecked on the coast of Spain. Several more fortunate vessels, immediately after their launching, took on cargoes of pipe staves, fish, and other products, and spread their sails for the Canaries.

The work of training apprentices in the shipbuilding trade was the specialty of Alexander Adams, a master-craftsman. Among the problems of shipbuilders were a scarcity of labor and a tendency among workmen to shift from one yard to another. Mr. Adams helped to stabilize conditions by training 30 apprentices between 1646 and 1675. The foundations of skilled workmanship laid by him brought benefits to the shipbuilding industry for the next hundred years. Foremost among Adams' successors was William Parker, his son-in-law, who followed him in the shipbuilding business. In later years, Parker specialized in mast building and became famous as the "mast merchant."

In Hull, in the latter part of the seventeenth century, the Captains Langlee, father and son, had a yard at the foot of Ship Street. The younger Langlee was succeeded by John Souther, whose sons, John and Leverett, later became noted for their schooners and square-rigged craft. Other prominent builders at the foot of Ship Street were Curtis and Barstow, Barnes, Litchfield, and William Hall. In Hingham, Thomas Barker was building ships at Goose Point by 1637 and, about a dozen years later, was in Boston, under contract to build a bark. In 1675 William Pitt held a shipbuilder's license, and in 1693 a James Blaney was permitted to build a "vessel or two" near "Mill Cove."

All manner of boats slid down the ways of the local shipyards. There was a continuous demand in the fishing and coasting trade for shallops fitted with mainmast, foremast, and lugsails. The Medford yards, in addition to brigantines and barks, which were built square and usually weighed less than 50 tons, sent out many sloops and ketches. The deck cabins of the sloops, placed at the stern, gave the appearance of the poop-deck of earlier date. Another characteristic of the sloop was the single mast carrying fore-and-aft mainsail boom and a yard or two of topsail. Broad-beamed sloops often did duty in carrying firewood to Boston and Charlestown. The ketch became the common type of vessel used by Bostonians in the West Indies trade—two-masted, rigged with a square sail on the mainmast and a lateen on the mizzen. Smaller sloops, called "lighters," used for river navigation, were built at Rock Hill Landing, near West Medford. Pinnaces were fashioned sharp at both ends, often having two masts, and sometimes built "open," with no deck or only a half-deck. They varied in size from a few tons to over 50 tons.

So rapidly did the shipbuilders develop skill and enterprise that, within 35 years after the founding of Boston, there were 300 New England vessels, mostly Boston owned, engaged in coastal and overseas trade. Thirteen hundred smaller craft were fishing off the coast. A variety of industries connected with shipping had been established on this side of the water. Even while huge supplies of cordage and sailcloth were emerging out of the holds of vessels from the mother country, John Harrison of Salisbury, England, had in 1641 opened his rope-walk in Boston.

Wharves, Ferries, and Forts

The increased maritime activity of Boston, with its need for improved waterfront facilities, necessitated the gradual "filling in" of marshes and swamp areas covering the Peninsula, and the pushing out of the water mark to the deeper waters of the harbor. The area of solid ground presenting navigable water frontage was limited, and the merchants early recognized that a more uniform waterfront was desirable than the many indentations and coves allowed. Bounties were established for persons who showed their public spirit by extending the shore line. In 1643, the town granted the North Cove (Mill Pond), the area now partly occupied by the North Station, to Henry Symonds, George Burden, and others, for the purpose of erecting "corn mills" on its shores. The new owners opened and deepened a channel from Mill Pond to the Great Cove on the other side of the Peninsula, which became known as Mill Creek.

The original waterfront and the center for shipping was principally in the vicinity of Dock Square, near the present Faneuil Hall. Here the first Town Dock was established in the early 1630's, and it was, for a considerable time, the focal point of all marketable produce. The merchant Edward Bendall was so prominently connected with the activities of this wharf that it became widely known as "Bendall's Dock." It was Mr. Bendall who contrived a primitive sort of diving bell, the first used in the harbor, and raised the *Mary Rose*, which had blown up in August 1641, from an explosion of gunpowder on board and had obstructed the harbor for almost a year.

Although the official records of Boston do not tell when the first wharf was built, many persons, even before 1650, had received permits to construct wharves at points along the waterfront. An ordinance had provided that beacons be placed at landing places to warn of stones or logs which, partially submerged in the tide or too near the water's edge, might be a danger to vessels. This measure was passed because of the damage suffered by vessels loading and unloading without wharf facilities. In 1641, Valentine Hill and others were granted a large tract near the "Dock" to develop wharves, with the privilege of collecting for tonnage. Scarlett's Wharf was established at the foot of Fleet Street by Samuel Scarlett, who received the land in 1669. It served as an important disembarkation point for troops. Thomas Clarke, a wealthy merchant, had a wharf whose outline corresponded to the north side of the present Lewis Wharf. The Clarke Wharf became particularly famous later when it was owned by Thomas Hancock and his nephew, John Hancock. Although wharves had to be built for unloading purposes, the lack of natural dock facilities was balanced by the advantages of the harbor, where 500 ships could easily ride at anchor.

Nor did colonial Boston neglect the ferry facilities necessitated by her situation. The rolling Charles separated the Shawmut settlers from the Charlestown people. A mile or two beyond the Charles, on the far side of the Mystic, lay Winnissimet (Chelsea). Inhabited Noddle's Island, completely cut off from the mainland, stood some little distance out in the harbor. By 1631, the "Great Ferry" was in operation between Boston and Charlestown. Seven years later, the General Court established a ferry to serve for connections with Chelsea, East Boston, and with ships in the harbor. In 1640, the famous "Penny Ferry" began carrying passengers across the Mystic near the site of the present Malden Bridge.

The first fortification in the harbor, an 80-foot eminence, was constructed on Fort Hill in 1632. Within 2 years elaborate fortifications were ordered for Castle Island. Beacon Hill derives its name from the signal light established there in March 1635, as a guide to mariners at sea and as a warning of hostile approach. Eleven years later, the North Battery was erected at "Merry's Point" in the North End. From its earth ramparts encased in timber, cannon commanded the harbor. The famous "Boston Sconce" (South Battery) was built in 1666, and stood guard where Rowes Wharf is now situated.

The celebrated sea wall, constructed partly for defense and partly for use as a wharf, followed the line of the present Atlantic Avenue, and extended from Captain Scarlett's Wharf to the Sconce. This sea wall was begun in 1673; in its completed form the timber and earth wall was almost half a mile long, 15 feet high and 20 feet wide, with emplacements for cannon, and with openings for ships to pass through. Along with these permanent defense arrangements, special precautions were taken on occasion, as when in 1649 the Deputies of the General Court established a military guard in Boston and Charlestown because of the multitude of strangers from the many ships in the harbor.

Rum, Slaves, Molasses

The building of fortifications along the waterfront reflected the increasing importance of Boston's shipping. Her earlier trading enterprise had been restricted largely to the collection of goods for export, the redistribution of commodities imported, and the barter of various colonial products. But when immigration lagged and "the scarcity of foreign commodities" increased at the Port during the Civil Wars in England (1642-49), a more extensive maritime commerce developed. Opportunely neglected by the mother country, Boston traders roamed the ports of the Western World, peddling and bartering. Islands of the sea and far-away coasts entered into the growing network of trade. Boston shipmasters brought back potatoes, oranges, and limes from Bermuda. Vessels sailed for Barbados and Jamaica with cattle, meat, butter, cheese, and biscuit. From Teneriffe came wines, pitch, sugar, and ginger—good exchanges for Massachusetts corn. Even Madagascar was not outside the range of the Boston sea captain.

In launching out into more distant trading in the 1640's, Boston found herself in the thick of the rum - slave - molasses traffic. Many Boston shipmasters would take on a cargo of rum from one of the numerous distilleries along the Massachusetts and Rhode Island shores and sail to the coast of Africa, where the product passed as currency. To slake their fierce thirst for the fiery beverage, the Negro chiefs sold their enemies, acquaintances, friends, and when those outside the family group had been carried away, even sold their wives, children, mothers, and fathers into bondage on West Indian plantations. After the slaves had been exchanged for molasses in the West Indies, the Boston sea captains headed north. In New England, the molasses was turned into the distillery for more rum, to be used for another voyage in this tri-cornered trade. The liquor was also sold in enormous quantities to fishermen engaged with net and harpoon in the biting spray and bitter winds off the Banks, to robust laborers on the docks and in the shipyards, and to the masters of Boston ships who were required by their bonds to serve rum to the crew.

Sometimes slaves were actually imported into the Colony. Captain William Pierce of the *Desire* on his return from a trading voyage in 1638 brought back, as a part of the general cargo, Negroes whom he had taken on at Providence, Barbados. John Hull sent two Negroes to Madeira in exchange for wine. In 1645, the first vessel in America authentically known to have been engaged in the slave trade, the ship *Rainbowe,* after being fitted out by Thomas Keyser and James Smith, the latter a church member, sailed from Boston to the coast of Guinea. There she found some British slavers tied up, waiting for business to improve. To hurry things along, the Yankee skipper concocted a scheme with the Britishers. Under pretense of a quarrel with the natives, the combined forces landed a cannon, attacked a village on a quiet Sunday, killed many of the inhabitants, and brought away captives, two of whom were the share of the Boston seamen. Public indignation was stirred at the spectacle of these slaves being brought into the Port. The owners of the ship were sternly rebuked by the authorities, and the slaves were sent back to their own country at public expense.

Romance and drama of the sea live in the simple accounts of the West Indies trade. As early as 1638, the *Desire,* one of the first vessels engaged in traffic with the islands, brought back a cargo consisting mainly of cotton and tobacco. In 1642, the *Trial* carried fish and staves to Fayal, in the Azores. The Catholics of these islands were large consumers of sea food, and their occupation as winemakers made the Massachusetts staves acceptable for the construction of casks. Picking up wine, sugar, and other articles in the Azores, the *Trial* exchanged these at St. Christopher's in the West Indies for iron from a wrecked ship, and for cotton and tobacco, and returned to Boston in the winter of 1643. Other Boston sea captains sailed to Jamaica, bringing back bars of silver and Spanish coin and plate. Many lost all they had to pirates, while others returned with so much money that they were themselves suspected of piracy.

More often than slaves from Guinea, the Boston shipmasters carried such New England foodstuffs as corn, flour, biscuit, and especially salt codfish, which formed the principal diet for thousands of slaves. In addition, hats, clapboards, pipe staves, lumber, and salt comprised the staples of Boston's export to the West Indies. The return cargo usually included cotton, indigo, ginger, dye-woods, tobacco, and molasses. The tobacco brought on one voyage was of such poor quality that John Winthrop pronounced the consignment sent by his son Henry, "very ill conditioned, fowle, full of stalks, and evill coloured." By the middle of the century, it had ceased to be an important commodity, and sugar became the chief medium of exchange in the Caribbean.

The seaman of the hazardous West Indies route, according to Charles E. Cartwright in *American Ships and Sailors,* was typical of the seafarer from colonial Boston. Born within the sound of pounding surf, playing as a boy on the rough waterfront swarming with riggers, ropemakers, and sailors, he had learned a love of the sea with his alphabet. Older boys had taught him to scull an oar and sail a dory. As soon as he was strong enough to heave a rope, he had shipped as an apprentice, since no vessel left port without two or three boys. Then he chanced his luck with roaring Hatteras gales and Caribbean buccaneers. In the long voyage, with no land in sight for weeks or even months, the Boston seafarer became a different breed of man, a native of the ocean rather than of the land. He strode about the ship in his wide canvas trousers, his broad belt supporting a vicious case knife. He wore rings in his ears, and his hair was gathered in a tarred pigtail. The Boston sailor lived on a hardy diet of salt pork, salt beef, hardtack, and lobscouse. He was subject to stern discipline aboard the little ships of the West Indies trade, and he might frequently be flogged with the rawhide cat-o'-nine-tails. Though as skilled with blunderbuss and cutlass as in handling the rope and marlin spike, though fond of rum and coarse revelry, the Boston seaman was still a jolly, generous chap.

The West Indies trade developed rapidly because it formed a natural complement to Boston's commerce with Europe. Local exports to the islands exceeded the purchases made there, whereas the imports from England were much greater than the exports to the mother country. Through the bills of exchange, the specie, and the tropical produce, obtained from the "sugar islands," Boston shipmasters obtained the cargoes required for successful trade with England. Neither the wars of England with France and Spain nor the threat of pirates and privateers on the Spanish Main could stop this profitable exchange, to which may be largely attributed the steady commercial growth of the Port. The small West Indies island of Martinique became more valuable to the merchants of Boston than the whole of Canada. Edward Randolph, the Collector of the Port, called Boston in 1679 "the mart town of the West Indies." In the 6 months from March 25 to September 29, 1688, out of 141 ships clearing from Boston, 84 were in the West Indies traffic. Nearly all these were Boston-owned and Massachusetts-built. Of the more than 140 arrivals during the same 6 months, 89 came with cargoes from the West Indies, 37 from other American Colonies, and 21 from England. One of the impulses for the establishment of the famous New England mint in 1652 was the need for coining and recording the bullion and currency which poured in from the southern islands.

John Hull, who became mint-master in 1652, was himself a large owner of shipping. His vessels, the *Friendship,* the *Society,* the *Dove,* the *Sea Flower,* the *Hopewell,* the *Tryall,* and the *Endeavor,* were carrying his ventures up and down the Atlantic coast and to European ports. He imported English goods and exported tanned hides and other colonial products. His own men cut timber on the Piscataqua for export. In trading with Spain, Hull usually consigned his goods to the ships of John Usher, Boston merchant and bookseller. While Hull's own vessels concentrated on the southern route, his assorted cargoes were often carried by "constant traders," ships that left Southampton or London in the early fall, dropping anchor at Boston between late October and early December. That part of his business correspondence which has been preserved reveals John Hull as a stern Puritan, who insisted that his seamen adhere rigidly to the rules of the church. In written orders, dated September 18, 1671, and sent to John Alden, son of the bashful John and master of the *Friendship,* Hull concludes,

leave noe debts behind you, whereever you goe, I know you will be carefull to see to the worship of God every day on the vessell and to the sanctification of the lords day and the suppression of all prophaines. . . .

Punctual in his dealings, Hull required the same rigid punctuality from others. He was extremely jealous of his reputation for honesty. When his cousin, Thomas Buckham, called him a "very knave" in company, the wrathful Hull wrote,—

I can through the grace of God bid defiance to you and all men to challenge any one action in my whole life in all my dealeings amonst men since I attained the yeares of a man, I thank God I have dealt honestly not in Craftyness nor in Guile but in the feare of God.

A prompt apology is called for, "else I shall desire I may have no more to doe with you in this world, for the sin of Backbiteing and slandering is to be hated by all good men." Nevertheless, John Hull was ingenious enough to make piety show on the right side of the ledger. He became one of the wealthiest and most respected merchant princes of Boston.

A Growing Colony

In 1660, Parliament passed, upon the demand of the English mercantile class, a series of Navigation Acts which amplified and enforced those enacted 9 years earlier to give protection from the disastrous competition of colonial traders. These acts provided, among other things, that all goods in overseas trade were to be carried in ships owned by Englishmen and manned by crews at least three-quarters of whom were English. The acts also enumerated a list of articles produced in the colonies which could be shipped only to an English port, or through English ports to other countries. In 1663, the Staples Act was passed. This act made England the exporter of all European goods to be sent to the colonies and forbade the colonies to import directly from France, Spain, or Holland. An exception was made in the case of salt for the fisheries of New England, which could be carried from any part of Europe, of servants, horses, and provisions, which could be imported from Scotland and Ireland, and of wines, which could be sent directly from Madeira and the Azores.

The Boston merchants received the news of the restrictions upon their liberties with anxiety. After a generation of independence, they found it extremely distasteful to limit their activities and onerous to pay tribute at the London Custom House. While the Crown appeared unwilling to bring matters to a head and followed a policy of peaceful persuasion, Boston shipowners determinedly ignored the Navigation Acts. The government of the Colony did not disdain conciliation and diplomacy on occasion. At a timely juncture in 1666, during a brief war between England and France, a shipload of masts at a cost of £2000 was sent from Boston as a present for His Majesty's Royal Navy. Ten years later, a direct appeal was made to the royal appetite with a large present of cranberries and codfish for His Majesty's table.

The larger part of Boston's trade between 1660 and 1675 was carried on illegally. Products from all over the world entered Boston duty free, and the Port outfitted ships to trade at will with all the nations. Boston shipmasters sailed to Newfoundland and Annapolis Royal, carrying provisions, salt, and rum; they bargained with New York, the Jerseys, Pennsylvania, Maryland, Virginia, the Carolinas, Bermuda, and the Caribbee Islands, carrying every native commodity— meats, vegetables, fruits, flour, oil, candles, soap, butter, beer, rum, horses, sheep, cows and oxen, staves and earthen ware. They received in exchange tobacco, sugar, molasses, salt, and wines. Routes, definitely established, were varied from time to time only in so far as was necessary to evade the English customs authorities. Boston traders sailed to Spain, Portugal, and Italy, trying one port after another,—Cadiz, Bilbao, Alicante, Cartagena, Marseilles, Toulon, Leghorn, and Genoa. From these ports, some went on to England and then back to Boston; others went from Spain or Portugal to the Azores and the Canaries off the coast of Africa, then to Senegambia, Goree, or the Guinea coast for beeswax, gums, and ivory, and finally home, in some cases by way of England. Still others sailed direct from Boston to Madeira, the Azores and the Canaries, sold their cargoes of New England staples, and returned by the same route with the wines of these islands.

The majority of Boston merchants sent their vessels to England with lumber, flour, furs, and naval stores, which were exchanged for cloth and iron wares. In some instances, the next objective, after touching in England, would be the Newfoundland coastal ports for fish; in others, the voyage would be directed to Lisbon or the Straits of Gibraltar for continental articles, and thence back home. Frequently, captains sold their entire cargoes and ships for cash to London or Bristol merchants, invested the proceeds in manufactured goods, and shipped the merchandise home on a returning vessel. Little wonder that, when the friendly Cromwell proposed during the 1650's that the people of Boston remove to Jamaica to better their living conditions, there were few in

Boston so dissatisfied with local prospects that they desired to leave.

Privateering

The normal course of Boston's trade with ports outside English jurisdiction was at times upset by the turbulent political and military situation. The feeling of loyalty to the mother country was so strong among the Boston people that England's quarrels became their quarrels—especially when profits were to be made thereby. While England and Holland were engaged in the first Dutch War in 1653, the General Court of Massachusetts forbade the exportation from Boston of such produce as corn, pork, peas, beef, and bread to the French and Dutch colonies of America. During these English wars, daring Boston sea captains turned from peaceful trading to privateering. Equipped with a commission from the General Court or with letters of marque and reprisal, the captain and the crew of a privateer shared adventure on the high seas and a rich prize. Wrought up by Holland's capture of the Boston shallop *Philip,* commanded by George Manning, when England and Holland were again at war in 1674, the Council at Boston ordered Captain Mosely out after the Dutch ships. Mosely had participated in the earlier Dutch wars as a Boston privateer. He sailed in the armed vessel *Salisbury* and roamed coastal sea lanes for the enemy. Joined by a French vessel, willing enough to cooperate in the search, as the French were anxious to recover Acadia from the Dutch, Captain Mosely met a Dutch fleet of three vessels. As he drew near with his French consort, he was gratified to see that one of the three ships flying the Dutch flag was none other than the shallop *Philip.* When Mosely and the French captain opened fire on the Dutch privateers, the captured *Philip,* still commanded by Captain Manning, turned its guns on the Dutchmen, who quickly surrendered. Captain Mosely returned in triumph to Boston with not only the recovered *Philip,* but also with two Dutch prizes, the *Penobscot* and the *Edward and Thomas.* He arrived in Boston Harbor on April 2, 1675, more than a year after England had made peace with the Dutch.

The honor of being the commander of the first Boston privateer in King William's War (1689-97) fell to Captain Cyprian Southack, who at the age of 10 had served in the

English Navy. His first privateering activity for the Colonies was on the *Mary,* a little vessel of eight guns. Shortly afterward, he was transferred to a more formidable ship, the *Porcupine,* and cruised in a campaign against the French along the coast of Acadia (Nova Scotia). On June 27, 1690, off Scilly Cove, Newfoundland, the *Porcupine* captured the *William,* originally an English ship and still commanded by her master, Jacob Chubb, of Weymouth, England, who had entered the French employ after seizure on the high seas. Southack convoyed the recovered *William* first to St. John's and later to Boston. The following month, again off Newfoundland, Southack seized the French ship *Gift of God,* 80 tons, laden with wine, brandy, fish, and salt, and brought the cargo to Boston. Another Boston privateer active in this war was the *Swan,* commanded by Captain Thomas Gilbert. In the St. Lawrence River, she captured a French flyboat of 300 tons, bound for Quebec with claret, white wine, brandy, salt, and linen paper. Since the French privateers continued to harass Boston shipping, the Council of the Colony, on June 8, 1691, made proposals to two privateer captains "to encourage their going forth on their Majesties' service to suppress an enemy privateer now upon the coast." One of the two privateersmen was Captain Leonard Walkington, who had served under Southack on the *Porcupine,* the other was the notorious Captain William Kidd.

Royal Control

Despite the outward loyalty of the Boston people to the mother country in her colonial wars, their smuggling activities led to stricter regulation for the Port. In 1675, Edward Randolph was appointed royal messenger and investigator by the newly created Lords of Trade and Plantations in London. The previous year, when Boston merchants had boldly entered the Yucatan logwood trade, all exceptions allowed to Boston shippers had been canceled, and they were ordered to touch at London or other English ports. Continual complaints of English merchants and shipowners, and the reports of agents in European ports, all pointed to gross violation of the Navigation Acts by the chief port of Massachusetts. Randolph was dispatched to Boston to deliver a formal letter of complaint and summons to Governor Leverett of Massachusetts, and to bring back a reply to the charges. The royal instructions were not obeyed and Randolph was treated as a hostile agent. He managed, however, to collect all necessary information to prove that the English customs revenue suffered a loss of £100,000 annually, and recommended revocation of the Massachusetts charter. In 1678, Randolph was appointed, at his own request, Collector and Surveyor of the Customs in New England. He tried to put an end to the evasion of duties. Taking observations on the waterfront in 1679, the distinguished visitor noted that the "corporation of Boston" was lording it over the whole region, and that the Port was a great clearing house and distributing center for the American Colonies.

The merchants had vigorously opposed Randolph each time he returned to Boston armed with new powers to enforce the Navigation Acts. Their European trade was prosperous, and they were agreed that English trade policies had no rightful application to the Port of Boston. When a British agent seized several vessels for illegal trading with Scotland and Malaga, he was imprisoned by the masters and seamen of the vessels. To frustrate the execution of Randolph's commission, Colonial naval officers were established at the Port in 1681 to record all inbound and outbound ships. Boats refused to register with the English authorities, taking their papers instead to the Colonial naval officer. Prohibited goods were unloaded outside the harbor, the vessels then securing an unquestioned entry from the local port officers. Bostonians decided to discourage any person from accepting the office of Collector of Customs without their consent. They were determined to maintain their free trade with the ports of the world and to make Boston the trading center for all European goods designated for southern plantations. The flagrant obstructions they opposed to English restrictions were interpreted by Randolph as final proof of the disobedience of the Boston people. In August 1681, he embarked for England with all evidence necessary to convict the Colony of Massachusetts of exceeding its powers.

When in the fall of 1684 the Charter of Massachusetts was annulled, English shipowners and merchants finally succeeded in abolishing the grave threat of Boston's competition as an independent port. Sir Edmund Andros was appointed Governor of the New England Colonies in 1687, a year after the frigate H. M. S. *Rose* had been stationed outside Boston harbor to apprehend smugglers. The Navigation Acts were so effectually enforced that Boston's trade was crippled. The

more profitable shipping routes with Europe and the West
Indies were entirely blocked, and the evasion of duties was
practically eliminated at the Port. A severe depression set in;
many boats idled at the wharves. The Andros government
lasted 2 years and 4 months and ended in the violent revolt
of the Boston people. Andros was deported, and once again
Englishmen in Boston were free to trade with the West Indies
and Europe.

Commerce again began to prosper at the Port of Boston,
even after Massachusetts became a Royal Province in 1692.
The first of the Royal Governors, Sir William Phips, did not
enforce the Navigation Acts. Sir William sums up in his
personal career the Boston traditions of the sea. Unlettered,
he had tended sheep until the age of 18, when he turned to
the building and sailing of coasters. At 22 he became a ship's
carpenter in Boston. Fearless and adventurous, he showed
rare enterprise and intrepidity in salvaging treasure valued
at more than £300,000 from a sunken Spanish vessel in West
Indian waters between 1684-86 and, for this exploit, was
knighted by the King. Phips' appointment had been intended
to conciliate the Boston merchants, but he became increasingly
unpopular. Complained against and summoned to England
in 1694 to answer charges, Phips died of illness a short while
after he had reached London.

The second Royal Governor, Richard Coote, Earl of Bellomont, received his commission in 1697, and arrived in Boston
2 years later. The Boston merchants protested to Bellomont
when new restrictions were imposed upon their commerce
by the Lords of Trade in London. They insisted that "they
were as much Englishmen as those in England, and had a
right, therefore, to all the privileges which the people of England enjoyed." Although Bellomont tried earnestly to end
the illegal practices which made the English trade laws a dead
letter, he found that the laws could not be enforced. The Boston people refused to restrict their commerce to English ships
and ports and regarded the five percent duty on imports and
exports as unjustifiable. The Royal Governor noted that there
were "more good vessels belonging to the town of Boston
than to all Scotland and Ireland." He listed the Boston-owned
ships for the year 1698 as 25 of 100 to 300 tons; 38 of 100 tons
and under; brigantines, 50; ketches, 13; sloops, 67; a total of
193 vessels. Bellomont's data included the statement that Boston was exporting annually about 50,000 quintals of dried

fish (112 pounds to the quintal), three-quarters of which was shipped to Bilbao. Local merchants claimed for Boston four times the commerce of New York.

Piracy

A main object of the King in the appointment of Governor Bellomont was the suppression of piracy, which had assumed scandalous proportions along the Atlantic seaboard. The cry of Boston merchants against piracy had reached the ears of Parliament. Following the success of Dixey Bull, lesser pirates continued to operate in the waters outside Boston Harbor. A story is told by Cotton Mather of how the sailors of the *Antonio* seized the ship, in 1672, off the Spanish coast, put the captain adrift in a longboat, and appeared in Boston with the ship and cargo. The Charlestown merchants were inclined to take the part of these mutineers; but, after the master himself had arrived to denounce the ringleaders, they were executed.

On the complaint of a New London sea captain in 1685 that he had been chased by a pirate right up to the harbor's mouth, the General Court ordered an expedition against the suspected parties, one Veale and his partner Graham. The 40 volunteers called for were in no haste to present themselves, and the Court offered free plunder as an inducement to anyone who would enlist. The expedition failed to find the pirates and returned home empty handed. In cases where a pirate was caught, the set procedure was to hang him on Bird's Island, now known as Nix's Mate. One victim, the mate of Captain Nix, in his dying speech predicted that the place of his execution, and the island where sheep were once pastured, would disappear as a proof of his innocence. Indubitably, it is now submerged at high tide.

In the summer of 1687, rumors spread through the town that the ketch *Sparrow*, just arrived from Barbados and Eleuthera, had taken on pirates as passengers. A search revealed 900 "pieces of eight" and some plate in the chest of Mate Danson, the only man left of the 18, aside from the captain, who had started with the ship at Eleuthera, the rest having disembarked at points along the way. Danson admitted that he had served 4 years previously on a privateer, and that he had later plundered what he could from Arabs and Malabars on the Red Sea. But nothing came of the lengthy investigation. The plate and money were returned to Danson, and no case could be found against the captain and two other suspects arrested on board the *Sparrow*.

After these lesser swashbucklers came some of the pirates whose exploits under the "Jolly Roger" gave to that sinister emblem a sure place in the annals of adventure—Joseph Bradish, William Kidd, and the rest of their marauding company. The first of these, apprehended in 1699, was James Gillam, who killed Captain Edgecomb of the *Mocha,* a frigate owned by the East India Company. A tip to the authorities led to the discovery of Gillam's mare at an inn, and, although the next morning was Sunday, Governor Bellomont called his Council together, and published a proclamation offering 200 pieces of eight for the capture of Gillam. His friend, pirate Knot, under pressure, admitted that Gillam, alias "James Kelly" had recently been sheltered in his house and had gone thence to Charlestown. There Gillam was apprehended. He first denied his identity and swore that he had not come on Kidd's sloop from Madagascar; but, when Kidd's own men identified him, the game was up.

The Cambridge pirate, Joseph Bradish, ventured into the harbor in his ship *Adventure* in April 1699, and was soon lodged in the stone gaol, together with his companions. By his good fortune, the gaolkeeper, Caleb Roy, was his kinsman. Roy kept him locked up, but without irons, until June 25. On that day the door of the prison was found open, and Bradish with his friend, Tee Wetherly, had fled. The faithless gaoler was dismissed, and on October 24 the recaptured prisoners were again under lock, well secured in irons. The money and goods taken from Bradish amounted to £30,000, not including the jewels. Another apprehended freebooter, John Halsey, who had started as a privateer with a commission from Governor Dudley, had more than £50,000 and two shiploads of merchandise in his possession.

The case of Captain Kidd and Lord Bellomont presents a more confused picture as to the innocence or guilt of the accused. Captain Kidd is believed to have entered into a private agreement for the suppression of piracy with Lord Bellomont and others, before Bellomont assumed his duties as governor. Kidd sailed in 1697 to the Indian Ocean to intercept pirates there, and little was heard of him for over a year. That little was sufficient, however, to cause the English Government to order his arrest for piracy and to make Lord

Bellomont act with great caution to avoid appearing as an accomplice of the captain. Kidd was accused of turning pirate and capturing the *Quedah-Merchant,* a vessel belonging to a country friendly to the English. In 1699 Kidd arrived in Rhode Island and communicated through an agent with Lord Bellomont. The agent produced two French passes which Kidd claimed were found on the *Quedah-Merchant,* thereby making that vessel legitimate prey. Lord Bellomont presented the case to the Council in Boston and, with its approval, sent a letter to the adventurous captain in which he said ". . . you may safely come hither . . . I assure you on my word and honor I will nicely perform what I have promised. . . ." Kidd came to Boston and was summoned before the Council on July 3. He pleaded for time to write an account of his voyage, and was given until the next day. The time was extended to the second day, but he was still unprepared. Lord Bellomont thereupon produced papers from London ordering the arrest of the captain, and on July 7 he was committed to prison.

He was placed in irons weighing 16 pounds, and his gaoler given a 40-shilling increase in pay per week to insure Kidd's remaining in prison. The pirate's loot was as fabulous as his adventures. An inventory of finds upon one of his ships, the *Antonio,* included 1,111 ounces of gold, 2,353 ounces of silver, 17-3/8 ounces of precious stones, 57 bags of sugar, 41 bales of merchandise, 17 pieces of canvas; the booty upon his ship *Quedah-Merchant* in India was estimated as worth £30,000.

When Kidd requested Bellomont to send him under guard to get the *Quedah-Merchant,* which had been left in Hispanola, the Governor would not trust him; this although, if the ship were a lawful prize, the share of the Governor and his friends would have been four-fifths of the value, under the terms of the original agreement with Kidd. In February 1700, Kidd was sent to England on the frigate *Advice.* The following year he was tried for murder and piracy. Lord Bellomont, apparently convinced that Kidd had departed from his original orders, did not send the French passes to England, and Kidd was deprived of his most important evidence. Kidd was found guilty and hanged.

As the century closed, though harassed by pirates and enemy privateers, Boston owned a fleet of nearly 200 vessels. Borne by favoring winds or struggling with Atlantic gales, these ships were playthings of more than wind and weather.

They and their rich cargoes were at the center of opposing pressures, westward from the Lords of Trade in London, eastward from the merchants and traders of Boston. And so, with the resultant of great forces still undetermined, Boston's shipbuilders, shipowning merchants, sea captains, fishermen, and sailors moved on to a new era.

~~~~~~

CHAPTER II

PROVINCIAL PERIOD, 1700-1783

~~~~~~

The Waterfront

WHILE A CHORUS of ringing hammers mingled with the screech-
ing of winches and capstans, Boston's waterfront echoed to
the tune of a popular ditty:

> Wide awake, Down-Easters,
> No mistake, Down-Easters,
> Old Massachusetts will carry the day!

Hoisting sail and anchor, crews shouted the challenging
chanty, proud in the knowledge that Boston's seagoing vessels
numbered 194 against New York's 124; that her skilled craftsmen, plying their trade in the town's 14 shipyards, were
constantly augmenting the fleet; that her fishermen were
reaping generous bounties from the Banks of the North Atlantic. The doggerel boasted Boston's faith that wealth and
riches would be won by sailing ships to the southern and
middle Colonies, to Europe and Africa, to the sugar plantations of the West Indies and many another tropical isle.

Successive improvements made the waterfront and harbor
area ever more commodious. Seventy-eight wharves, in 1708,
jutted into the harbor along the Boston and Charlestown
waterfront. The most impressive, Long Wharf, undertaken
by Oliver Noyes, Anthony Stoddard, John George, Daniel
Oliver, and other businessmen, was completed in 1710 and
set a new standard in the Port's facilities. Enabling vessels
of any draught or burden to load and unload without lighterage, the finished structure extended from the bottom of King's
(now State) Street 800 feet out into the harbor. More than 30
years later, after the wharf was doubled in length, an English
traveler spoke in admiration of this engineering feat, "a fine
wharf about half a mile in length."

Another epochal event in the development of the harbor
was the establishment of Boston Light, the first lighthouse in
the Colonies. Headed by the Boston merchant, John George,
the enterprise had been set in motion by a petition addressed

to the General Court. The details of the sponsorship and completion of Boston Light appeared in the *Boston News-Letter* of September 17, 1716:

By virtue of an Act of Assembly made in the First Year of His Majesty's Reign, For Building and Maintaining a Lighthouse upon Great Brewster (called Beacon Island) at the Entrance of the Harbor of Boston, in order to prevent the loss of Lives and Estates of His Majesty's subjects; the said Light House has been built; And on Friday last the 14th Currant the Light was kindled, which will be very useful for all Vessels going out and coming into the harbor of Boston, or any other Harbors in the Massachusetts Bay . . .

Early pictures show that Boston's first lighthouse was a tall, commanding structure with a tower of rough-cut stone. The rays proceeded from wicks immersed in fish or whale oil within large lamps. The chief difficulties with this lighting device were excessive smokiness and the fire hazard from dripping oil. It is doubtful whether the first beacon in the harbor was even provided with reflectors. Maintenance costs for the lighthouse were derived from charges imposed on incoming and outgoing vessels; the fees were one penny per ton for ships in overseas trade, 5 shillings per year for fishing vessels and ships in local trade, and 2 shillings for coasters on clearance only.

The early annals of the lighthouse record the drownings of the first two keepers and the weathering of a severe gale. In November 1718, Captain George Worthylake was sailing with his wife and daughter near Noddle's Island, when a sudden wind capsized their boat, and all three perished in the choppy waters. Stirred by this accident, 13-year-old Benjamin Franklin wrote "The Lighthouse Tragedy." While the piteous fate of the Worthylakes was still fresh in the public mind, Robert Saunders, a sloop captain, was ordered to take over the duties of lighthouse keeper. Before his appointment had been officially confirmed, he too was drowned at sea. Five years later the Great Storm of 1723, regarded locally as perhaps the most violent in the century, lashed the Massachusetts coast. Blowing up on February 24, it raised a record 16-foot tide, which loosened the walls of the lighthouse.

The early keepers of the light performed the additional functions of pilot and collector of fees. The fourth lighthouse keeper, Mr. Ball, was sometimes too busy with his other duties, however, to be available for the pilotage of an incoming ship. Tricksters saw in this an opportunity of building up a profitable occupation for themselves. Watching for their chance, they would run their boats ahead of Mr. Ball's, represent themselves as pilots and collectors of imposts to some richly laden vessel, and pocket a handsome fee. Mr. Ball ended this practice by appearing before the General Court and having himself appointed official pilot of the Port. The Court assigned for his boats certain insignia which were not to be copied— broad red vanes for all craft authorized to conduct ships in and out of Boston Harbor.

The erection of Boston Light undoubtedly helped to prevent such serious wrecks at the entrance to the harbor as had happened in previous years. On the last day of January in 1702, the brigantine *Mary,* loaded with logwood from the Bay of Campeachy, had come to grief on the rocks off Marblehead. In November of the following year, the ship *John of Exon,* with wine and salt from Lisbon and Fayal, struggling homeward in mountainous seas, abruptly ended her voyage on the rocky teeth of Pemberton's (Georges) Island. Quickly filling, she sank almost within sight of the Port, her cargo a total loss. Shortly before the construction of the lighthouse, His Majesty's sloop *Hazard* was wrecked on the Cohasset Rocks. The manner in which the first lighthouse keepers stood by in emergencies was demonstrated in a terrific gale on September 15, 1727, when a North Carolina sloop grounded on Greater Brewster Spit. Captain John Hayes, the lightkeeper, pulled the sloop loose and piloted her safely into the inner harbor. Two sailors from the endangered vessel, following in the lighthouse boat, ran on the rocks near South Battery (Rowes Wharf), and the damage resulted in a sizable repair bill for the General Court.

The Town

Boston had become the principal mart of North America, and symbols of commercial activity marked every quarter of the town. Numerous countinghouses and warehouses shadowed the wharves. Scores of sumptuous mansions lined King's Street. The English traveler Joseph Bennett, who came to Boston in 1740, observed:

A great many good houses, and several fine streets little inferior to some of our best in London, the principal of which is King's Street; it runs upon a line from the end of the Long Wharf about a quarter of a mile, and at the upper end of it stands the Town House or Guild Hall, where the Governor meets the Council and House of Representatives; and the several Courts of Justice are held there also. And there are likewise walks for the merchants, where they meet every day at one o'clock, in imitation of the Exchange at London, which they call by the name of Royal Exchange too, round which there are several booksellers' shops; and there are four or five printing-houses, which have full employment in printing and reprinting books, of one sort or other, that are brought from England and other parts of Europe.

Life took on new style and color in Boston as the eighteenth century developed. The rich merchant families enjoyed ease and luxury with their Negro servants and fine coaches; they were the exclusive patrons of the tailoring, wig-making, and silversmithing establishments set up by indentured servants from the mother country. Scarlet uniforms, gold braid, powdered wigs, ruffles, and hoopskirts superseded the somber garb of the Puritan. The Royal Governors created an English atmosphere in the fashionable North End, where "How is this done at Court?" became the question on the lips of wealthy shipowners and their wives. The Boston traders enjoyed life to the full in their mansions at Boston and their roomy country places at Milton, Cambridge, or even in far-off Hopkinton. They derived pleasure from cruises along the coast and found relaxation in trout fishing. Owning the goods, the factories, and the ships, the mercantile "quality" expected and received deference from the lower classes. They were inclined to rule the community according to the law of the sea; but traders could not impose upon the populace the unquestioning obedience seamen gave to shipmasters.

Despite the more lavish mode of living, many of the older Puritan habits of conduct and demeanor remained rigidly in force in the early 1700's. Sunday travel and amusement were forbidden. Strolling along the streets and on the mall was taboo; all unnecessary public conversation was forbidden. Whatever orders the Boston merchants might give to the masters of their ships, ashore all showed uniform dignity, business integrity, and benevolence. To a man, the shipowners were staunch church members. Some outsiders, however, dared to question the sincerity of conviction beneath the Bible-reading and churchgoing of the Boston people. One Englishman even asserted that there were more "religious zealouts than honest men" in the town, and added that the citizens, "though they wear in their Faces the Innocence of Doves, you will find them in their Dealings as subtile as Serpents."

Peter Faneuil (1700-43), a leading merchant of the times and donor of Faneuil Hall, lived in a style that blazoned his lofty position in society. His magnificent estate was centrally located near King's Chapel, his appearances in public were in "the handsomest manner," his household furnishings revealed his refined bachelor tastes and included the latest European importations. He ordered from a London firm three gold watches, one dozen French knives, one dozen silver spoons, one dozen silver forks, "with three Prongs, with my arms cutt upon them," and half a dozen razors. His palate was never long neglected; tripe, bacon, and citron water were often on the list. Faneuil gravely asked Lane and Smithhurst of London to send him "the latest best book of the severall Sorts of Cookery, which pray let be of the largest character for the benefit of the maids reading." When he shipped a pair of gray horses to St. Kitts, the proceeds were returnable, partly in sweets for his sister Mary Ann, and partly in sugar and molasses. He bought a chariot and demanded from his London agent four horses "right good or none." A sybarite and yet an unstinting benefactor, his gifts to private charity were large, his public ones more lasting.

After a training in the best mercantile tradition of careful yet enterprising trade, Faneuil carried on a general commission and shipping business. Operating the vessels *Providence, Friends Adventure,* and *Rochelle,* he received goods from agents in Bristol, London, Bordeaux, Cadiz, Hamburg, and Kingston (Jamaica), and exported cargoes of rum, fish, produce, as well as newly constructed ships. Faneuil engaged extensively in coastal commerce, especially in New York. Whenever he ventured both ship and cargo, the enterprise was almost always shared with his brother, uncles, friends, or correspondents. He charged 5 percent for handling a consignment, whether it was fish, oil, or a bag of gold. An early advocate of modern business methods, Faneuil stationed near the fishing grounds agents who were constantly kept informed as to the price of fish in Massachusetts markets. His emissaries also acted as advertising men in extending his commercial connections. Seeking to protect his wealth from a fluctuating currency, Faneuil exhibited genuine business acumen in the purchase of Bank of England stock amounting to £14,800. His meticulous account books reveal that, though he dunned debtors with proper vigilance, he submitted reluctantly to the 2½ percent charged him by his friend and New York correspondent, Gulian Verplanck. His eyes always remained open to see that men everywhere "act the Honest and Just part by me." Making large profits from the sale of smuggled European commodities, Faneuil considered a Judge of the Admiralty who scanned too closely his shipping operations "a Ville man."

Charles Apthorp, Thomas Boylston, and Thomas Amory also stood out among the wealthy shipping merchants of the town. They operated vessels sailing to the Mediterranean, West Indies, and Europe, as well as fishing boats, whalers, and coasters. Supplementing their maritime activities, they underwrote insurance, speculated in land on a grand scale, and engaged in private banking. Some indication of the magnitude of Boston's trade was seen in the great fortunes amassed by these men. Through his maritime ventures, Thomas Boylston became one of the richest men in Massachusetts, with extensive possessions estimated in excess of £80,000. Charles Apthorp, when he died in 1758, aged 60, left to his heirs an estate of £50,000. Thomas Amory, rum-distiller, shipbuilder, bold and able trader, accumulated by shrewd management investments valued at £20,000, aside from a brewery, a wharf, a beautiful home, and large land holdings in Carolina and the Azores. Ever wary for his good name, he was explicit in his counsel to agents abroad. To his representative in the Azores he wrote: "Now if the above people send for these effects sell anything that belongs to me, or take money at interest on my account so that you continue to discharge them, for I had rather be a loser any way than have my reputation in question abroad."

Pillage on the High Seas

Much of the wealth of socially eminent Boston families was founded upon privateering—a form of pillage on the high seas honored in time of war. The news of Queen Anne's declaration of hostilities against France and Spain in 1702 brought a quick response from Boston. On June 20, the Boston ketch *Endeavor,* in command of Captain Thomas Dowling, sailed to warn the other Colonies along the coast; and within 10 days, the *Province,* in charge of Captain Cyprian Southack, was sent to spread anti-French propaganda among the Indians. The sloop *Seaflower* was taken into the Colonial service, equipped with 6 guns and a crew of 50 men, and employed to search for French privateers and to convoy coasting vessels into Boston Harbor. Coastguard service was maintained by Captain Andrew Wilson of the *Greyhound,* later used as an express boat. Captain Peter Lawrence obtained a commission from Governor Dudley, and set forth, with a crew of 40 men, on the Boston sloop *Charles* in search of prizes. He sent a number of captured vessels into the Port. Pleased with such booty, the Governor wrote on August 5, 1702: "We have three privateers with about 60 men each, who have last week sent in a French ketch and three sloops laden with fish and salt, taken upon the coast of Cape Sables, and we hope for better prizes by those that are abroad." Six weeks later he triumphantly announced:

I have sent out four small sloops with about 50 men each, who have in 30 days past brought in four sloops and five ships, the least ship above 100 tons, one of them a mast-man bound to Port Royal to load: the other are bankers, some with fish, others with salt, etc. for a fishing voyage, and the sloops are abroad again for one cruise more, by which time our seas will be governed by the northwest wind too hard to abide.

Boston privateers joined in the three naval expeditions against Port Royal, whose conquest finally placed Nova Scotia under the dominion of the British. The first expedition had decided at a council of war that its force was insufficient to take the Port. After ravaging the surrounding country in the summer of 1704, the fleet returned to Boston. The second Port Royal invasion was undertaken in May 1707, men-of-war and privateers sailing from Nantasket Roads. Reenforced by additional vessels from Boston, the armada reached the Port Royal basin the same month; they were repulsed in their attempt to storm the Port, and sailed for home on August 24. Three years later, after an expedition finally captured Port Royal, vast preparations were made for the invasion of Canada; Quebec, the key to the French possessions in America, was to be reduced by an English fleet. To accomplish this objective, Sir Hovenden Walker set sail for the St. Lawrence River on July 30, 1711, after having been charged with delaying unnecessarily in Boston Harbor. In a sudden gale followed by a thick fog, 8 of his vessels were dashed to pieces on the rocks of Cape Gaspé, and more than 800 men were lost. The privateers turned back without prize or plunder.

Yankee daring displayed in the seizure made by the *Bethel* was characteristic of Boston skippers during the troubled days of England's war with Spain (1739-48); the story of her adventure was only one of many similar tales of ships whose prows swept past the headland of Nantasket bound for Europe or southern ports. Excitement touched the crew of the *Bethel,* out of Boston for Europe, as she approached the Azores in the dusk of a June day in 1748. The *Bethel,* carrying a Colonial letter-of-marque, was authorized to capture any Spanish vessel that came into view, and hopes of sighting a prize ran high. When the lookout's jubilant shout announced a sail ahead, the *Bethel* packed on canvas. The stranger tacked, as though preparing to fight, but unfalteringly the Boston vessel drove toward her. When the prey took to flight, Captain Isaac Freeman, scanning the pursued vessel in the failing light, saw that she was armed with 24 guns. Since the *Bethel* carried only 14 guns, besides 6 dummy ones of wood, Freeman ordered his crew of about 38 on deck, and instructed them, in order to hide the real number of fighting men, to rig sham figures with their spare clothing. When darkness fell, lanterns were hoisted in all parts of the *Bethel,* and she closed in on the fugitive. "After a serenade of French horns and trumpets," stated Freeman in a letter to Messrs. Quincy and Jackson, part owners of the privateer,

we demanded from whence she came and whither bound. When, after a few equivocations, . . . she announced she was from Havana for Cadiz . . . we gave them a hearty cheer, and ordered . . . her captain on board immediately. He begged we would tarry till morning . . . but we threatening him with a broadside which he much feared, he complied. By daylight we had the last of the prisoners secured, (there were 110 of them) who were ready to hang themselves on sight of our six wooden guns, and scarce men enough to hoist topsails.

The *Boston Evening Post* of August 29, 1748, carried the full story of the capture and summed up the incident by saying: "the Spanish Don may truly be said to have been jockey'd out of a prize worth the best part of an hundred Pounds Sterling."

A line of demarcation between legitimate privateering and piracy was difficult to establish. The notorious John Quelch, hanged in Boston, June 30, 1704, with five of his men, had considered himself a privateer while attacking Portuguese commerce off Brazil. Upon arriving at Marblehead he learned of the treaty of peace which made his acts piratical. The last words of Quelch on the execution stage must have pleased the Puritan ministers consoling his soul. "I am not afraid of Death, I am not afraid of the Gallows, but I am afraid of what follows; I am afraid of a Great God, and a Judgment to Come." Two decades later Boston was afforded another mass hanging, when a group of young men sailed a captured pirate ship into the harbor on May 3, 1724. They had been impressed into piracy along the Newfoundland Banks, but overpowered the pirate crew and killed the leader, John Phillips, and some of his gang. In due course, six of the pirates were condemned to death. Bills for the hanging of the two freebooters, Archer and White, on June 2, 1724, provided not only for all expenses connected with digging the graves and burying the dead, but even for the cost of "cheering drams" after the work of the executioners had been finished. An especially vicious ravager of the sea, surnamed Fly, had his neck stretched with great pomp in Boston in 1726. A contemporary gravely observed that, on the following lecture day, Dr. Cotton Mather in giving out the Sixteenth Psalm did not mention Fly "otherwise than in a bold scorn" by reading the line, "My lips their name shall *Fly*." It is not to be doubted that there were many substantial merchants in Dr. Mather's congregation who regretted the passing of Fly, for pirates were good customers and paid in silver and coin.

Ships and Shipyards

During the first half of the eighteenth century, while piracy in the Atlantic was slowly passing into romantic memory and the sea lanes were becoming comparatively safe, Boston experienced a "golden age" of shipbuilding. Twenty-one ships of an aggregate tonnage of 1,530 were launched from Boston in 1710, almost half of the entire Province's output of 56 ships, which weighed 3,720 tons. Thirteen years later, 700 vessels slid down the ways of New England shipyards, the greater portion of which were probably fitted in Boston. Graceful and swift-sailing, the first Boston schooner was completed in 1716; a pronounced departure from the traditional square-rigged type, the schooner came into great favor among Boston seafarers engaged in the carrying trade. In a single year, the Province as a whole constructed 150 ships aggregating 6,000 tons, principally for foreign sale, and in 1720 it owned approximately 190 sailing and 150 fishing boats. In 1741, John Oldmixon, in the second edition of his book, *The British Empire in America*, wrote that there were "at one and the same time, upon the stocks in Boston, forty top-sail vessels, measuring about 7,000 tons."

Changing conditions of ocean trade made for the increased size of ships. Earlier commerce had consisted of mixed cargoes, sent in small consignments, and for this purpose a vessel of less than 100 tons was most convenient. In 1726, however, Thomas Amory, in noting the requirements of advancing

business, spoke of a demand for a larger type of merchant
ship. Jealous of the growing dimensions of Massachusetts
ships, Governor Wentworth of New Hampshire reported to
the Lords of Trade in London in 1724 that his unruly neighbors along the Massachusetts coast were building a veritable
leviathan of 1,000 tons, for use in the contraband lumber trade
to Spain or Portugal. Either this complaint exaggerated the
facts or the ambitious builders abandoned their project, for
the largest ship built for some time in the Massachusetts
Colony, a 500-ton vessel, was completed at Mr. Clark's shipyard in the North End of Boston in the fall of 1732. The pre-
ponderance of clearances over entrances for the Port of Boston
in the year 1748 was one indication of a policy on the part
of merchants and sea captains to sell smaller craft in some
foreign port at the end of the voyage, bringing back only the
larger vessels. Ships, in fact, comprised one of the chief items
of Boston's trade with England and her colonial possessions.

Already in the winter of 1724-25 London shipwrights had
become vocal in protest against the growing competition of
the Massachusetts builders. Shipbuilding, according to the
official statement of the Lords of Trade issued in 1721, was
the most important and best managed among the many profitable lines of manufacture in Boston. Pointing out that the
Massachusetts rate of construction was ruinous to them, the
London people called for drastic limitations on the size of
ships built in the Colonies. They realized that vessels could
be produced in Boston and neighboring coastal towns for
about £8 per ton, while in England the cost was between
£15 and £16 per ton. Although crusty protectionists, the Lords
of Trade were unable to answer the prayers of their peti-
tioners, and, despite recurrent periods of inactivity, Massachusetts shipbuilding continued in a fairly prosperous condition. In Boston, however, ship construction declined after
1741, and only 15 vessels were launched from the town's yards
in 1749.

Boston capital probably supplied the driving power behind
the shipbuilding industry, even after the bulk of operations
had been transferred to smaller shipyards along the coast,
where the absence of rigid inspection permitted the use of
inferior materials, and where mechanics, fishermen, and seamen were available for the workmanship and manning of the
vessels. As the need for heavy timber pushed the center of
shipbuilding farther and farther up the Bay, much of the

shipping under Boston registry was built along the north-eastern shore of Massachusetts and in New Hampshire and Maine. Yards along the Piscataqua River brought out no less than 200 vessels a year. Shipbuilders sometimes sent gangs of shipwrights into forests 7 and 8 miles from the water, where they constructed craft of 100 tons and more. In the winter, these vessels were mounted on sledges and dragged by a team of as many as 200 oxen to the frozen surface of a navigable stream, down which they were towed to the sea when the ice melted.

The "Mosquito" Fleet

Such small vessels trading along the southern coast in the ports of New York, Pennsylvania, Maryland, Virginia, and the Carolinas, and as far north as Canada, effectively riddled the Navigation Acts and brought to Boston such varied and substantial maritime commerce that Edmund Burke aptly called them "the Dutch of America." Augmented by cockleshell fishing smacks of 30 to 40 tons, which were forced off the Banks by winter storms, this "mosquito" fleet loaded its holds with rum, flour, fish, beef, port, European products, whale oil, horses, livestock, salt, sugar, hats, cloth, and ironware and went on peddling trips to the South, returning with tobacco, grain, and naval stores of pitch and tar. During the 3-year interval from June 4, 1714 to June 4, 1717, Boston clearances to other seaports in America numbered 390, while for about an equal length of time New York's departures amounted to less than half of the Boston tonnage.

When it promised profitable returns, no voyage appeared too difficult or hazardous to these coastwise traders. In 1729, an exploratory cruise under Captain Henry Atkins, beyond the Canadian Maritime Provinces to Labrador's frozen wastes, extended Boston's commerce to "the Eskimeaux coast." Touching the mainland at several points near Davis' Inlet in his sturdy ship, the *Whale,* Captain Atkins found an abundance of fish and seal and great forests of pine, alder, birch, and hazel. The natives encountered near the shore were terrified at the sight of the large vessel, and only after considerable reassurance was Atkins able to bargain with them. They dressed in beaver and seal skins, and their ignorance of the value of these pelts convinced him that they had never bartered with agents of the French of Hudson Bay posts. At one place he exchanged files, knives, and other small articles amounting to 10 shillings for a quantity of whalebone which brought £120 sterling in Boston. This pioneering trip established a lucrative commerce with the Belle Isle Straits, from which Boston was soon importing large cargoes of fish and furs.

While a great number of Boston mariners doubtless made it a point to avoid the observant eyes of the customs officials, sparse and scattered figures give an approximate picture of the coastwise trade. In the year 1720, according to the *Boston Gazette,* departures outnumbered arrivals 368 to 277. Trade with the Southern Colonies was more than twice as large as that with the Canadian Provinces. Boston vessels sailing to nearby New Hampshire, Rhode Island, and Connecticut comprised two-thirds of the total outgoing shipping. Receiving English goods and paying with fish and lumber, New Hampshire alone in 1725, had a coastal traffic with Boston equal to well over £5,000. The week of May 8-14, 1741, was a busy one for the import of foodstuffs into the town of Boston. In 7 days her wharves received from incoming vessels 6,650 bushels of corn, 200 bushels of peas, 180 bushels of beans, 534 bushels of flour, 291 barrels of beef, 278 barrels of pork, and 79 bushels of rice. In 1760, entrances into the Port of Boston from other North American towns had increased to 441, while the clearances to coastwise points had advanced to 357. By this date, shipping to the Canadian Provinces, which totaled 165 arrivals and 123 departures, had surpassed by 50 percent traffic to the Southern Colonies. This increasingly important Canadian trade almost equalled the established routes with the New England towns, from which, in 1760, 163 vessels dropped anchor in Boston, and to which 145 departed. With the neighboring emporium of New York, Boston's direct commerce was still small in that year, only 8 vessels entering, and 9 clearing. Indicating a rapid gain during the preceding 40 years, Boston's coastwise traffic in 1760 reached the grand total of 798 voyages.

The Harvest of the Sea

Since the slaves in the southern plantations and the West Indies consumed ever-increasing quantities of fish, coastal Massachusetts, in an effort to maintain a supply of the commodity, took to reaping the rich harvest of the sea on a vast scale. As early as 1636, the sacred cod had been officially declared the symbol of Massachusetts, and, by 1700, dried codfish had become the mainstay of Boston's export commerce. Daniel Neal in the *History of New England,* written in London in 1720, states that Boston merchants export "about 100,000 Quintals of dried Cod-fish yearly, which they send to Portugal, Spain and the Ports of Italy, the Returns for which . . . may amount to the Value of about 80,000 l. [pounds] annually." Growing rapidly, the fisheries along the coast were producing for export 10 years later 230,000 quintals of dried fish, which sold in southern Europe for about 138,000 pounds sterling. Some 400 Massachusetts vessels, averaging 40 tons and a crew of 7, serviced the codfisheries alone. For the curing of the fish, each boat required three or four additional men on shore. Although Boston fishermen were credited with only 30 percent of the total annual catch, their port served as the main distributing center for the whole New England fishing fleet.

Five trips were made every year by the Boston fishing fleet; the first to Sable Island early in March; the second to Brown's Bank for spring fish; the third and fourth to Georges' Bank, where large schools spawned during the summer; and the fifth trip to Sable Island again for winter cod. To prevent fishermen from deserting their vessels, the General Court, in 1755, enacted a law which provided that no member of a fishing crew could demand his share of the profits until the contracted term of service had been completed. Faring on a diet of salt port, biscuits, and rum, hardy Massachusetts fishermen worked "on their own hook," the individual's catch determining his portion of the receipts. Although mackerel and herring, at first used for bait, soon found a ready market in the West Indies, the highest prices were commanded by the silvery cod. To encourage the codfisheries, Boston citizens, according to the *Boston Evening Post,* February 18, 1754, offered to award $60 to the vessel returning with the largest catch in proportion to the size of the crew, $50 as a second prize, and $40 to the third-place winner.

Next to the codfisheries in economic importance, the Massachusetts whaling industry played a prominent role in Boston's shipping activities. As the whale supplied fuel for more and more lamps in Europe, local merchants foresaw the possibilities of handsome profits to be derived from purchasing whale oil at nearby ports, arranging for delivery in Boston, and then shipping it to London and other European markets. Eager to monopolize the available supply, agents were dispatched posthaste to Nantucket, already famed for its intrepid whalers, and in the year 1745 they obtained 10,000 barrels of oil for Boston's export. As early as 1720, a direct shipment to London of Nantucket oil cleared Boston with a quaint bill of lading:

Shipped by the grace of God, in good order and well conditioned, by Paul Starbuck, in the good ship called the *Hanover*, whereof is master under God for the present voyage, William Chadder and now riding in the harbour of Boston, and by God's grace bound for London; to say:—Six barrels of traine oyle, being on the proper account & risque of Nathaniel Starbuck, of Nantucket, and goes consigned to Richard Partridge merchant in London. Being marked & numbered as in the margin & to be delivered in like good order & well conditioned at the aforesaid port of London (The dangers of the sea only excepted) unto Richard Partridge aforesaid or to his assignees, He or they paying Freight for said goods, at the rate of fifty shillings per tonn, with primage & average accustomed.

In witness whereof the said Master or Purser of said Ship hath affirmed to Two Bills of Lading all of this Tener and date, one of which two Bills being Accomplished, the other to stand void.

And so God send the Good Ship to her desired Port in safety. Amen!

Articles & Contents unknown to—(signed) William Chadder

Date at Boston the 7th 4th mo. 1720.

Although steady profits from the far less hazardous freighting of oil proved more attractive than whaling itself to Boston seamen, attempts to develop a local whaling fleet met with a fair degree of success. Encouraging the industry, the *Boston News-Letter* in July 1737, announced that "Capt. Atherton Hough took a whale 'in the Straits' ", and in a later issue stated that "there is good prospect of success in the whale fishery to Greenland this year for several vessels are come in early deeply laden and others expected." At no time, however, did the number of Boston whalers operating in northern and southern waters exceed 20. Averaging 100 tons in size and carrying a crew of 12, these ships accounted for an annual take of 1,800 barrels of spermaceti and 600 barrels of whale oil.

One of the whalers, returning to Boston in 1766, reported a harrowing variation of the Biblical Jonah story:

Capt. Clark, on Thursday Morning last discovering a Spermaceti Whale, near George's Banks, mann'd his Boat, and gave Chace to her, & she coming up with her Jaws against the Bow of the Boat struck it with such Violence that it threw a Son of the Captain's; (who was forward ready with his Lance) a considerable Height from the Boat, and when he fell the Whale turned with her devouring Jaws opened, and caught him: He was heard to scream, when she closed her Jaws, and part of his Body was seen out of her Mouth, when she turned, and went off.

Ocean Trade and Travel

Boston commercial voyages were often so incalculable in their range, so diverse in their turnings and windings, that one may question whether the itinerary was really fixed at the time of departure. If the Boston captain returned with the ship in which he had embarked, his wines from Madeira, Fayal, and the Canaries, his sugar, molasses, and often specie from the West Indies were a clear indication that he had traveled wide, and that trading had been good. Another variation of successful voyaging was the return of the captain as a passenger, having sold both ship and cargo in England. In such a case, he brought home either the cash proceeds of the sale, or a shipment of English manufactured goods purchased with the funds derived from the sale of ship and cargo. Maritime records showed that in the 3 years from June 4, 1714 to June 4, 1717, a total of 1,267 foreign-bound vessels sailed out through the Narrows of Boston Harbor—518 for the West Indies, 25 for the Bay of Campeachy, 58 for "foreign plantations," 45 for Newfoundland, 43 for Europe, 34 for Madeira, the Azores, etc., 143 for Great Britain, 390 for the English colonies of North America, and 11 for unknown ports. These outgoing ships aggregated nearly 63,000 tons, and employed between 8,000 and 9,000 seamen. While these 1,267 vessels departed from Boston, only 232 set sail from the rival port of Salem.

Relatively few changes took place in Boston's import trade between 1717 and 1770. From the Canary Islands, the Iberian Peninsula, and Southern France came ever larger cargoes of salt, wine, brandy, fruit, oil, silk, lace, and fine linens. As Boston vessels more frequently took a southerly course to Mediterranean ports-of-call, the Colony of Massachusetts purchased proportionately less from the mother country. While in 1700 London had supplied a major part of the shipments which weighted the holds of Boston-bound vessels, by 1769 only two-fifths of New England's imports came from England. Among the products most frequently sent by England were linens, serges, bays, kerseys, and stockings. In addition, the mother country sent ship rigging, the best grade of refined sugar, lead, paper, and glass.

The Province of Massachusetts enjoyed an ever-growing export trade. The best grade of packed codfish, "dunfish,"— mellowed by alternate burying and drying—commanded a high price in the Catholic countries of Portugal, Spain, and France. The principal Massachusetts exports in 1763, shipped largely from Boston, were codfish valued at £100,000; whale and cod oil £127,500; whalebone, £8,450; pickled mackerel and shad, £15,000; masts, boards, staves, shingles, £75,000; ships—70 sail at £700—£49,000; naval stores, £600; potash, £35,000; horses and livestock, £37,000; pickled beef and pork, £28,500; beeswax and sundries, £9,000. Ten years later, New England as a whole was credited with exporting 911,000 gallons of rum, of which 419,000 gallons went to Africa, 361,000 gallons to Quebec, and 111,000 gallons to Newfoundland.

Ocean travel in Boston's early shipping days was a dangerous undertaking, and only urgent business forced landsmen to entrust their lives and comfort to the Atlantic. The price of passage to Europe before 1700 was quoted at £5 and this moderate figure proved a poor bargain for the accommodations offered during the month-long voyage. Nevertheless, almost every ship that made the crossing carried merchants, Government officials, military men, clergymen, and scholars. Few of the passengers were prominent; only 18 of them were mentioned by name in the Boston newspapers of 1737.

What the trans-Atlantic traveler could sometimes expect may be learned from the diary of Jacob Bailey, a graduate divinity student who sailed from Boston for London in 1760. Arriving on board, he found himself

In the midst of a most horrid confusion. The deck was crowded full of men, and the boatswain's shrill whistle, with the swearing and hallooing of the petty officers, almost stunned my ears. I could find no retreat from this dismal hubbub, but was obliged to continue jostling among the crowd above an hour before I could find anybody at leisure to direct me. (. . A young gentleman) invited me down between decks . . .I . . . followed him down a ladder into a dark and dismal region, where the fumes of pitch, bilge water, and other kinds of nastiness almost suffocated me in a minute. . . . We entered a small apartment, hung round with damp and greasy canvas, which made, on every hand, a most gloomy and frightful appearance. In the middle stood a table of pine, varnished over with nasty slime, furnished with a bottle of rum and an old tin mug with a hundred and fifty bruises and several holes, through which the liquor poured in as many streams. This was quickly filled with toddy and as speedily emptied by two or three companions who presently joined us in this doleful retreat. . . . This detestable apartment was allotted by the Captain to be the place of my habitation during the voyage!

The company was in keeping with the surroundings. The "young gentleman" who had invited Bailey "had fled his native country on account of a young lady to whom he was engaged." Everyone seemed to swear roundly, especially one swashbuckler, described as "the greatest champion of profaneness that ever fell under my notice," continually "roaring out a tumultuous volley of stormy oaths and imprecations." Another member of the company, a "lieutenant of marines . . . distinguished himself by the quantities of liquor he poured down his throat."

A boy was called to bring supper.

Nothing in human shape did I ever see before so loathsome and nasty. He had on his body a fragment only of a check shirt, his bosom was all naked and greasy, over his shoulders hung a bundle of woolen rags which reached in strings almost down to his feet, and the whole composition was curiously adorned with little shining animals.

The cuisine was correspondingly elegant:

beef and onions, bread and potatoes, minced and stewed together, then served up with its broth in a wooden tub, the half of a quarter cask. The table was furnished with two pewter plates, the half of one was melted away, and the other, full of holes, was more weather-beaten than the sides of the ship; one knife with a bone handle, one fork with a broken tine, half a metal spoon and another, taken at Quebec, with part of the bowl cut off.

The sleeping accommodations consisted of

a row of greasy canvas bags, hanging overhead by the beams . . . Into one of them it was proposed that I should get, in order to sleep, but it was with the utmost difficulty I prevented myself from falling over on the other side.

Molasses

Engaging more than one-half of Boston's foreign shipping, the West Indies route provided the most profitable market for local merchants. During a 3-year period beginning June 4, 1714, clearances of barks, sloops, and other vessels from Boston for the West Indies numbered 518, most of them bound for the British islands. Commerce, however, with the Spanish, Dutch, and French possessions in the Caribbean assumed increasing proportions after the Peace of Utrecht in 1714. Seeking to protect the native brandy industry, the French Monarchy had decreed that no rum could be brought into the country, and in order to block her enemies' food supply she forbade the reexport of raw sugar. Since sugar found a poor demand in France, its price in the French West Indies tumbled downward, and the French planters were willing to dispose of their molasses at half the exchange rate received in the British islands. Ever alert for the ingredients of rum manufacture and for new areas in which to unload their local products, Boston ships swarmed to the French islands. There the planters, discovering that their molasses could be exchanged for good lumber, horses, oxen, and provisions, increased their acreage by leaps and bounds until production reached 122,500 hogsheads of sugar in 1744, as compared with 60,950 hogsheads produced in the British islands. In 1731 Boston had imported 20,000 hogsheads of French molasses, which were distilled into 1,260,000 gallons of rum, selling for 2 shillings per gallon.

The famous Molasses Act of 1733 was Parliament's answer to the angry protests of the British West Indies planters, who demanded legislative protection from the large importations of "foreign molasses" into the Northern Colonies. Prohibitive duties of ninepence per gallon were imposed on rum and spirits, sixpence per gallon on molasses and syrups, and five-pence per gallon on sugar, when these commodities were imported from other than the English West Indies. Rigidly enforced, this act would have destroyed Boston's rum trade, injured her fisheries, and cut off her indispensable source of specie in the French islands. After vain appeals by the local merchants, the act was completely ignored, and molasses flowed into Boston with no duties paid. This illegal commerce reached unprecedented heights after 1740, when the entire production of the British West Indies amounted to only one-eighth of the molasses brought into American ports. During King George's War (1744-48), Boston ships, together with those from other Colonial towns, carried on so extensive a trade in the Caribbean with England's enemy that they constituted a major cause for the failure of British naval operations in that area. While Boston privateers were fighting to oust the French from Canada, local merchants were engaged in supplying fully the trade demands of the French in the West Indies.

Boston ships of the West Indies route operated in a complicated manner. The vessels were often compelled to take roundabout trips before they could obtain a cargo which would find a ready market in Boston. One local ship of 40 tons went to Rhode Island, Barbados, Guinea, back to the Barbados, and then to Antigua before returning home. Another record of a chartered vessel provided for a 10- to 12-month voyage, evidently with the intention of doing a seagoing huckstering business. The means employed in circumventing British restrictions in the West Indies spoke well for the daring and ingenuity of the smugglers. One picturesque device was the "Jew's Raft," which consisted of timbers, chained together in the rough outline of a vessel. Exempted from British restrictions on ships, these suicidal contrivances were sailed to the West Indies by their reckless crews. Duties were often evaded directly from Boston through connivance with the local customs officers and the port officials of the French West Indies. In wartime, ships known as "flags of truce" carried contraband. A vessel of this type would sail from Boston, carrying a few prisoners for legitimate exchange, but as soon as a French Indies port was reached, a valuable cargo of molasses would be poured into her hold.

The Molasses Act proved a grave British blunder, for because of it the smuggling of contraband lost all taint of illegitimacy and acquired a respectable status in Boston. The growing sentiment that every merchant had a natural right to exchange his property with whom he pleased had taken root, and, when in 1756 British revenue cutters were pressed into service to enforce the act, the erstwhile evader became the pillar of commercial propriety. His political strength later gave him a position of dominance in Boston.

British naval commanders were empowered to serve as customs officers after 1763 and were permitted to retain the usual percentage of profits from seizures. When this measure failed to put a stop to smuggling, English port officers began to use writs of assistance—extraordinary search warrants which authorized the holder to seize suspected goods anywhere and *without notice,* even to break into homes to search for contraband. In 1760-61 vigorous protests had been lodged against the legality of the writs, on the ground that they were tyrannical. Although the Boston people were ably represented by James Otis, a young attorney, the Colonial Court, headed by Thomas Hutchinson, Lieutenant-Governor of the Colony, declared the writs legal according to an act of Parliament. Moreover, Governor Bernard claimed that Massachusetts opposed them because she wished to engage in the French West Indies trade as freely as did the charter colonies of Rhode Island and Connecticut, where the customs house officials "did virtually nothing to enforce the law."

Despite the zealous attempt at enforcement of the Molasses Act by British patrols along the coast, Boston smugglers, with the help of every dodge that Yankee cunning could invent, swept merrily on to the French West Indies. Cargoes were landed in the dead of night at isolated coves, and then hauled into Boston by horse and team. From the neutral ports of St. Eustatius and Monte Cristi, where as many as 50 Boston vessels dropped anchor at the same time, came hold after hold of French sugar and molasses. Other Boston sloops stopped at the French port of New Orleans for contraband cargo. Two-thirds of the molasses that entered the Port of Boston in 1760 could be traced to French origin, and in the following year this illicit flood had grown to three-quarters of the total import.

The Boycotts

Well aware of the mounting loss of revenue occasioned by the persistent smuggling of the Boston traders, George Grenville, head of the Crown's Cabinet, and an advocate of colonial participation in expenses of British Empire defense, decided to adopt more intelligent measures. His Sugar Act of 1764 cut the molasses duty by one-half, to threepence a gallon, but, on the other hand, implemented the law by providing that all cases arising under a writ might be tried in any vice-admiralty court in America—even in Canada—since Grenville well knew that no Colonial jury would ever convict in a smuggling trial. The lowered tax was still a great concession to the West Indies traders, and in itself it did not raise as much resentment as was created by the methods adopted to enforce the collections. Rewards were offered to informers, ships were boarded and searched, homes and warehouses were ransacked. The easygoing ways of the men in the West Indies trade were proscribed to an extent that made profit well-nigh impossible.

When the odious Stamp Act was passed a year later, the principal merchants of Boston agreed to import no more manufactures from England, and even countermanded orders already sent over. Like the heaping of insult upon injury, the new tax kindled their smoldering resentment into a flaming outburst of opposition. On the night of August 7, 1765, under the cry of "freedom from revenue taxation and imperial control of justice," milling crowds of Boston patriots and roisterers hanged in effigy Andrew Oliver, the Massachusetts collector, destroyed his home, and tore down his office. When the first of November arrived, not a stamp was offered for sale, since no royal official could enforce the act. John Hancock sent the *Boston Packet* to London without stamped clearances, but with a certificate from Boston port officers that no stamps could be procured within their jurisdiction. Arriving in the

Thames, she passed the customs without delay. The following year, on the petition of London merchants, the law was repealed.

In 1767, guided by the new ministry of Charles Townshend, England's colonial policy underwent a drastic revision, disastrous for the Colonies. The Townshend Acts levied new import duties on wine, oil, glass, paper, paint, lead, and tea. The merchants called for a non-importation policy. The Massachusetts Assembly was not slow to protest the duties and called upon all the Colonies for united action. Their activities caused Governor Bernard, in compliance with Royal instructions, to dissolve the General Court for its scornful insolence. The customs service was strengthened by placing a board of commissioners in the colonial ports. The Boston commissioners, now that molasses smuggling had ceased with the reduction of the duty to one penny a gallon, attempted to stop the illicit trade in Madeira wine, which had increased to avoid the excessive impost of £7 a ton. They met with the organized resistance of 98 Boston merchants. The climax came when a mob interfered with the seizure of a ship belonging to John Hancock. In the rioting that followed, the commissioners were forced to flee to the fort on Castle Island, from which they appealed to Admiral Hood at Halifax for protection. Obviously a dangerous situation had developed; on September 28, 1768, a thousand British regulars landed in Boston.

The Townshend Acts, with the exception of the duty on tea, were repealed in 1770. Since the principle of taxation remained, the merchants were not wholly appeased, but they attempted to carry on in the usual trade channels. The period of non-importation had had an adverse effect on Boston's foreign trade and placed her in a position inferior to both New York and Philadelphia. Trade with Great Britain and Ireland was still strong, with ship chandlery, drugs, woolen materials, and tea among the leading imports and whaling products, pearl ash and potash, hides, fur, and lumber figuring prominently in the exports. The Mediterranean and African trades dropped to a low point when a total of only 13 entries and 13 clearances were recorded in 1773 for both areas together. The West Indies trade was still Boston's best, leading in the importation of salt and molasses but running below rival ports in some exports. In the coasting trade, Boston was still supreme, the leading items including shoes, rum, and food products.

Tea and a Party

As long as the price of tea continued to be comparatively low, it was consumed duty-paid. But when the price advanced sharply in 1771, the smuggling of Dutch tea became immensely profitable. The contraband was concealed in rice barrels, in wine casks, in every possible receptacle. Despite constant seizures and penalties and Boston's standing as the leading importer of dutiable tea, within a year much of the tea drunk in Boston was of Dutch origin. In a blundering attempt to destroy Dutch competition, Parliament decided in 1773 to provide Boston with cheaper tea by permitting the East India Company to export tea directly from India, thus avoiding the payment of a tax in England. The immediate effect of this new policy was to drive Boston merchants, who saw their smuggling profits endangered, into the ranks of the radicals; at fiery mass meetings they urged the people to boycott "monopolized" tea. Nevertheless, the cargoes continued to be shipped to Boston.

The dumping of the tea into Boston Harbor has become a famous incident in American history. On Sunday, November 28, 1773, the tea ship *Dartmouth* joined shortly afterward by the *Eleanor* and the *Beaver,* had moored at Griffin's Wharf. Refusing to permit the vessels to unload their tea, the agitators placed them under a citizen guard. If the tea was not unloaded in 20 days it would be taken over by the collector of customs, a situation desired by neither the merchants nor the importer. The owner of the *Dartmouth* was urgently requested to return his ship to London, for the Boston merchants anxiously desired a peaceful removal of this threat to their prosperous trade; but the customs officials refused to issue clearance papers. On the nineteenth day, after the arrival of the ships, December 16, 1773, confronted with the possibility that the tea would be landed on the morrow, 7,000 citizens gathered at the largest protest meeting hitherto held in Boston. After listening to the bitter denunciations which poured from the lips of Samuel Adams, Josiah Quincy, Jr., and other merchants, and after learning that Governor Hutchinson had refused a permit for clearance, the aroused multitude advanced upon the waterfront. There a patriotic band of Sons of Liberty and traders, covered with Indian war-paint and brandishing tomahawks, staged the Boston Tea Party. A vast assemblage, silhouetted in the moonlight, watched in solemn silence,

View of Boston Harbor and British war ships landing their troops in 1768. Line engraving by Paul Revere. *Courtesy of the Society for the Preservation of New England Antiquities.*

The Province Sloop passing Boston Light. *Courtesy of the
Mariners' Museum, Newport News, Virginia.*

while the "Mohawks" unsealed the hatches and piled the tea on deck. Three hundred and forty-two chests were ripped open, dumped overboard, and carried by the wind and the tide to every part of the harbor.

Thoroughly aroused, England retaliated with the Boston Port Bill, which went into effect on June 1, 1774. The act provided "for discontinuing the lading and shipping of goods, wares, and merchandizes, at Boston or the harbour thereof, and for the removal of the custom house with its dependencies, to the town of Salem" until compensation should be made to the East India Company. Boston was designated as the rendezvous of all British men-of-war in American waters, and seaborne commerce came to a standstill. The good citizens of Salem, however, declined to take advantage of a situation that would have greatly increased their wealth. Marblehead, which had been declared the major Massachusetts port, graciously permitted Boston merchants to enjoy the free use of its wharves and storehouses, while its inhabitants offered to load and unload goods consigned to Boston.

Revolution and Ruin

The year 1775 found Boston a town of despair. All her privileges as a seaport had been annulled, her warehouses emptied; her ships and workers were idle, her foreign trade throttled. Every means of water communication, even with Charlestown and Dorchester, had been severed. In the face of a serious shortage of commodities and the ominous prospect of war, her population had begun to scatter. An 11-month siege had reduced the town to about 6,000 inhabitants, food was almost unobtainable, and the cost of living doubled. Finding it impossible to force payment from debtors by law, merchants closed their shops. Although privateering on a grand scale was carried on by vessels from less beleaguered ports, not a Boston boat moved, not a raft or a lighter was allowed to approach the town with merchandise. Even after the British withdrawal on March 17, 1776, conditions were desperate, for along with General Howe went several hundred Tories and a large portion of Boston's wealth.

Boston's business was slow to revive. The first efforts were concentrated on the outfitting of privateers; 365 vessels were commissioned during the Revolution, and in some cases fortunes were made. By 1777 Boston privateers had roamed the coast from the British provinces in the north to the West

Indies in the south, had crossed the ocean and plundered British vessels on the coasts of Spain, France, and England. Upon a petition to the Council, which had taken over the duties of the Governor, the theoretical embargo on all vessels except those engaged in fishing was lifted, and permission for a restricted export was granted. Articles for trade, however, were limited to lumber, dry and pickled fish, and the cargoes of captured vessels. Three types of commercial venture could be attempted from Boston: by unarmed merchantmen on coastwise and West India voyages, by armed letter-of-marque vessels, and by ships owned or chartered by the State. Under letter-of-marque commissions, cargoes of rice picked up at the Carolinas, or tobacco at Virginia were traded with Spain, France, and their possessions for salt, sugar, naval stores, clothing and brandy. No embargo hindered the official State ships, which were dispatched at will to obtain necessities of life, but the harassing British cruisers made their voyages so precarious that the few returning vessels hardly alleviated the general depression.

As the War shifted south, normal commercial activities increased and more vessels entered and sailed from Boston than from any other Massachusetts port. In fact, Boston became the point of departure for most of the Cape Cod ships, as well as those of Maine and of states as far to the south as Virginia. Yet as late as 1780 the town continued to feel the distress; there was nothing to export, import credit was strained, and prices were rising continually. While the cost of outfitting a privateer was great, the chances of success had become slight; strongly convoyed British craft could not easily be taken, and Boston losses were heavy. The British patrol on the Atlantic coast became increasingly efficient, and while food abounded in the Southern States, transportation to Boston was almost impossible. Local merchants were forced to keep their vessels abroad, where they harassed British commerce on the coasts of Spain, France, and England, and sent their prizes into friendly foreign ports. Thereupon, in the manner of men whose profit was gained from precarious adventure, officers and crews lingered, caroused, and squandered fortunes. Anticipating the post-war depreciation of currency, others invested their privateering profits in real estate in France and Spain. One of the last exploits of Boston privateers occurred in the summer of 1783, when five Boston merchants joined in an expedition, attacked and took the little town of Lunenburg, Nova Scotia, and plundered its stores of foodstuffs. Goods to the amount of £8,000 were brought away and sold in Boston.

The town had paid dearly for having commenced the Revolution. Pestilence, privation, and military occupation had reduced her population. Trade, industry, and commerce had been destroyed. Privateering had succeeded only in establishing a class of *nouveaux riches* who, in the hungriest days of the war, conducted themselves with a degree of ostentation never before seen, while the destitute in the almshouses went without bread. Many years were to pass before the social, financial, and political components of sound commerce were to be balanced.

CHAPTER III

BETWEEN THE WARS

The Critical Period

THE YEARS immediately following the cessation of hostilities, from 1783 to 1789, are rightly known in American history as the "critical period." Fundamental among the problems to be met was the inadequacy of the Articles of Confederation, which provided a loose political union with no federal control of customs. Offering a trade treaty to the British ministers, the Boston statesman, John Adams, was rebuked with the contemptuous observation that 13 political groups, rather than one, must be dealt with, and that some States already had signed individual tariff agreements. Adams well knew that separate commercial treaties for the various States only added to the general confusion of trade in the United States, since imports forbidden in one were frequently transshipped through a neighboring State as domestic articles. The new nation also felt the loss of the privileges and protection accorded to the commerce of British colonial possessions. Even France, willing enough to aid the Colonies in their struggle against her ancient enemy, would not extend that friendship to a potential commercial rival. Another handicap to business in the United States was the lack of a sound national currency. Worthless paper bills had driven "hard" money into hiding, and American credit abroad was at an end.

Severely hit by the post-Revolutionary decline of American commerce, Massachusetts experienced a prolonged depression, and Boston suffered more than any other port on the Atlantic seaboard. Her merchants lost their valuable West Indian fish markets when a London Order in Council, on April 17, 1784, directed that the products of the West India Islands be carried to the United States only in British bottoms. As late as 1786, when the exports of Virginia had passed pre-war figures, Massachusetts had regained only one quarter of her earlier trade. Her lumber and wood products were unable to find a profitable market, and her ships had been eliminated from the international carrying trade. Even Nantucket whale oil could not be sold abroad, since England was determined to develop her own whaling industry. To offset shipping losses, the General Court in 1784 imposed a duty on foreign manufactures. Two years later, the tariff was increased to 25 percent, and leather goods, foods, luxuries, and novelties were actually prohibited from entering the Commonwealth.

With the advent of peace, a flood of foreign goods had poured into Boston. Ships flying the flags of Britain, France, the Netherlands, Germany, and Sweden filled the harbor as European manufacturers eagerly sought to recapture the Boston market. Once again English firms stationed agents in Boston, and British merchantmen direct from London anchored in the Port. In 1783, from May to December, 28 French vessels and as many British docked at the local wharves, unloading cargoes valued at half a million dollars. Piece goods, hardware, Cheshire cheese, and assorted luxuries arrived from abroad in such large quantities that prices fell rapidly. Paul Revere, temporarily an importer, advertised on November 13, 1783, that he would "sell hardware and cutlery at a very low advance for cash."

The Boston traders found themselves hard pressed to match exports for imports. They had no furs or rum to exchange, and the long years of warfare had depleted their stock of flax, lumber, naval stores, and general provisions. Foreign manufactures had to be paid for in specie, and its constant flow outwards depreciated the currency still further. Determined to relieve the Boston merchants, the General Court placed stricter limitations upon the movement of British shipping through the Port, and so effectually banned the carrying of Massachusetts products in British bottoms that during the summer of 1785 not a London merchantman dropped anchor in the harbor. In their domestic trade, Boston sea captains had suffered for several years from another handicap—they lacked the essential West Indian sugar and molasses for exchange in the Southern States. Although the Dutch, Swedish, and Danish West Indies again became contraband centers for the British islands, Boston skippers managed to regain only a small part of their bartering trade in the field and forest produce of the South.

A Federalist Seaport

By 1788 the depression in Boston was breaking, and commerce began to regain its vigor. Once more, as in pre-

Revolutionary years, Boston sloops and fishing vessels, loaded with bricks, potatoes, rum, fish, butter, salt, molasses, wooden and earthen wares, and axes, set out for Chesapeake Bay, Albermarle and Pamlico Sounds, and Cape Fear, where they peddled and bartered for corn and tobacco. Boston sea captains had learned to outwit the Barbary pirates, and bravely they sailed to Mediterranean ports. Competing successfully with the Dutch and the British, they recaptured a large part of the carrying trade from Lisbon. For the 12 months ending August 1788, the expanding overseas shipments from Boston included fish valued at £66,000; rum, £50,000; whale and cod oil, £34,000; pot and pearl ashes, £30,000; flour, £15,000; flaxseed, £10,000; and furs, £10,000. Boards and staves, candles, leather and shoes, tea, coffee, and molasses were other commodities shipped in sizable quantities. Already on February 28, 1788, the *Independent Chronicle* had announced that "subscriptions were filling up to build three ships," and urged the establishment of a Chamber of Commerce "for the purpose of promoting an extensive trade upon such principles as will lastingly cement the union of the whole confederacy."

When the first Congress convened in July of 1789, customs regulations were immediately adopted to make Boston the leading port of the United States. Dictating the nation's financial and foreign policies, local merchants saw to it that no other section of the country was as strongly favored as maritime Massachusetts. American shipping was given a 10 percent reduction of duties on all imports, and vessels carrying tea direct from the Far East were obliged to pay only one-half the impost levied upon British merchantmen. Port charges for American ships were reduced to 6 cents a ton, payable once a year, while foreign-built and owned ships were required to pay 50 cents a ton at every port of entry. By an Act of July 31, establishing districts for the collection of import and tonnage duties, the Port of Boston was designated as one of 20 Massachusetts areas.

Stimulated by legislative protection, Boston's commerce entered a period of vigorous expansion. Over a thousand local vessels, averaging less than 75 tons in burden, crowded the Atlantic coastal routes. Prosperity had also returned to the South, and Boston sloops again distributed imported goods along the coast, interchanged domestic products, and collected commodities for the overseas trade. From foreign shores the Port was visited in 1790 by 60 ships, 7 snows (modified brigantines), 159 brigs, 170 schooners, and 59 sloops—a total of 455 vessels. An article in the *Independent Chronicle* on October 27, 1791, boasted: "Upwards of 70 sail of vessels sailed from this port on Monday last for all parts of the world." Vessels calling at the Port in 1793 numbered 119 from the West Indies, 11 from England, and 163 from other foreign lands, while during a single day a year later 450 craft of all types rode at anchor in the harbor. For the decade from 1790 to 1800 the annual arrivals from abroad averaged 569.

When the wars engendered by the French Revolution began in 1793, the French extended a boon of incalculable value to enterprising Bostonians. The National Convention promulgated a decree granting American vessels the rights of French shipping. During the hectic years that followed, however, trade with France took on an uncertain aspect, for although provisions could be sold at profiteer rates, it became increasingly difficult to collect payment. The *Jane* of Boston, under Captain Elijah Cobb, was captured by a French frigate and brought into Brest early in 1794. Upon her release by order of the prize court, Captain Cobb sold his cargo of rice and flour at a profit of 200 percent, but to obtain his money had to go to Paris during the Terror and interview Robespierre. Due to the "paper" blockade of the British and French coasts, European trade became very hazardous in 1798, when both warring nations seized Boston ships on the slightest pretext. While French vessels captured Boston vessels for carrying contraband, British men-of-war claimed the right to search American ships for His Majesty's subjects. Impressment and seizure notwithstanding, the number of Boston vessels engaged in the reshipment of goods to European countries and in the European carrying trade continued to increase.

Wharves and Shipyards

Despite the vicissitudes of war and peace, of depression and recovery, the appearance of the town had changed little since the early part of the century. As reconstructed by Samuel Eliot Morison in the *Maritime History of Massachusetts,* Boston in 1790

seemed "almost to stand in the water, at least to be surrounded by it, and the shipping, with the houses, trees, and churches, have a charming effect." Beacon Hill, a three-peaked grassy slope, still innocent of the gilded dome, dominated the town. From its base a maze of narrow streets paved with beach stones, wound their way seaward among ancient dwellings; dividing around Copp's and Fort Hills to meet again by the water's

edge. One of them, to be sure, led to "landward to the west," but at spring
tides even that, too, went "downward to the sea." Buildings crowded out
to the very capsills of the wharves, which poked boldly into deep water.
The uniform mass of slate and mossy shingle roofs pointed, hipped, and
gambreled, was broken by a few graceful church spires, serene elders of
the masts that huddled about the wharves.

In November of 1794, Thomas Pemberton noted that at
Long Wharf "vessels of all burdens load and unload; and the
London ships generally discharge their cargoes. It is the general resort of all the inhabitants, and is more frequented, we
think, than any other part of the town." He added that "the
harbour of Boston is at this date crowded with vessels. Eighty-
four sail have been counted lying at two of the wharves only."
Congress took further cognizance of the importance of the
Port in 1797 by appropriating $1,600 for buoys to be placed
in and near Boston Harbor. Within a decade the total merchant shipping of Massachusetts had tripled, and the Boston
fleet, second only to New York City, had grown to three times
that of Salem. Affiliated maritime enterprises were carried on
in the new seven-story Exchange Coffee-House, and at the
novel India Wharf structure of stores, counting-rooms, and
warehouses. Designed by Charles Bulfinch, the famous Boston
architect, India Wharf was considered the foremost waterfront
development in the United States. Before the close of the
century, a semaphore telegraph system with semaphore stations at Woods Hole, Edgartown, Sandwich, Plymouth, Marsh-
field, Scituate, and Hull was bringing Boston shipowners news
of the passage of their vessels through Nantucket Sound.

Boston and Charlestown shipyards hummed with the repair
of vessels and the construction of naval craft. Rotted planks
were removed, bottoms were caulked, and decks were scraped
and painted. In 1794 the keel of the renowned *Constitution*
was laid in Edmund Hartt's yard, near the present site of Constitution Wharf. Nicknamed "Old Ironsides" because of the
exceptionally heavy timbers in her frame, the *Constitution's*
lower beams were of white oak, the floor under her guns of
solid oak, and the deck of selected Carolina pitch pine. Paul
Revere furnished the copper for her hull, and her spikes were
forged by a secret process. The only place in Boston large
enough to make her sails was the Old Granary Building at the
corner of Tremont and Park Streets, where the Park Street
Church now stands. After two unsuccessful attempts at launching, the frigate was finally christened on October 21, 1797,
and in 9 months was made ready for her maiden voyage. Two

years later President John Adams watched the 28-gun frigate
Boston slide down the ways of Hartt's yard, and then on behalf of the Federal Government graciously accepted this gift
from the citizens of Boston for the defense of American shipping on the high seas. The vessel so pleased the Boston merchants that they rewarded Mr. Hartt with an inscribed silver
service, and the *Columbian Centinel* boldly asserted that "a
more excellent piece of naval architecture cannot be produced
in the United States."

After investigating the entire New England coastline, the
Federal Navy Department in 1797 established a Government
shipyard at Charlestown. The choice of the location received
widespread approval, since the Port of Boston, so it was maintained, could never be effectively blockaded. A site of 43 acres,
"little more than an unpromising mud flat," was purchased at
a cost of $39,214. Appointed naval constructor at the Yard,
Josiah Barker held this post for 34 years, and trained several
young men who later became prominent shipbuilders. One of
his pupils, Thatcher Magoun, was to achieve a reputation as a
leading American ship designer. Commodore Samuel Nicholson served as the first commandant of the Navy Yard, but his
administration of 11 years was marked by few improvements.
When Commodore William Bainbridge took charge in the
spring of 1812, "the Yard possessed hardly a convenience for
building or repairing vessels, or laying them up in ordinary."
The new commandant succeeded in obtaining large sums of
money, principally for the repair of vessels during the War of
1812. These repairs were usually done at daily wages of $4 for
master carpenters, $1.50 for sawyers, $1.25 for joiners, and $1
for laborers. The working day began at sunrise and ended at
sunset.

The booming Federalist era saw banks and insurance offices
spring up on State Street. Although insurance on Boston vessels had been underwritten locally since early shipping days, it
was a marked advance in the field when three marine insurance companies were officially incorporated in Boston. Between 1799 and 1805 Peter C. Brooks, great-uncle of the cru-
sading Phillips Brooks, amassed a huge fortune in this shrewd
business of weighing chances of success against failure. From
September to December 1796, the insurance rates from Boston
to other United States ports ranged from 1½ to 2 percent, to
any European port from 2¼ to 3 percent, to Baltic and Mediterranean ports from 3 to 3½ percent, to Mauritius from 5 to

6 percent, to China out and back from 10 to 12 percent. Two months later, due to French spoliations, all insurance rates from Boston had practically doubled.

Distress in the West Indies

The flood tide of commerce again carried a goodly half of Boston's vessels to the "Sugar Islands" during some stage of each voyage. Swiftly taking advantage of a legal loophole which permitted West Indian governors to suspend the embargo on American ships in cases of emergency or disaster, Yankee sloops began grounding on reefs and unloading cargoes before becoming sufficiently light to float off. Strict enforcement of the ban on Boston vessels had proved a costly affair to the British islanders. After 15,000 slaves had died from starvation, pressure from the planters became so strong that governors found it convenient to see almost constant "distress" in the islands. A disabled ship could not be refused admittance, and emergencies and disasters grew to epidemic proportions. By similar connivance of His Majesty's northern subjects, Boston vessels suddenly took on a "British" character in Nova Scotia. Even the Spanish ports of Trinidad and Havana served as smuggling centers for the British islands, which remained officially closed to American ships until 1830.

The opening of the French West Indies in 1783 brought great joy to Boston, even though trade was limited to the export of certain enumerated articles and the import of rum and molasses. The slanting sails of many newly rigged Boston ships dotted the ocean pathway to the Indies, crowding the harbors of Guadeloupe and Martinique. The trade was uninterrupted until October 1793, when England, which had that year declared war on France, ordered the seizure of any ship bearing the produce of a French colony or carrying provisions to such a colony. During the next 3 months, the English seized 250 American vessels and condemned 150 of them. In January 1794, the British Government exempted the American trade with the French West Indies from the prohibitory order of October, and Boston ships again took up the profitable trade. The conclusion of Jay's Treaty between the United States and Great Britain the same year, settling the differences arising from nonobservance of the peace of 1783, caused the French to regard the United States as unfriendly and to take retaliatory measures, declaring any American vessel submitting to search by English men-of-war subject to capture. This action led to an undeclared naval war between the United States and France which lasted until 1800 and resulted in the capture of 84 French ships.

Baltic and Mediterranean Routes

Hampered by trade restrictions in the West Indies, harassed by French and British cruisers, Boston shipowners turned to new and safer markets. In the spring of 1784, the *Light Horse* had already carried a cargo of West Indian sugar from Salem to Kronstadt, the port of St. Petersburg, and shortly afterward George Cabot of Beverly had opened trade with Russia by dispatching his ships the *Bucanier* and the *Commerce*. In 1786 and 1787, two vessels brought cargoes of hemp, iron and duck linen to Boston from St. Petersburg. By 1788 the *Astrea,* owned by "King" Derby and captained by James Magee, with his brother-in-law Thomas Handasyd Perkins as supercargo, was disposing of New England rum, Virginia flour, tobacco, imported tea and coffee at the Baltic ports of Gothenburg and Kronstadt. A decade later, more than 50 Massachusetts and New York vessels were sailing to northern European waters, and by 1799 they were transporting cargoes valued at more than a million dollars. Although the bulk of the new Baltic trade was carried in Massachusetts bottoms, not until after 1802 did Boston merchants wrest the lead from Salem.

William Gray became the principal American engaged in the Russian trade. Making Boston the center of his activities, he reshipped Russian duck, sheeting, cordage, and iron to Philadelphia, Charleston, and New Orleans. In southern ports, ships of his fleet took on tobacco, sugar, and cotton for the Baltic market. Other Gray vessels carried lumber and coffee direct from Boston to Algiers, thence going dead freight to Gallipolis, where olive oil was loaded for ports in the south of Russia. Boston vessels also arrived at Baltic seaports by way of Lisbon, Cadiz, the West Indies, Amsterdam, and Bremen, bringing pepper, sugar, fruits, coffee, tea, rum, wine, cotton, indigo, and tobacco. The imports from Russia contributed significantly to Massachusetts preeminence in shipbuilding during the first half of the nineteenth century; hemp, cordage, and duck were used in the manufacture of sailcloth, and the iron was turned into nails, anchors, and ship fittings. The iron plates and anchors, in particular, were utilized extensively until the Civil War, when they were replaced by superior products from the mines of Pennsylvania.

By 1806 the trade with Russia had become so important that George Cabot wrote to a London friend:

> In our trade with Spain and the south of Europe, we sell much more than we buy. There is a loss often by the ships returning *dead* freighted. There is also a loss on the balance of this trade, which must be received in money or bills which are ordinarily of a correspondent value. Thus, when money cannot be extracted from Spain without a loss of five percent . . . there will be a loss of about five percent on bills. . . . In Russia, we sell little or nothing, and buy to a great amount. We go there *dead* freighted, and pay all in cash or rather in bills on London, *better to us than money,* having cost us a considerable premium in Spain or elsewhere; yet who, among those that think no trade so important to the buyer as to the seller, will dare to deny that the trade with Russia since 1783 has been for its amount the most useful trade to the country?
>
> The hemp, iron, and duck brought from Russia have been to our fisheries and navigation like seed to a crop. Had it so happened that the trade of Spain and Russia were united, the time and expenses of a middle passage and other losses would have been avoided.

When the ports of Western Europe were closed to neutral shipping by orders of Napoleon in 1806, Boston's commerce with Russia yielded fabulous profits. In 1809 the 281-ton Boston ship *Catherine,* worth only $7,000, was said to have cleared $115,000 in a single voyage. During the winter of 1810-11, scores of Boston shipmasters swarmed about Riga and Kronstadt; of the 200 American ships trading in Baltic waters, over one-half hailed from Boston and nearby ports. Yankee skippers took part in the gay social life of the Russian nobility, attended sumptuous dinners, brilliant balls, sleigh rides, and skating carnivals. A number of Boston traders, however, at first shrank from such high living and, partly to escape the Danish privateers which were then seizing American ships, they sailed all the way round Norway to Archangel, whence their goods were carried fully a thousand miles overland to Moscow. But, according to Morison, few made a second trip to Archangel, since their Russian customers expected them to stay up and drink vodka throughout the bright summer nights.

Though at no time did Boston's eastern Mediterranean trade reach such spectacular heights as her Baltic traffic, the results were profitable and gave Boston contacts with a large number of ports. Usually, salt fish and sugar were sold in Spanish and Italian ports, and the cargo was replaced by cheap European goods, which commanded a high price in the Near East. In order to purchase Turkish opium for the Canton market in 1795, the Perkins Company of Boston established a residential agent at the busy port of Smyrna, on the Levantine coast of Asia Minor. For a number of years, Ebenezer Parsons of Boston brought coffee to Smyrna from Mocha on the Red Sea. After sailing around Africa, he disposed of his cargo for three or four times the price he had originally paid. Most Boston vessels obtained Mediterranean produce for distribution in the United States by the transfer of domestic cargoes at Gibraltar and Fayal. Their return ladings comprised oranges and lemons, figs and currants, nuts and raisins, wine and olive oil, corkwood and wool, and Oriental cloths and carpets.

Round the World

A bold aggressiveness carried Boston skippers into strange waters. With characteristic Yankee acumen, Captain Hallet in 1783 had been sent from Boston to China in the 55-ton sloop *Harriet* with a cargo of ginseng, believed by the Chinese to possess miraculous healing powers and to be capable of restoring virility to the aged and the infirm. Although inferior in quality to the plant raised in China, the ginseng growing wild in New England commanded a high price at Canton. When Captain Hallet put in at the Cape of Good Hope, he fell in with some British East Indiamen who, alarmed at possible future competition, bought the *Harriet's* cargo for double its weight in Hyson tea. In July of 1784, an advertisement in the Boston papers announced that "fresh teas taken out of an Indiaman, and brought by Captain Hallet from the Cape of Good Hope," were to be had at the Dock Square store of Penuel Bowen. Hallet had made a good bargain, but thereby lost to a New York ship the honor of hoisting the first American ensign at Canton.

The Boston merchants inaugurated and dominated a commerce which carried hardy young Yankees in fragile barks around the Horn to the Northwest Coast, where the Indians were given cheap New England manufactures in return for valuable furs. From there the course was set to Canton, where the pelts were exchanged for the treasures of the Orient. The publication in 1783 of the journals of John Ledyard, a traveler who accompanied the great navigator, Captain Cook, had called the attention of the commercial world to the immense number of sea-otter found on the northwest coast of America. Ledyard advocated the opening of a fur trade between that region and China but he failed to convince New York merchants of the advantages of such an enterprise. Possibly local traders had learned from a young Bostonian, Samuel Shaw, who had sailed as supercargo on the *Empress of China* of New York, the first American ship to reach Canton, that several English vessels already had sold Alaskan sea-otter furs for amazingly high prices at that port. Before his return to Canton to establish the first American commission house there, and full of enthusiasm about the China trade, Shaw proposed that the merchants of Boston equip a ship to compete with the British and Dutch traders. Favorably impressed, Charles Bulfinch, John Derby, John Martin Pintard, Joseph Barrell, Samuel Brown, and Crowell Hatch raised $50,000, and assembled a crew which included "an expert furrier, a surgeon, and an artist."

Two ships were fitted out, the 83-foot *Columbia* of 212 tons and the *Lady Washington* of 90 tons. Captain John Kendrick was placed in charge of the expedition, and Captain Robert Gray commanded the accompanying sloop. The vessels left Boston for the Northwest Coast on September 30, 1787, and doubled treacherous Cape Horn the following April. Encountering severe gales enroute, the two ships became separated. Eleven months out of Boston, the *Lady Washington* entered the still waters of Nootka Sound on the Northwest Coast. There the adventures of her crew demonstrated the wisdom of heavily arming the trader and choosing a former privateersman as commander. After a shore party had been ambushed by Indians and one of the seamen had been killed, the scene of the attack was named Murderer's Harbor. The *Columbia* finally joined the other ship; her crew was so stricken with scurvy that the sailors of the *Lady Washington* had to aid in hauling down sails and dropping anchor. Since it was too late to attempt any trading, the winter was passed in Friendly Cove on Vancouver Island, where the seamen lived ashore in log huts. They occupied themselves with fashioning rough chisels, which the natives had been reported as willing to trade for furs. When spring came, a large cargo of pelts was collected in exchange for copper, iron pots, pans, and trinkets. A few shiny nails or several chisels often obtained from the Indians a prime sea-otter skin which later sold for $30 in the China market. Running short of provisions, Captain Kendrick decided to remain behind in the sloop and dispatch the *Columbia* under Captain Gray.

The *Columbia* set sail for Canton on July 30, 1789. Stopping for provisions at Hawaii—the first American vessel recorded as calling there—Captain Gray took on a young native named Attoo as cabin boy. After many weeks, the vessel finally arrived at Canton, where the furs were readily exchanged for tea. The following February the *Columbia* weighed anchor and hoisted sails, maintaining a westward course. After an absence of nearly 3 years, having navigated 42,000 miles by her log, the *Columbia* entered Boston Harbor on August 10, 1790 —the first American vessel to circumnavigate the globe. Her return called forth fervent enthusiasm; salvos of artillery were fired, and "a great concourse of citizens assembled on the various wharfs . . . with three huzzas and a hearty welcome." A rumor spread throughout the crowds that a native "Ouyhee" was on board, and

before the day was out, curious Boston was gratified with a sight of him, marching after Captain Gray to call on Governor Hancock. Clad in feather cloak of golden suns set in flaming scarlet, that came halfway down his brown legs; crested with a gorgeous feather helmet shaped like a Greek warrior's, this young Hawaiian moved up State Street like a living flame.

That evening the weather-bronzed faces of the captain and crew surrounded a festive table provided by the Governor in honor of the signal achievement of Boston's own seamen, and later Congress struck off a medal in commemoration of their remarkable voyage.

The China Trade

Although the *Columbia's* first trip, like most pioneering ventures, proved a financial failure, four of her sponsors showed their continued faith in the enterprise by preparing the vessel at once for another voyage. On September 28, seven weeks after arriving home, Captain Gray sailed again for the Northwest Coast. Meeting this time with more favorable weather rounding Cape Horn, the *Columbia* rejoined her consort in 9 months, the *Lady Washington* having in the interim returned from a trip to China. During the tense trading season which followed, the two vessels were often attacked by hostile natives, and four men, including Captain Kendrick's son, were slain. On this second trip, Captain Gray discovered a great river, which he named Columbia after his sturdy ship. Loaded with valuable pelts, Gray proceeded to Canton, disposed of his skins for a mixed cargo of chinaware, sugar, curios, and tea, and returned to Boston on July 29, 1793. To find something salable at Canton was the riddle of the China trade, and the *Columbia* had solved this problem with the beautiful black fur of the sea-otter, which was plentiful on the northwest coast of America and in great demand at Canton.

Even before the *Columbia* had returned from her first voyage, the Boston vessel *Massachusetts* had started on the direct route around the Cape of Good Hope to India and China. Modeled after a British East Indiaman, the 800-ton *Massachusetts* was armed with 20 guns and measured 116 feet in length. Since this merchantman was the largest yet built on this continent, her venture excited great interest in Boston. When the ship set sail from Hancock's Wharf at 4 o'clock on Sunday afternoon, March 28, 1790, vantage points nearby were crowded with spectators. As she made way down the harbor, her anchor snapped a hook on the catblock and returned to the bottom. After a few embarrassing moments, the ship's officers managed to continue on a voyage which was to prove a series of misadventures. Sailing eastward for a month, the *Massachusetts* reached the coast of Guinea without mishap, and then pursued a southerly course along the African shores. Curiously enough, the vessel carried no chronometer, and none of her officers, including Captain Job Prince, could make a lunar observation. The discolored waters off the coast of Barbary and Guinea were often used as guide-marks by mariners, but, despite this substitute for nautical instruments, the officers of the *Massachusetts* found themselves so far off the course that the ship nearly ran aground on the barren shores of South Africa. An uneventful passage across the Indian Ocean was broken only by the cry of "Man overboard!" when three seamen were catapulted into the water by a freak accident, and one of the unlucky trio drowned. Another miscalculation in the sighting of Java Head compelled the *Massachusetts* to make 15 degrees extra "easting" and lose 3 weeks' time. Dropping anchor at Pigeon Island a month later, a second fatal accident occurred when a midshipman, handling the mainsail aloft, lost his hold and went tumbling to his death on the deck below. The *Massachusetts* finally moored at the Dutch island of Batavia, where her cargo had been scheduled to be exchanged for goods salable at Canton, but the authorities only permitted her to take on water and provisions.

When the *Massachusetts* arrived off Canton, at the Whampoa River anchorage, on the tenth of October, her frame and planking, injudiciously constructed of green wood, were found to be rotting away. Moreover, because of poor judgment in stowing the holds, the cargo had spoiled beyond salvage. Green masts and spars covered with ice and mud had been placed with 400 to 500 barrels of beef in broken stowage, the deck hatches then hermetically sealed by caulking. When the holds were opened, after a passage under blazing tropical skies, the beef was found to be almost boiled, the hoops on the masts rotted and fallen off, and the interior of the vessel covered with a blue mold more than half an inch thick. Despite her decayed green timbers, the *Massachusetts* was greatly admired by Cantonese shipmasters and was bought by the Portuguese Government for $65,000. This unsuccessful venture only stiffened the determination of Boston merchants to develop the Northwest fur trade route to China.

Ushered in by these notable voyages, the Pacific trade from the Port of Boston rapidly increased. Early in 1790, the 70-ton brigantine *Hope,* followed in November by the 157-ton brigantine *Hancock,* left Boston for China via the Northwest Coast. A few months later the 150-ton copper-bottomed *Margaret,* commanded by the veteran James Magee, set sail for the same region on a "voyage of observation and enterprise." Described as "the best provided of any that ever sailed from this port," the ship's crew managed to collect during a single trading season 1500 sea-otter furs, which sold at Canton for as high as $40 apiece. So many Boston traders appeared on the Northwest Coast that the fur-trapping Indians named all Americans "Boston men." From 1790 to 1818, 108 vessels from the United States, as compared with 22 from England, reached the Northwest, and a list giving the names of 63 of these ships reveals that 53 came from Boston. The cargoes of 12 vessels clearing Boston for the Northwest between 1797 and 1800 were invoiced at between $7,500 and $19,700 each.

In *A Narrative of Voyages and Commercial Enterprises,* published in 1842, Captain Richard J. Cleveland mentioned four Boston sloops he had seen on the Northwest Coast during the season of 1799, and added that 10 more were due from Boston. Of 16 vessels trading on the Northwest Coast in 1801, 10 were Boston ships. All sea-otter skins imported at Canton from June 1800 to April 1801, were brought by Boston Nor'westmen; 14 Boston vessels entered Canton in 1802, and 11 in 1803. During these 3 years over 34,000 skins, worth about $20 each, were shipped to China, and of this number almost nine-tenths arrived in Boston ships.

There is a dramatic story of the maritime trade between Boston and ancient China in every voyage via the savage northwest coast of North America and the romantic islands of the Pacific. It was customary to clear Boston in the autumn in order to round Cape Horn during the Antarctic summer. "The passage around Cape Horn from the Eastward I positively assert, is the most dangerous, most difficult, and attended with more hardships, than that of the same distance in any other part of the world," wrote Captain Porter of the frigate *Essex*. Although many a great ship met its doom off the Horn, not one of Boston's Nor'westmen, so far as is known, failed to round with safety. To stock fresh provisions and thus prevent scurvy, the Nor'west traders interrupted their voyage twice and sometimes three times, at the Cape Verde Islands, the Falklands, the Galapagos, or Hawaii. They usually arrived on the Northwest Coast the following summer, anchored off the nearest Indian village, and bartered as long as they could. Putting in at every Indian village, Boston traders were accustomed to spend one or two seasons on the coast, sometimes even 2 years. Often a trading vessel lost several of its crew in battles with the Indians, and rocky coasts, fast tides, heavy fogs, and long calms added to the hazards of a voyage. The insurance rate for the Northwestern trade was 17 percent covering risk "against the Natives as well on shore as on board."

Every Boston Nor'westman carried certain staples: cutlery, ironware, tin, chisels, knives, nails, clothing, blankets, beads, molasses, sugar, rum, and muskets. But the Indians often proved fickle; sometimes they scorned blue cloth, demanding only red, or insisted upon greatcoats at a rate of exchange that made trading impossible. On the other hand, the very next village might be willing almost to give furs away. At one place, green glass beads were so coveted that the Boston traders offered only two for a skin, while on another occasion 60 skins were traded for a moderate quantity of spikes. When Joseph Ingraham arrived off Queen Charlotte Island on the *Hope* from Boston, he noticed that all the Indians were wearing jackets and trousers. His cloth could not be traded until he hit upon the brilliant idea of sewing on brass buttons. To add to the fantasy, Ingraham ordered the ship's armorer to make iron collars, and so established a vogue that became popular on the Coast. He sold these collars for three skins apiece. When the Boston ship *Jefferson* anchored off the Alaskan coast with virtually nothing to offer the natives in return for their cache of some 800 sea-otter skins, the crew used their wits. Everything loose or not absolutely essential to the voyage was transformed into trading material. A Japanese flag and the cabin mirror were articles the seamen could do without. The ship's carpenter was put to work making rough boxes, which passed with the natives as trunks. To the delight of the local women, old sails were fashioned into garments, and unsalable bar iron was hammered into bangles. The Yankees were so busy trading that they forgot to celebrate the Fourth of July. Only the arrival of the bark *Phoenix* of Bengal with more acceptable articles put an end to the flurry.

As the profitable Northwest fur trade attracted more ships, operations spread southward. In violation of Spanish regulations, Boston skippers seized opportunities for contraband trading along the South American and California coasts. Captain Ebenezer Dorr, Jr., sailed the first American vessel into California waters in 1796, when he anchored the Boston ship *Otter* at Monterey. Four years later Charles Winship, captain of the Boston brigantine *Betsy,* defied the Spanish officials by dealing directly with the Indians. A novel scheme first carried out by Captain Joseph O'Cain of Boston was an agreement with the Russian authorities at New Archangel (Sitka) whereby he borrowed 75 canoes and 120 Indians. O'Cain transported these Indians to the California coast, put them off his vessel in their canoes to hunt sea-otter, and in a single season filled all his holds.

Pioneering in the Pacific

Most of the present insular possessions of the United States in the Pacific were visited by Boston Nor'westmen before 1800. Captain Ingraham in the *Hope* had touched the Marquesas as early as 1791 and named two of the islands Washington and Adams; 12 years later Amasa Delano, the Boston skipper from Duxbury, called at the Wake Islands. The Sandwich Islands became an ideal stopping place, where the natives supplied hogs, yams, and green vegetables for the long voyage to Canton. The *Columbia* touched at these islands on her first and second voyages, and the *Hope* called there in May 1792.

For South Sea trading, every Nor'westman carried an assortment of whale's teeth, glass bottles, calico, needles, and looking-glasses—the last having an invariable appeal to the natives. The South Sea Islands were searched for products to bring to the China market; they yielded tortoise-shell, mother-of-pearl, edible bird's nests, shark's fins, and *bêche de mer,* a slimy sea slug prized by the Chinese for soup. Sandalwood was contracted for at Hawaii, where Captain Kendrick had discovered it growing wild on the island of Kanai. Kendrick's keen eye did not even overlook the beeswax that had drifted ashore.

The Boston sea captains in the South Sea Islands acquired a reputation as bold traders. They were willing to buy or sell anything, even—as the *Jefferson* had proved—their ship's equipment. Often a Boston trader would ceremoniously make an agreement with a Fiji chief, who promised to sell all native articles only to him. Captain Reuben Brumely signed a treaty with a native chief, whereby sandalwood was to be sawed in lengths and the bark shaved off at a cost of about one cent a pound; he sold the wood at Canton for 34 cents a pound. King Kamehameha I of Hawaii repudiated a contract with the Winship Brothers of Boston for all the sandalwood grown in his territories; he termed the knives, hatchets, and nails inadequate. When Captain Richard J. Cleveland of Boston gave the King a horse, Kamehameha was skeptical; he could not see that a horse's ability to transport a person faster than he could walk was sufficient compensation for all the food that the animal would eat.

Crossing the vast Pacific without charts or proper nautical instruments, Boston vessels made their way up the China coast in the autumn, approaching Canton from the south. After obtaining a "chop" (official permit) at Macao, their ships were again examined at the mouth of the River Pearl before permission was granted to proceed to Canton. At first the Chinese experienced difficulty in distinguishing the Bostonians from the British, but later named them the "New People." The "Hong" merchants trafficked in Bohea, Souchong, and Hyson tea; they sold the finest silk, and exchanged their nankeens, crepes, and chinaware for furs and ginseng. The lading completed during the winter months, Boston vessels were carried by the monsoon down the China Sea. Off the coast of Borneo there were dangerous shoals, reefs, floating islands, baffling currents, and treacherous winds. Often the vessels stopped for fresh food and water at Java. If a Nor'westman were becalmed, or ran on a reef in the Strait of Sunda, between Sumatra and Java, native pirates would suddenly appear ready to plunder the cargo and massacre the crew. Safely beyond these straits, the Nor'westmen caught a southeast wind across the Indian Ocean to the Cape of Good Hope, from which they headed directly toward Cape Cod. The passage from Canton to Boston usually required 6 months.

This commerce from Boston to the Orient did not fit into a stereotyped pattern; rather, the Boston shipowner followed the fortunes of trade as an adventurer would follow the fortunes of war. If a captain were unable to purchase a sizable cargo at Canton, he could always carry merchandise for an agent, or he might increase his profits by freighting goods to Ceylon and Calcutta. Then he could either return to Canton for more goods or stop at Mauritius to complete his cargo.

When vast herds of fur seals were discovered on the barren wastes of Patagonia and along the Chilean coast, a new variation in the China trade developed. As early as 1783, Lady Haley, an Englishwoman living in Boston and sister to the political reformer John Wilkes, had dispatched her ship *States* to the Falkland Islands in search of sealskins and sea-elephant oil. After uninterrupted days of chasing and clubbing seals, the crew collected 13,000 skins. When the pelts were brought to New York City, they fetched only 50 cents apiece. In the hope of obtaining a higher price, these furs were shipped to the Orient, where the Chinese merchants eagerly offered $5 a skin. Three and one-half million seal pelts were brought to Canton between 1783 and 1807. The search for seals led the Boston sea captain, Mayhew Folger, on the ship *Topaz*, to Pitcairn Island in 1808. Instead of finding seals, he was met by a canoe filled with natives who spoke perfectly good English. When they came aboard, Folger learned that there were descendants of the mutineers of H.M.S. *Bounty*. Their story was so amazing that Captain Folger later communicated it to the British Admiralty.

Boston's Nor'westmen

One of the most courageous Nor'westmen of the age was Captain William ("Bill") Sturgis. Coming from Barnstable in 1796, he had entered the Boston counting-house of his wealthy relative, Thomas Handasyd Perkins. At the age of 16, the youth sailed to the Northwest Coast and China as foremast hand on the Perkins' ship *Eliza,* then served as chief mate on the *Ulysses,* returning to Boston 5 years later as master of the *Caroline.* Noticing in 1802 that the Indians used ermine pelts for currency, Sturgis purchased 5,000 of them at the Leipzig Fair and brought them to the Coast. There he traded one ermine for one sea-otter skin, until the Indians obtained so many they lost their value as currency. Making his third voyage to Canton in command of Theodore Lyman's veteran ship *Ata-*

hualpa, with $300,000 in specie on board, Sturgis was attacked at the mouth of the Canton River by Apootsae, a notorious Chinese pirate. As the junks approached, Captain Sturgis ordered a shot across their bows "just to show how soon it will bring them about on the other tack." But the warning went unheeded, and the marauders continued their advance. The resolute captain, noted for his bushy eyebrows and fierce expression, lit a cigar and ordered a keg of powder brought to him.

Knowing the terrible cruelty of these pirates, Sturgis declared he would blow up the ship rather than surrender. Everyone on board believed he meant it and put up a fearful battle. Several small cannon, which Sturgis had taken on board in violation of Mr. Lyman's express orders, as well as boarding pikes, Brown Bess muskets, and horse pistols, were used effectively. The captain's cousin, James Perkins Sturgis, a passenger on the *Atahualpa,* and "yellow as a cornflower" from jaundice, was restored to his normal complexion by the fright of the battle. While the Chinese pirates, to the accompaniment of a terrific banging of gongs and the howls of their wounded, hurled hand grenades whose sulphurous powders caused them to be dubbed "stink pots," Captain Sturgis skillfully maneuvered the *Atahualpa* within range of the Macao forts, which poured their shot down on the pirates, and put them completely to rout. Sturgis was a hero in the eyes of the Chinese, and the mandarin ordered the pirate leader Apootsae killed by the torture of the "thousand cuts."

William Sturgis became a leading citizen of Boston. At the age of 28 in 1810, he organized the firm of Bryant & Sturgis, which for the next 30 years controlled more than half the Pacific trade of the United States. "Next to a beautiful woman and a lovely infant," Captain Sturgis once remarked, "a prime sea-otter fur is the finest natural object in the world." When he occupied a seat in the Massachusetts General Court, one of the professional orators of that body declaimed a long Greek quotation, to which the Captain replied in one of the Indian dialects of the Northwest Coast. When his nephew, Robert Bennet Forbes, went to sea at the age of 12, he boldly admonished the boy to "always go straight forward, and if you meet the devil cut him in two, and go between the pieces; if anyone imposes on you, tell him to whistle against the northwester and to bottle up moonshine."

Another gallant Nor'westman was Captain John Suter.

After privateering against the French, imprisonment in a Brest dungeon, and impressment by the British, he shipped from Boston at the age of 19 on the *Alert,* bound for the Northwest and Canton. Promoted to master of the *Pearl,* with a cargo and outfit not exceeding $40,000, he sailed again for Canton. In spite of difficulties with the Indians, Captain Suter managed to collect enough furs and sandalwood to purchase $156,743 worth of merchandise at Canton. His return cargo consisted of 50 blue and white chinaware sets of 172 pieces each, 480 tea sets of 49 pieces each, 30 boxes of enameled cups and saucers, 200 chests of Souchong tea, 395 chests of Hyson tea, 400 chests of other teas, cassia oil, 191,000 pieces of nankeens, 92 cases of silk, and sundries. When the cargo was sold at auction in Boston in 1810, the net profit from the voyage amounted to $206,000.

John Suter, like other New England sea captains of his time, was a deeply religious man. Following a regular routine, he read chapters of the Bible to his crew. This daily habit was a great source of amusement to one member of the ship's company, who delighted in setting back the marker until the day when Captain Suter remarked that he seemed to be running into headwinds through the Book of Daniel. Captain Suter proved an able successor to Sturgis as commander of the *Atahualpa.* Offered a "primage" of 10 per cent, with the usual "privilege" and salary, and a sixteenth share in the ship and cargo, Suter returned to the Northwest. While the vessel was carrying on a brisk trade with the Indians, a native chief came on board, presumably to barter. But no sooner had he set foot on deck than a flotilla of dugouts, containing 2,000 warriors, rushed out and surrounded the ship, prepared to massacre Suter and his men. Instantly the captain seized the chief as a hostage, forced him to order his savages to return to shore, and did not release the crestfallen leader until the *Atahualpa* had reached the open sea. This happened to be the same Indian chief who had previously captured the *Tonquin,* sent out by John Jacob Astor. After Suter arrived at Hawaii, after the War of 1812 had begun, and was informed of the proximity of British men-of-war, he sold his ship and later managed to send his valuable furs to Canton. When peace was concluded, he shipped a cargo from Canton to Boston and realized for the owners a net profit of $120,000.

The Boston seamen in the China trade were extremely young. High wages and lure of the ocean called Yankee lads

from the villages of Cape Cod and the farms of New England
to the Boston waterfront, and a berth at sea. When a ship returned, some boys went back to their homes, while others
stuck to the sea and soon became officers. On her first voyage,
the *Columbia* had paid ordinary seamen $5 a month, able
seamen $7.50, but she sailed in a time of unemployment. In
1790 the *Massachusetts* carried a crew of 14 petty officers and
44 boys from New England villages. At the ripe age of 19, as
master of the 60-foot sloop *Union* of Boston, John Boit, Jr.,
started on a voyage which was perhaps the most remarkable
youthful exploit of the period. On the Northwest Coast his
crew of 22 beat off an Indian attack; at Hawaii they found
"the females were quite amorous"; they exchanged sea-otter
for silks at Canton; and successfully weathered a 4-day gale en
route to the Cape of Good Hope. Seized and then released by
a French cruiser, fired upon by a British frigate, the battered
craft dropped anchor in Boston Harbor after an absence of 2
years, probably the only sloop-rigged vessel ever to encircle the
globe. By 1799 youths were being paid $8 to $10 a month, able
seamen $18, and petty officers up to $24 a month in the Northwest fur trade. Completing a voyage to Canton, the young
crew of the *Sea Otter* received from $500 to $600 each. Clever
seamen could make an extra couple of hundred dollars by
judicious purchases at Canton, stuffed into their seachests.
Many a young man went to sea in a Boston vessel merely to lay
aside a little money to get married on, or to buy a farm. But
sometimes he never returned; there were Indians to contend
with in the Northwest, fever in the tropics, pirates and canni-
bals in the Pacific, and raging storms on the Seven Seas. And
always the dangerous uncertainty of European warfare threatened to make Boston vessels the prize of a combatant.

Impressment and Embargo

By the year 1800, the Port of Boston had reached unprecedented prosperity. It had passed Philadelphia in both the
coasting and foreign trades, and Boston's total tonnage was
second only to that of New York. The increased activity was
the outgrowth of Europe's absorption in military rather than
agricultural matters, which resulted in the curtailment of the
usual sources of supply and a heavy demand for provisions
from America. Since Boston vessels were the chief carriers of
American foodstuffs, their number in the overseas route increased sevenfold; by 1807, Massachusetts had become the

Map of Boston, *circa* 1800. *Courtesy of the Society for the
Preservation of New England Antiquities.*

A Down East paddle steamer heading out to sea. *Courtesy of the Society for the Preservation of New England Antiquities.*

largest shipowning State in the Union. Many Boston ships participated in the carrying trade between the warring nations and their colonial possessions, some even maintaining a "ferrying trade" between London and Copenhagen. By means of banking connections in London, a Boston shipmaster could leave an outward cargo with a commission merchant practically anywhere, and draw a bill against his London account, which served as a "letter of credit" in any port. Such commodities as sugar, tea, and coffee, formerly shipped directly to European ports, were first brought to Boston, and then reexported to Europe.

Although the harbor was crowded with shipping and Boston's merchants were unusually prosperous, her citizens had been forced for some years to endure a mounting list of abuses at the hands of the English and the French. When the continued seizure of ships and cargoes at sea and the British practice of impressing American seamen culminated in the *Chesapeake* outrage, public opinion in the United States reached the boiling point. On June 22, 1807, the 50-gun British ship *Leopard* demanded the surrender of seamen aboard the United States frigate *Chesapeake,* alleging that they might be British deserters. Upon the Captain's refusal to permit a search of his vessel, the *Chesapeake* was fired upon, 21 of her crew killed or wounded, and 4 unharmed seamen impressed on board the *Leopard.* The merchant shipowners of Boston and Salem attempted to condone this shameful attack, but the injured nation cried out for the "defense of national honor."

Maritime Boston had been compelled to swallow a bitter pill when Thomas Jefferson defeated John Adams for the Presidency. Mindful of the grossly inadequate military preparation of the United States, President Jefferson replied to popular indignation over the *Chesapeake* affair with the Embargo. The act, passed by Congress on December 22, 1807, ordered British men-of-war to leave United States ports and forbade all commerce with foreign countries. Despite the speed of its enactment, the Embargo Act was known in advance to Boston merchants, and the Port buzzed with the breakneck loading of cargoes, as vessels were hurriedly cleared. Owners ordered ships already at sea to stay away from American ports. While the "stress of weather" was usually given as the reason for landing these absentee craft in Nova Scotia or the West Indies, they really operated in the carrying trade for belligerents. Renegade Boston sea captains conspired with the

British Admiralty, forwarders, and shippers in innumerable misrepresentations and evasions. Great profits came out of the "bad weather" and the studied apathy of British naval officers.

American naval vessels were stationed at the entrances to the harbor in an attempt to stifle the lucrative foreign commerce of Boston. Coastwise sailing and fishing were permitted only when bonds had been posted to guarantee return to the United States; certificates were even necessary for shipments from one State to another. The credentials issued by Governor Sullivan of Massachusetts, however, were so numerous that they sold in New York at high premiums. Many Boston ships engaged in the overseas trade remained abroad where American laws could not affect them. A number of blockaded vessels managed to obtain the necessary papers to leave Boston, after customs officials were intimidated and threatened by irate mobs. Furthermore, the nearby Canadian border offered tempting opportunities for illegal trading; goods were shipped overland or run up the coast in small craft and loaded at Canadian wharves for trans-Atlantic passage. But the embargo temporarily ended the boom in Boston's overseas shipments.

The resentment of the Boston populace against Jeffersonian policy rose to such a pitch that early in 1809 a town meeting went on record as refusing to aid in the enforcement of the embargo. In a series of resolutions, the General Court asserted that the act was "unjust, oppressive, and unconstitutional, and not legally binding on the citizens of this State." One especially destructive effect of the stoppage of commerce was the skyrocketing of prices in Boston, so that necessaries of life could be obtained only at "luxury" figures. Whether brought in by costly wagon routes, or by dodging the ubiquitous revenue cutters, flour selling for $4.50 a barrel at Richmond commanded $11.87 in Boston; rice costing $4 a hundred pounds at Charleston retailed for $8 in Boston; and upland cotton purchased at Savannah for 9 cents a pound yielded 20 cents in Boston. Wearied by the continued agitation of 14 months of ineffective embargo, Jefferson finally capitulated. Since the smaller ports of Massachusetts had been ruined by the blockade and deserted by their merchants, the net result of Jefferson's Repeal Act was to increase the preeminence of Boston as the maritime gateway of New England.

Three years of profitable commerce followed. In 1809 the value of articles of American growth and manufacture exported from Boston reached the huge sum of $4,000,000, and rice, flour, cotton, tobacco, staves, and naval stores accounted for more than half of the total shipments. A year later the value of domestic exports amounted to $3,500,000, more than twice that of all other Massachusetts shipping towns put together. In 1811, shipments had dropped to $3,000,000, but tar, pitch, turpentine, rosin, and the farm and field products of the South still headed the export list. Boston's trade with China, the West Indies, South America, and the Baltic and Mediterranean countries continued to flourish.

"Mr. Madison's War"

The early months of the War of 1812 found Boston still an active shipping center. Regarding open warfare as an unwelcome interruption, independent Boston men shook off this latest annoyance with their habitual disregard for restrictions. Maritime Boston was bitterly aware that the slogan "Free Trade and Sailors' Rights" was a misnomer, and openly pledged sabotage to "Mr. Madison's War." A few Boston skippers even went to the extent of taking out Portuguese papers so that they might engage in neutral shipping. Prices soared as the foreign demand for provisions continued while the supply diminished. Through the medium of licenses from the British blockading squadron, Boston merchants at first carried on a brisk trade with England. But soon the licenses were revoked, and the blockade progressively tightened. British men-of-war patrolled the coast, on the lookout for any vessel foolhardy enough to enter Boston Harbor. Occasionally a sloop slipped into the Port, but the risk of capture was too great for any vessel flying the Stars and Stripes to put to sea. Coastwise shipping became inactive, and even fishing in small craft became too dangerous.

By the fall of 1813, Boston Harbor was a picture of desolation. Wearing "Madison's night-caps," as the inverted tarbarrels and canvas bags placed over the mastheads were dubbed, about 250 ships lay slowly rotting at their wharves. Large numbers of seamen were out of employment, capital and ships lay idle, prices of imports rose rapidly, and domestic products were sold at such a high price that 44 vessels departed from Boston to foreign ports. Wagon traffic commenced between Boston and the South, and the "Horse Marine" supplied the only comic relief to an otherwise grim drama. Boston skippers had to weather gales of laughter as they plowed their way through seas of mud, while customs officials literally boarded their wagons. Once more, as 30 years before, Boston became a sealed port.

Opposed to the war, Boston furnished less than her share of privateers. As against 58 from Baltimore, 55 from New York, and even 40 from Salem, Boston fitted out only 31 armed vessels. The most famous Boston privateer, the *True Blooded Yankee,* operated from French ports and struck terror in the British Isles. In company with another Boston vessel, the *Bunker Hill* of 14 guns, she cruised the Irish and English Channels and captured many rich prizes. One seizure brought into Brest was reputed to have been worth half a million dollars. Another captured vessel, laden with dry goods and Irish linen, was safely piloted to the United States, while a third was sent to Bergen, Norway, and sold there. A single voyage of little more than a month, in 1813, netted the *True Blooded Yankee* 27 vessels and 270 prisoners; her exploits even included the burning of seven ships in a Scottish harbor.

If the "thunders" of any one American warship "shook the mighty deep" during the War of 1812, that vessel was Boston's own frigate *Constitution.* When Captain Hull received news of the formal declaration of war, he lost little time in gathering a doughty crew and setting forth. With the Stars and Stripes proudly floating from her masthead, the *Constitution* sailed from Boston on July 12 to join the squadron of Captain Rodgers in southern waters, lest by operating alone she encounter a superior enemy force. With 44 guns in her portholes, and a crew of 475, largely untrained except for her officers, who were among the best in the service, Captain Hull confidently directed the sturdy craft. Twelve miles off Barnegat, New Jersey, on the afternoon of July 17, four ships were sighted directly ahead. The *Constitution* was up against Captain Philip Broke's blockading squadron, comprising the 38-gun frigate *Shannon,* the 32-gun *Æolus,* the 36-gun *Belvidera,* and the 64-gun razee *Africa.* Still another sail, also flying the Union Jack, appeared from the north. Confronted with the formidable squadron on one side, and the 38-gun *Guerrière* on the other, the lone *Constitution* wisely came about and packed on canvas. The chase that followed is one of the most thrilling incidents in naval history. Upon shifting winds, frequently dying down to dead calm, depended the fate of the *Constitution.* Luffing first to starboard, then to port, veering, and dodging, and alternately widening and closing the gap, the *Constitution* and her pursuers kept up the struggle for 3

days. Becalmed at one stage of the flight, Captain Hull out-
witted the enemy by "kedging," a process of sending ahead a
long towline in small boats, and dropping anchors at regular
intervals. The crew then seized the inboard end of the hawser,
pulling slowly at first until the ship began to move, then
gradually increasing the rate of haul, finally running aft with
the line. To lighten the load, 2,300 gallons of drinking water
were pumped out. At last, on the morning of the twentieth,
the British fleet gave up the chase, and Captain Hull and his
exultant crew returned to Boston.

Determined to bring the fight to a different finish, Captain
Hull quietly eased the *Constitution* out of Boston Harbor on
August 2, in rank disobedience of orders. After recovering the
American brig *Adeline* from the British sloop-of-war *Avenger,*
he headed southward for Bermuda. On the way, Hull was
informed by the American privateer *Decatur* that the *Guerrière* was hovering nearby. A day later the two formidable
warships met, and Hull found Captain Dacres of the *Guerrière* no less anxious than himself to engage in battle. At 5:45
in the afternoon, the encounter began. Captain Orne, an
American prisoner on board the *Guerrière,* later narrated:

At 6:30 I went on deck, and there beheld a scene difficult to describe.
All the *Guerrière's* masts had been shot away, and as she had no sails
to steady her, she lay rolling like a log in the trough of the sea. Many
of the men were employed in throwing the dead overboard. The decks
were covered with blood, and had the appearance of a butcher's slaughter-
house. And what with the groans of the wounded, and the noise and
confusion of the enraged survivors on board the ill-fated ship, the scene
was a perfect hell.

After the remnants of the British crew had been transferred
to the *Constitution,* the battered *Guerrière* was blown up.
On August 30, the victor in the first important naval engagement of the war, gayly bedecked with flags and bunting,
appeared off Boston Light. Cannon boomed and great rejoicing spread throughout the town as she passed up the harbor.
That evening, at a banquet to Captain Hull and his officers in
Faneuil Hall, the pride and delight of the Boston people
knew no bounds. Shortly afterward Congress voted an award
of $50,000 to the officers and men of the valiant man-of-war, a
gold medal to Captain Hull, and silver medals to his officers.

But the victories of the *Constitution* did not bring the war
to a quick conclusion, as the people of Boston had fervently
hoped. When hostilities continued for another year, dissatis-
faction in Massachusetts ports reached the "secession" point.

Boston's soldiers were fighting in Canada; her seacoast was left defenseless; and her ship carpenters, sailmakers, and seamen were deserting for inland regions where work could be obtained. Boston was in distress, but the demands of maritime interests were powerless to alter the policy of the Federal Government. With the deliberate intention of considering secession, the General Court of Massachusetts summoned a New England convention to meet at Hartford, Connecticut, in the autumn of 1814. Such eminent merchants as Thomas H. Perkins, William Sturgis, Daniel Sargent, and Israel Thorndike were among those members of the legislature who favored withdrawal from the Union. But secession was disapproved in the report the Convention issued on January 6, 1815, after a turbulent session. Five weeks later, news of peace reached Boston, and the citizens of the town enthusiastically celebrated their return to the freedom of the seas.

CHAPTER IV

PORT OF THE WORLD

"From Wharf to Waterfall"

AT THE CLOSE of the war, commercially-minded Bostonians rushed to their vessels with all the enthusiasm of an East Indiaman's crew feeling the first faint puff of wind after days of calm under a tropical sun. Sailors swarmed up masts and released acres of gleaming canvas; the harbor reawakened to the familiar sights and sounds of a great trade. In 1815, during a single month, 144 ships slanted down the Bay, bound again for the far-distant ocean reaches. Carefully selected cargoes were sent to China, the East and West Indies, the Mediterranean, the South Seas, South America, and the Baltic. The sudden restoration of the American market, however, led to an alarming increase in imports; quantities of British goods were dumped on Boston wharves at prices below production costs, in a vain attempt to stifle the young factories called into being by the war. Coastwise trade grew in proportion, for the extraordinary new volume of imports had to be distributed.

The War of 1812 materially changed the economic structure of Massachusetts. Gloucester, Provincetown, and New Bedford remained loyal to the cod, mackerel, and whale fisheries, but they exported their products through Boston. The nearby towns of Salem, Marblehead, Newburyport, and Beverly gradually turned away from the sea and sought financial salvation in the development of manufacturing. Capital, previously tied up by embargo, non-intercourse, and war, was cautiously diverted to industry. Francis C. Lowell and Patrick T. Jackson, members of well-known shipping families, "prepared against peace" by establishing at Waltham, in 1814, the first complete cotton factory in America. Within a generation, fishermen by the score put aside their nets and applied weather-toughened hands to the making of shoes. Progress in the State was altered, rather than arrested; by 1840 the center of interest had shifted "from wharf to waterfall."

Despite the new industrial development, Boston's ocean commerce steadily expanded. Between 1820 and 1830 the annual arrivals from foreign lands averaged 787 ships; in the same decade the number of coastwise vessels arriving at the Port exceeded any previous record. As Boston absorbed much of the shipping of Massachusetts ports that were themselves unable to provide vessels large enough for successful competition, the city—for Boston became a city in 1822—established over some trade routes a national supremacy that was not to be challenged for years to come.

In 1817 Congress had passed a tariff designed to protect American manufacturers and exclude foreign vessels from the coasting trade. The following year British ships were even forbidden to handle commerce between the United States and the Canadian Provinces. But the duties imposed were so low and so easily circumvented by false sales and invoices that British manufacturers continued to flood the Boston market. Foreign products were also smuggled in by sea captains eager for a high profit. Often the tariffs hurt the foreign trade of Boston's merchants, especially in England and the British West Indies. When import duties on cotton and woolen goods were increased, Boston's shipowners and merchants succeeded in obtaining low tariff schedules on noncompetitive Oriental goods, which had no effect on New England's "infant industries." Already local textile manufacturers had begun to export to world markets, sending goods to South America and the Far East, as well as to southern and western communities where gradually growing urban centers provided ever larger commercial outlets.

As Boston's maritime prosperity came to depend on manufacturing, protectionist principles became essential to Massachusetts. By 1830 the number of Boston ships engaged in domestic trade was more than twice that employed in overseas commerce. To stop the unrestrained boosting of tariff schedules, however, the United States signed a treaty with Great Britain opening American ports to English vessels and granting American ships, whether carrying raw materials or manufactured articles, similar concessions in British colonial ports. In substance, the treaty made it possible for the more efficient carrier to obtain the larger share of the trade. At first Boston benefited from the agreement, later her mercantile development was injured by it. Discriminatory tonnage taxes against foreign vessels docking at American ports, imposed since the ratification of the Constitution, were of course abrogated by the new treaty. The removal of those taxes forced local shipping to compete on an equal footing with British vessels; it was eventually to succumb under the onslaught of British steamship development. Clearsighted members of Boston's merchant families might have realized the city's glorious deep-water career was facing hard weather, but the storm warnings seemed distant, and few had time to study the omens, so busy were they in sailing the course their ancestors had charted.

Merchants and Icemen

Typical merchants of the time were the Cunningham brothers, Andrew and Charles. Methodical almost to a fault, the partners arrived at their counting-rooms on Rowe's Wharf promptly at 7 o'clock every morning. Once Captain John Codman returned from China with a cargo of tea, against the explicit orders of Andrew Cunningham. Although there had been a change in conditions since the sailing, and the tea realized a handsome profit, Mr. Cunningham called the captain into his office and gave him a verbal lashing for disobedience; he then handed him an envelope containing a check for $1,000. Another enterprising Boston merchant, Benjamin C. Clark, built the schooner-yacht *Mermaid* in 1832, the first decked-over boat in the harbor, and later created the *Raven*, winner in 1845 of the first yacht regatta in Massachusetts Bay. Clark, like the Cunninghams, was successful in the West Indies and Mediterranean trade; he sent his vessels to Sicily for oranges, lemons, macaroni, and sulphur, and he imported wines, fruit, and whale oil from Fayal in the Azores.

Comparable was the business of Supply Clap Thwing, an India Wharf commission merchant who engaged chiefly in the New Orleans trade. He imported and exported portions of the cargoes of some 300 ships, all chartered except a few which he owned personally. Osborn Howes of Boston, the first American captain to set foot in Turkey, formed with his brother-in-law the firm of Howes & Crowell, trading with China, Western Europe, California, and Australia. The original Siamese twins were brought to America by a junior officer of Captain Daniel C. Bacon, who obligingly lodged them in the woodshed of his Temple Place home. Captain Bacon was the owner of the *Gamecock,* then one of the fastest vessels afloat. Enoch Train occupied a very prominent position in the maritime community, sending his ships *Dorchester, Cairo,* and *Governor Davis* to South America, and then, in the thirties, entering the Baltic trade with the famous Water-man-and-Ewell-constructed *St. Petersburg,* a square-sterned vessel 160 feet long, 33 feet wide, and of 814 tons burden, with spacious accommodations for passengers: a packetship in all respects. In the forties, Train started a packet line between Boston and Liverpool in competition with the Cunard steamers, diverting four vessels to the Atlantic crossing while his new ships were being built.

William H. Bordman, Jr., took full advantage of the opportunities offered in the many-cornered and unspecialized trade typical of the period. One of his ships, the *Arabella,* went to Calcutta in 1826, laden with cigars, paint, currant-jelly, shaving soap, cider, oakum, ham, pineapple, and native cheese. When his father's ships brought pepper and Bourbon cloves from Sumatra, part of the cargo was left with Perkins and Saltonstall in Baltimore in exchange for flour, and some was traded for sugar in Haiti and Havana. Three years afterward, Bordman's vessels carried sugar from Havana to Gothenburg for Swedish iron, and in 1830 he shipped a pepper cargo to the Mediterranean ports, the exact destination being left to the supercargo, who was to be advised at Gibraltar as to the possible price to be fetched by pepper at Antwerp, Leghorn, Genoa, and Trieste. Bordman was also interested in the South American, Northwest Coast, and Canton trade.

Another phenomenon of these booming days was the ice man with perhaps the longest route of his trade. Young Frederic Tudor was seized with the "crazy notion" of shipping ice from his father's pond in Saugus to the West Indies. Added to his conviction that the enterprise held vast commercial possibilities, Tudor was motivated by a humanitarian impulse. Reports had come to his ears of communities depopulated by yellow fever. The thought that there was no ice at hand to relieve the sufferers aroused his determination to provide a palliative for future epidemics. In 1805, Bostonians laughed and newspapers jeered when he sent to Martinique a 130-ton cargo of "crystal blocks of Yankee coldness." Tudor had a difficult time persuading a crew to sail on his brig *Favorite,* since pessimistic critics had predicted that the melting ice would swamp the vessel. Financially the first venture was a dismal, dripping failure. In the face of this defeat, however, Tudor wrote in his journal that one could not be a hero in love, war, or the ice business by turning back; by 1812 he had developed a regular ice trade with the West Indies.

Soon Tudor owned ice-houses in Cuba, Jamaica, and the southern United States. To accomplish this he had to teach crusty sea captains never to leave the hatches open, to experiment with such insulators as rice, hay, and coal dust before settling upon pine sawdust, and to educate the people to the use of ice by first giving it away. Once the public's fancy was caught, however, he could name his own price. At Charleston, ice brought 1½ cents a pound, at New Orleans 2 cents, at Havana 3 cents; and at Rio de Janeiro, where the bark *Madagascar* successfully brought the first shipment of ice across the Equator in 1833, Tudor obtained a Spanish dollar for 12 pounds. In the same year the *Tuscany* had plowed through the waters of Calcutta Harbor with a cargo of ice which had twice survived crossing the Equator, only one-third of the 180 tons placed aboard her in Charlestown having melted. Puzzled by the cold white blocks, the natives became indignant and demanded their money back when their purchases disappeared after having been left in the sun. Several even wanted to know whether ice was grown on trees or shrubs and inquired how they should go about starting a crop. But the European communities in the Far East quickly took to iced drinks, and the ice business advanced at an amazing rate.

To meet the increasing demands, ice from almost every pond in greater Boston was brought by pung or train and loaded on brigs or barks at Tudor's Wharf in Charlestown. Thoreau waxed lyrical at the thought of water from his beloved Walden being sent to the far-off Hindu, whose mystic philosophers he so much admired. As for Tudor himself, although forced by 15 competitors to lower his retail price to 1 cent a pound, he was able in 1841 to pay off a debt of $250,000 incurred during his early endeavors.

These and kindred leaders in the shipping industry towered above the common waterfront throng, moving with sober dignity along their wharves and conducting business in a stately manner. They dealt shrewdly and kept careful records of every penny that passed through their fingers. To all appearances they symbolized decorous living combined with adventurous financial activity.

The Town and the People

Boston had grown into a city of towering masts, staunch hulls, and impressive buildings. Fort Hill had yet to be leveled, and Atlantic Avenue was still a development of the future. Proud vessels crowded India and Long Wharves. They lay so close to shore that passers-by had to walk under the extended bowsprits, and merchant owners, glancing through the multi-paned windows of busy counting-houses, were able to see the trim, dark outlines of their own vessels' riggings silhouetted against the sky. Stevedores bustled about the docks; off in the distance, mates boisterously ordered sail on outgoing ships. Permeating this confusion came whiffs of pungent fragrance from Eastern imports, the aromas of spice, coffee and incense, the reek of copra-filled holds, and the sharp tang of salt cod.

In the center of mercantile Boston stood the Old State House, at that time the home of the new municipal offices and the post office. On the first floor was Samuel Topliff's News Room, a subscription club for Boston merchants, where newspapers, periodicals, marine registers, and bulletins from all corners of the world were on file. In the morning the Boston trader usually drove to the post office and then adjourned to Topliff's where he might learn of the previous night's happenings, for news of foreign arrivals was quickly wig-wagged to the habitues of the reading-room by a signal system from Long Island, in the harbor. Departing from Topliff's, the merchant usually walked to his office on one of the wharves. There he superintended the loading of his vessels, directed his "wharfinger," or general manager, and sent verbal orders by messengers to other docks. Before 2 o'clock he was picked up by his carriage and whisked home for an elaborate meal. In the late afternoon he went driving with his wife, and in the evening dined in the company of other merchants.

Narrow, cobblestoned Purchase and Broad Streets echoed to the rolling steps of brawny seamen ashore for the first time in months, pockets heavy with the wages of a voyage. Bent on finding the nearest brothel or cheap dance hall, the sailor "on the beach" sought solace from the brutal, dangerous life aboard ship. Rum-mills of the day knew how to part a man from his pay just as effectively as any of the modern "dives." Often the proprietor robbed his drunken victim and then promptly delivered him to some ship's captain, along with a padded bill for lodgings. Eventually the sailor awoke to the dismal discovery that he was at sea again. Worse still, when he returned to Boston, his erstwhile host was on the dock waiting to collect the lodging bill from the man's newly earned wages.

Bostonians were aware of existing conditions and took action to provide better conditions for the sailor ashore. On May 11, 1812, the Boston Society for the Religious and Moral Improvement of Seamen was formed to "establish a regular divine service" aboard merchant vessels. Before the organization was 6 weeks old, however, war with England broke out, and the Boston merchant marine was disrupted. The well-intentioned reformers had to content themselves with missionary work on a few of the wartime frigates. By 1820 the Boston Society for the Religious and Moral Instruction of the Poor had taken the place of the original association and was devoting a good share of its attention to seamen. The Reverend William Jenks, a fastidious, prim-looking Boston pastor, preached to them from a sail loft on Central Wharf, carrying on his work until the close of 1826, when the society broke its connection with the sailors.

Some months later Dr. Lyman Beecher and a group of Congregational ministers organized the Boston Seamen's Friend Society. They appealed to the public for funds and interested a number of prominent shipowners in the welfare of the sailors. Incorporated in 1829, they erected a 60-foot brick church for mariners on the eastern slope of Fort Hill, in clear view of vessels entering the Port. Some 70 feet above the ground floated a flag bearing the single word "Bethel," assuring a welcome to sailors from the furthermost points of the globe. Soon the society owned a lodging-house on Purchase Street, built at a cost of $19,000 and capable of accommodating a hundred seamen.

Other organizations also undertook to improve the tastes of Jack Tar ashore. The Boston Port Society functioned first in a little church on Hanover Street and then, in 1833, built the Seamen's Bethel in North Square, on the site of the present Italian Roman Catholic Church. Here, for nearly four decades, the ex-seaman Edward Thompson Taylor, better known as Father Taylor, walked the pulpit "like a quarter-deck," telling his sailor audiences that they came from "below—from under the hatches of sin, battened down above you by the evil one," and that they were going

aloft—with a fair wind—all taut and trim, steering direct for Heaven in its glory, where there are no storms or foul weather, and where the wicked cease from troubling and the weary are at rest.

Edward Thompson Taylor had visited Boston in 1810 and been converted in the Park Street Church. Years later his

sermons, spiced with nautical references and full of vivid
figures of speech, made the Bethel one of Boston's most popular resorts for the hardbitten men who sailed on ships. He
never minced matters. Once during a spirited sermon a member of the congregation started to leave. Father Taylor
stopped, leaned forward and said, "Sh! Sh! Keep still all of
you and don't disturb that man walking out." Another time
he noticed a woman talking and scowled down at her: "If that
lady on the third row, sitting in the end seat, with a yellow
bonnet, don't stop whispering, I'll point her out!" With the
passing of the years he became almost a legendary character,
as much a part of Boston as the Old State House. The only
preacher in the city whom Charles Dickens cared to hear, his
sermons also attracted Jenny Lind, Emerson, and Walt Whitman. Mourned by humble folk all over the world who had
never heard of Emerson or Whitman, Father Taylor died in
1871, "going out on the ebb as an old salt should."

An important service to sailors was offered by the Savings
Bank for Seamen, now known as the Suffolk Savings Bank for
Seamen and Others, located at the corner of Tremont Street
and Pemberton Square. Distinguished Bostonians served as
founders and officers of the bank, which first opened its doors
on the morning of May 1, 1833. The aim of the institution,
which was jointly sponsored by the Boston Port Society and
the Seamen's Friend Society, was entirely benevolent. Its
promoters hoped that the sailors, a notably spendthrift lot,
would place their money in the bank. The opening announcement stated that

more than a million of dollars are paid every year to seamen in this
port, and considering, too, these lavish habits of expenditure, it is
reasonable to calculate that a great proportion of this sum is diffused in
this city to support idleness, intemperance, debauchery and crime.

Change in the physical character of the town was evident.
The steady increase in population had compelled Boston to
expand at the expense of the harbor. By filling in the old
Town Cove, space for six new streets was provided; Commercial Street, one of the six, was built on the north side along
the wharves' heads. Where the town dock had formerly stood,
the million-dollar Quincy Market was erected in 1826. Beacon
Hill was partially leveled, and the dirt deposited in Mill Pond,
(North Cove) adding several acres to the city's area. This
growth of the town, and the resulting noise along the waterfront, drove prosperous merchants out of their homes near

the Bay back to "The Hill," while middle-class Boston established strongholds in the West End, Charlestown, and in the reclaimed territory. The recent immigrants poured into South Boston, East Boston, and the land that had once been the South Cove. The sailors' boarding-houses, dance halls, and barrooms were concentrated in the North End, east of Hanover Street and along Broad Street.

Wharf Activity

Along with the physical development of the city came improvement in the docking facilities of the harbor. Warehouses on the north side of Long Wharf gradually extended to the mainland and up State Street. Dignified Commercial Wharf, the finest waterfront business block in the city, attracted merchants whose ships touched the Cape of Good Hope, the Spanish Main, India, China, and the shores of California. In 1819, Central Wharf was erected with a brick three-storied warehouse running down its center for a full quarter-mile. Here 3 great auction rooms, countingrooms, and 54 wholesale stores provided businessmen with unexcelled facilities for handling their cargoes. In a cupola high above the structure was the office of the old Semaphore Telegraph Company, where advance news of arriving vessels was received from Telegraph Hill in Hull.

Wares from the Far East and the South were brought to India Wharf for disposal in the stores on the pier. The wharf was also used by boats bound for New York, Hartford, New London, New Bedford, and Nantucket. Nearby stood Lewis Wharf, home of Enoch Train's packet line and later one of the centers of the San Francisco clipper trade. T Wharf served coastwise shipping and saw the start of the first packet line to New York, as well as the beginning of an extensive Canadian service. The erection of Granite Wharf, the first modern all-stone dock, gradually attracted the East Indian and South American business. Equally important was Gray's, later named Tudor's, Wharf, in Charlestown.

Meanwhile vessels had grown to such dimensions that it became difficult to accomplish repairs below the waterline. The earlier method of beaching proved impracticable. To solve the problem, the first drydock in the United States was completed at the Boston Navy Yard, Charlestown, in March 1834. Built of Quincy granite at a cost of $972,000, it has since been enlarged and is still in use as Dry Dock No. 1. Between

Long and Central Wharves, on the site of the present Custom House tower, the "new Custom House," constructed with granite pillars, was dedicated in 1848.

Shipwrecks and Lifesaving

Numerous shipwrecks led Boston merchants to lodge complaints with the Federal Government about the inefficiency of lighthouses. In 1838 Lieutenant Edward W. Carpenter reported that Boston Light had a "revolving light, consisting of 14 argand lamps, with parabolic reflectors," about the size of "similar lamps in family use." A year later Boston Light was refitted with a new bronze lantern of 16 sides, instead of the previous 8, with larger windows, and with a range officially listed as 22 miles. By 1842 the light was making a revolution every three minutes, including two periods of illumination and two of darkness. Twelve years later the revolving time was a minute and a half, while today the light flashes white at 30-second intervals. The lighthouse received several permanent improvements in 1844, including the erection in the tower of a circular cast-iron stairway, spiraling around an iron pipe at the center and protected by a guardrail of the same material.

The dangers of the southern approach to Boston Harbor led to the establishment of Minots Light. Resting on iron piles 8 inches in diameter, the octagonal-shaped tower, begun in 1847 and costing $30,000, rose to a height of 75 feet. It first sent its rays out over the water on New Year's Day of 1850. But the "Minots Light Gale" of April 14-16, 1851, with violent easterly winds, rain, hail, snow, and an extraordinarily high tide of 15.62 feet, proved too much for the structure. Keeper Joshua Bennet was in Boston at the time, unable to return because of the hurricane force of the storm. Though by the morning of the sixteenth, the waves had torn away portions of the wooden structure, the two assistant-keepers, Joseph Wilson and Joseph Antoine, faithfully lighted the lamps as usual that night. Anxious watchers reported the light visible until 1 o'clock in the morning. At daybreak nothing remained but twisted fragments of the iron piling. The two men were drowned in a vain effort to reach the mainland.

The death of the two assistant lighthouse keepers followed upon a series of disastrous shipwrecks and bold rescues. From 1799 to 1825 the most outstanding rescuer of Boston Bay was William Tewksbury, a resident of Deer Island. Probably the most notable of his rescues occurred on May 26, 1817, when he and his son set out in a sailing canoe through choppy seas toward a capsized pleasure boat. Shipping water continually, they yet managed to reach the scene of the disaster and take seven of the eight survivors aboard their canoe, leaving the eighth clinging to the jolly boat of the overturned craft. When they returned, the last man had disappeared. Between 1817 and 1825 the father and son rescued 31 persons and received numerous medals, including one from the Massachusetts Humane Society.

The Great Hurricane of December 1839, however, completely overwhelmed the efforts of any individual life saver. Between December 14 and 16, howling gales ravaged shipping, and on December 22 and 23 a second storm struck, wrecking the schooner *Charlotte* at Nantasket and driving the bark *Lloyd* ashore at the same point. Six of the *Lloyd's* crew drowned attempting to launch a lifeboat, and 2 others were swept from the rigging where they had lashed themselves near Captain Mountford. Although eventually the *Charlotte's* sailors brought Mountford ashore, he died shortly afterward. The third phase of the hurricane was marked by tempestuous winds and an exceptionally high tide, which destroyed shore property and shipping in the inner harbor, and sent the ice-laden *Columbiana* on a wild rampage. Breaking loose from her berth at Swett's Wharf, the vessel crashed clean through the old Charlestown bridge, hit the Warren Avenue Bridge wharf, demolished the drawtender's house, narrowly missing his sleeping family, and ended up against the bridge. There might have been a worse disaster had not the mate leaped to the wheel and held the *Columbiana* to some sort of course during her zig-zag journey. All told, these three December storms caused damage of $1,000,000 in Boston Harbor, and tossed more than 20 vessels upon the shore.

In 1842, twenty-seven youthful members of the Farm and Trades School on Thompson's Island were returning aboard the *Polka* from a fishing trip, under the supervision of Oakes, an experienced sailor, and Mr. Peabody, one of the school's teachers. Tacking against a headwind for a landing on the island, the boat tipped over and sank almost immediately. Four boys managed to cling to a wooden bait box. The other 23—half the enrollment of the institution—together with the 2 men, were drowned.

The Massachusetts Humane Society obtained a $5,000

appropriation from the General Court in 1840 and placed 11 lifeboats in strategic positions along the coast. Volunteers manned these boats in cases of emergency, demonstrating their efficiency and bravery during the winter storms of 1841 and the "October Gale" of 1844. On December 17, 1841, the Boston-bound *Mohawk*, entering Massachusetts Bay, encountered an easterly wind of gale proportions. Her sails ripped to shreds, she drifted helplessly through the night, striking Point Allerton Bar the next day. The regular Nantasket lifeboat was damaged during the launching, but a smaller craft was utilized and the ship's company safely removed.

On the seventh of October 1844, the brig *Tremont*, bound for Boston, grounded at Point Allerton, and began to break up in the pounding surf. Moses B. Tower and two others hitched a team of horses to the Hull lifeboat and hauled it a mile and a half to a point opposite the ship, 5 other men joining them on the way. After a hard struggle the lifeboat was launched and inched its way through the rollers to the *Tremont*, and the captain and crew were rescued from their shattered vessel. Two months later the Nantasket lifeboat crew saved Captain Berry and 11 of the crew of the *Massasoit* after the Indiaman hit off Point Allerton. All night thundering seas washed over her and by morning the waves were still running so high that the shore lifeboat swamped 6 times before a successful launching. Everyone was taken off except a passenger, Stephen C. Holbrook of Roxbury, who had fallen down a hatchway in the excitement and was not missed until the rescuers had reached shore. Immediately the lifesavers manned 2 small boats and started back for him. Holbrook was seen creeping from the hatchway, as the ship broke in two and disappeared beneath the waves. The Humane Society awarded $10 to each of the lifesaving crew and $15 to 7 others. By 1845 the Nantasket lifeboat had rescued 36 persons. Inspired by this and other lifesaving records, the society continued to place more lifeboats around Massachusetts Bay.

The town of Hull became something of a "wreck center," and a brisk business sprang up from the ruins of Boston vessels. Thrifty citizens bought the wrecks and then broke them up, using the wood for fuel and saving the iron, copper, and other parts of value. The shell of the *Favorite* served as a stable until the sands buried it too deeply for such use; the roundhouse of the proud Indiaman *Massasoit* became a countingroom. Many an "old salt" might well have preferred a berth in Davy Jones' Locker rather than living to see the ignoble use to which his craft was put.

Port Fees and Charges

Damage to vessels entering Boston harbor was lessened by the establishment, in the 1840's, of definite rules regarding pilotage. A ship became liable to a $50 fine if it refused to take the pilot aboard after being hailed within 1½ miles of the outer light. This regulation applied to every craft bound for the Port, except fishing boats, intrastate shipping, and coastwise vessels under 200 tons. Ingoing ships were charged more than outgoing; the winter rates were higher than the summer. Thus an outward-bound craft drawing 14 feet had to pay $15.40 for pilotage between November and May and only $13.30 between May and November; incoming $26.18 in the winter and $18.90 in the summer. If a master preferred to pilot his own vessel, he might do so, providing he paid the full pilotage fees specified in the warrant. However, if no pilot appeared before his vessel passed a line from Harding's Rocks to the outer Graves and thence to Nahant Head, he could enter the Port without being liable.

Aside from pilotage, port charges were the same in Boston as in New York, with an entering fee of $5.70 and a clearing fee of $2.70. Customs charges payable to the collector of customs were $2.50 each way for a vessel of 100 tons or upward and $1.50 for less than 100 tons. The harbor master received 1½ cents a ton from vessels unloading; double that for vessels subject to foreign duties and tonnage, the sum payable within 48 hours after arrival. Schooners and sloops in the coasting trade were charged $2 by the harbor master, while an additional $2 had to be given for adjusting any difficulties respecting anchorage. Wharfage charges were 50 cents a day for ships under 50 tons and 12½ cents more for every 50 tons additional. There were additional fees for permits to land goods or load goods, debenture, and for the work of the port surveyor.

The Building of Ships

Shipbuilding became increasingly important in Boston as commerce expanded and the performance of Boston craft drew attention to the yards that produced them. Designers had developed new types of vessels: ships' hulls had increased their length and depth in proportion to their breadth, affording a cleaner, smoother run through the water and more speed per square foot of canvas. Building materials cost relatively little; higher wages and steadier employment attracted skilled shipwrights from England and the Continent and encouraged local craftsmen to greater efforts. As a result Boston vessels were usually better built than those found anywhere else in the world. Often the vessels were black-hulled, with a white band around the side; usually they were armed or at least had painted gun ports as a camouflage against pirates and privateers. Such was the speed, strength and durability of these Boston vessels that generally they completed four voyages to every three by a British or Dutch merchantman.

The productive Medford shipyards put out a great variety of small craft as well as many trim, admirably proportioned East Indiamen, seldom over 500 tons burden and able to "tack in a pint o' water." From 1783 to 1846, 375 vessels of 133,225 tonnage and a value of nearly $6,000,000 slid down the ways of the various yards along the Mystic River. One Medford craft was put together, then dismantled and shipped to the Hawaiian Islands aboard the *Thaddeus,* while another was launched without benefit of rum, as much a requisite of the shipwright's trade as the very tools he used. A construction record was established when the 400-ton *Avon* was completed in 26 days. Waterman & Ewell turned out the 620-ton *Paul Jones,* one of the fastest vessels of the time, as well as the large and beautifully appointed *St. Petersburg.*

But it was Thatcher Magoun who really spread the fame of "Medford built" vessels to every navigable body of sea water. Although George Fuller, Samuel Lapham, Jotham Stetson, Paul Curtis, and Sprague & James also played important roles in Medford shipbuilding, they are not to be compared with Thatcher Magoun. Born on June 17, 1775, the day of the Battle of Bunker Hill, Magoun followed the trade of ships-carpenter, worked with Enos Briggs in Salem, and then assisted in designing ships at Mr. Barker's yard in Charlestown, the present Boston Navy Yard. In 1802 he selected a site on the Mystic River for his shipyard, and there built the *Mt. Aetna,* the first Medford ship to come off the ways after the Revolution. In succeeding years he launched a large number of merchant vessels.

South Boston shipbuilding originated at the close of the War of 1812, when Lincoln and Wheelwright began working under the supervision of Samuel Kent. In 1822, Noah Brooks, Kent's brother-in-law, took over the business, and set up a yard at the foot of F Street. Since his interests were civic as well as commercial, Brooks managed to serve in the Legislature and the City Council; he petitioned for the establishment of the Mechanics Bank, and acted as a member of its Board of Directors. For a while E. & H. Briggs maintained a partnership with Brooks, but the company was dissolved in 1847, the Messrs. Briggs moving to the Point.

For years the Weld family had devoted much of their energies to the sea, and William Fletcher Weld was no exception. At Charlestown in 1833 he built the *Senator,* the largest ship then afloat. Soon afterward Weld moved his office and shipyard to Boston, and continued to send ship after ship down the ways. Over each completed craft floated the "Black Horse Flag," insignia of the firm of William F. Weld & Company. His sails "whitened every sea," and there were those who said that his company of shipowners was the largest in the world. Weld himself was hospitable and kindly; his Beacon Hill home was a Mecca for down-and-outers. He handled his business with meticulous care, attending to the most trivial matters, even hiring the cooks. An applicant for the position of sea cook was inevitably asked: "Can you make soup out of rope yarn?" If the man said yes, he got the job. All told, some 50 barks, brigs, and clippers were owned by William F. Weld & Company, and in later years a fleet of steamships sailed under the Black Horse Flag.

But Donald McKay, a young Nova Scotian with an uncanny eye for perfection of line, excelled the achievements of all other shipbuilders in America. Even in childhood he was fond of playing about the docks and shipyards of Shelburne, Nova Scotia, watching seamen at their multiple tasks alow and aloft, studying the slant of a vessel and the set of her sails as she departed from the harbor. Early in his 'teens, he and his brother constructed a small fishing boat; in 1826 at the age of 16, he was off to New York to learn the trade of shipbuilding from Isaac Webb. Fourteen years later he helped build the *Delia Walker* for John Currier, Jr., in Newburyport. The following year he formed a company with William Currier and in 1842 built the *Courier,* which is said to be his first production as a designer and builder of ships. By this time the name of Donald McKay was beginning to be known along the Boston waterfront. Enoch Train was persuaded to give McKay a trial, and the result was the *Joshua Bates.* So gratifying was this vessel that Train induced McKay to establish a shipyard at East Boston. Here McKay created his first Boston-built vessel, the *Washington Irving,* the finest, fastest, and most comfortable of the New York packets, and watched it glide smoothly down the ways in 1845. Soon afterward he launched the 1,301-ton *Ocean Queen,* and the smaller *Daniel Webster,* of 1,187 tons. These vessels firmly established McKay as a master builder, and paved the way for the glorious culmination of Boston shipping in the following two decades.

Mackerel, Cod, and Whales

Increased shipbuilding resulted in an extensive development of the fishing industry throughout the State, with Gloucester finally surpassing Boston in the 1840's. Until then Boston held first place in Massachusetts in the number of barrels of mackerel inspected annually; a total of 139,519 barrels were graded on the waterfronts in 1825. Boston's export of cod ran into large figures, especially when Gloucestermen sent their catches of halibut and cod, as well as mackerel, over the newly completed railroad. Although there were years of depression, the period as a whole was one of prosperity, and Boston, as the principal market, benefited accordingly. But the fisherman's share was desperately small, averaging only $62.31 a year in the cod fishery between 1840 and 1850. To relieve such distress, Congress passed a law paying a "bounty" to fishing masters and crews who devoted 4 calendar months a year exclusively to the catching of cod. The Government allowance brought the average income from codfishing up to $76.89, still far from enough to support a wife and family. Work on shore during off months, and the making of fishnets by women and children helped; yet even so the fisherman's income remained painfully below the standard of living for the day.

Few vessels actually sailed from Boston in search of whales; not more than a dozen voyages were recorded during the 30 years between 1816 and 1846, and several of them were far from successful. The Boston whaler *Telemachus* was lost at sea in 1826, after the crew had been rescued by an English brig. Off Brazil, first mate Phillip Russel and a member of the crew of the *Grand Turk* were killed by a whale on January 9, 1828. The Boston brig *Margaret,* of 125 tons burden, sailed on a whaling expedition and then disappeared. Other vessels fared somewhat better, returning with cargoes ranging from less than 100 barrels of sperm and whale oil to the cargo of the *Hope,* which docked in Boston on November 4, 1823, with 1,100 barrels of sperm and 300 barrels of whale oil. Undoubtedly, more money could be made in other phases of the shipping industry, and the Boston merchants realized this.

Packets, Sidewheelers, Railroads

By 1817, individual "packets" were sailing from Boston to New York, Philadelphia, Baltimore, Richmond, and the larger Maine ports. The approximate dates of departure were advertised in the *Columbian Centinel,* Boston's semiweekly newspaper; on July 12 appeared: "For New York and Albany, The good stanch sloop, *Traveller,* a regular packet, will sail in four or five days (wind and weather permitting); for freight or passage apply to the master on board, opposite 23 Long Wharf, or Messrs. John Barnard & Co." These vessels provided passengers with small comfortable staterooms and excellent meals, but they were not packetships in the real sense of the term, since their departures were made only when "wind, cargo and master were willing," and their destinations were by no means regular. Often such traders diverted their routes in the late summer and early fall to Savannah, Charleston, Mobile, or New Orleans, where they obtained profitable cargoes of cotton.

Such erratic sailings made it difficult to leave Boston for a particular destination at a definite time. To remedy the situation, a group of enterprising Salem and Portsmouth gentlemen attempted to establish a regular steampacket line between Boston and Salem. In 1817 the *Massachusetts* steamed down Boston Harbor, just 10 years after Fulton's initial voyage down the Hudson River. About 100 feet overall, 120 tons burden, equipped with a "walking beam" type engine, propelled by a series of paddles arranged like oars, the vessel boasted a curved stovepipe smokestack with the end fashioned into a devil's head, spouting flames. As a precaution, she carried a single mast and sails for auxiliary power. On her first trip, an excursion, the *Massachusetts'* engines broke down, and the passengers had to be sent home in stagecoaches. Subsequent delays and the apprehension aroused by boiler explosions on other lines contributed to the financial failure of three companies which successively tried to operate the steamer.

The second steamboat to appear in Boston Harbor was the *Eagle,* much smaller than the *Massachusetts,* and designed to maintain a schedule between Salem and Boston. Her first voyage, on September 17, 1818, was remarkable in that she was equipped to carry 200 passengers and only 2 persons availed themselves of the opportunity. At the end of the summer of 1821, the *Eagle* was broken up, the sale of her copper boilers, so it was claimed, bringing the owners more than the original cost of the steamer. During this same season the second *Massachusetts* also made the Boston-Beverly run, stopping at Nahant, and Marblehead, and Salem; it then ran between Boston and Nahant only until 1825. The summer colony at Nahant attracted a steady flow of visitors and the Nahant Steamboat Company, which was formed out of the ruins of the Massachusetts Steam Navigation Company, became the oldest steamship company on the bay, operating regularly from 1817 to 1893, with the sole exception of 1884.

Gloucester likewise availed itself of steamboat service. Operations of the Boston & Gloucester Steamboat Company were irregular, however, until 1859, when year-round service lasting until the 1920's was started. In the meantime, the south shore of Massachusetts Bay was not neglected. The Boston & Hingham Steamboat Company, which later became the Nantasket Beach Steamboat Company, was organized in 1831 and operated the Philadelphia-built *General Lincoln,* 95 feet long. In 1845 came the *Mayflower,* followed in 1857 by the *Nantasket,* names still used on the company's steamers. Provincetown was also connected to Boston by steamer when the *Naushin* was put on the run in 1848.

Steamships connected Maine ports with Boston as early as 1823, when the Kennebec Steamship Company began operating the *Patent* and *Maine* to Bath. Six years later the *Victory* added Portland to her itinerary. By 1830 the Boston, Portland, and Kennebec Steamboat Line sent the 351-ton *Connecticut* to Portland, where she connected with the *Patent* for Bath, Hallowell, Gardiner, and Augusta. The company boasted that the *Connecticut* was "copper fastened and coppered, with copper boilers and low pressure engines," and charged $5 for cabin passengers and $2.50 for deck passengers from Boston to Portland. Boston established connections with Penobscot ports 2 years later, when the *Bangór* was put into service. After 1836 these lines were operated by the Eastern Steamship Mail Line (the present Eastern Steamship Lines, Incorporated) which maintained a daily service, except Sundays, between Boston and Portland. Cut-throat competition marked the rivalries of the various companies on the same route. When Captain Samuel H. Howe attempted to operate an independent steamer service to Bangor in 1842, the Eastern Line reduced its fares to Portland as low as 50 cents, driving the new company out of business.

A combination stage and steamboat route from Boston to New York was inaugurated in 1827, when the steamboat *Long Branch* left New London for New York on Sundays and Wednesdays upon the arrival of the stages from Boston and Providence. During the same year the Fulton Steamboat Line placed its *Washington, Connecticut,* and *Fulton* on the Providence run, maintaining daily departures, except Sundays, at 3 p.m. Regular sailing packets also operated from Boston in the 1830's. Both the Despatch Line and the New Line advertised voyages to New York on Wednesdays and Saturdays of each week, wind and weather permitting. The sloops of the Despatch Line and the schooners of the Regular Line offered weekly sailings to Albany and Troy, forwarding freight "to any place on the Western or Northern Canal, Lake Champlain, or Montreal." Every Saturday three Boston lines, the Union Line, and Regular Line, and the Union and Despatch Line sent brigs to Philadelphia, while two companies maintained sailings to Baltimore, Norfolk, Alexandria, Charleston, and other southern ports. But much of this commerce would have died a premature death had not the "sailing packet" lines plied between Boston and every tidewater village along the New England coast, transporting freight and passengers at regular intervals.

Early in the 1840's the rivalry between the trains and the stagecoaches for steamer connections grew to considerable proportions. After a train ride from Boston to Springfield, the passengers were transferred to a stagecoach line to Hartford, by train again to New Haven, and thence by water to New York. The new Independent Line via Providence advertised that "the elegant and commodious steamboat, *New Haven,* will leave Providence on the arrival of the three o'clock train from Boston, on Tuesday's, Thursday's and Saturday's." Another route passed through Worcester and Norwich, Connecticut, with a train leaving Boston daily at 4 o'clock in the afternoon and meeting the boat at Norwich, "before 8¼ P. M." Through fare was $6, the same as on the Providence route, and the freight rate was 35 cents per 100 pounds, with no cotton being carried on passenger boats. In April of the same year, when Commodore Vanderbilt placed his *Cleopatra* on the Providence Line and lowered the rates, the Norwich

Line cut the through cabin fare to $2 and the deck fare to $1.50, successfully meeting the Vanderbilt competition.

The opening of the Erie Canal in 1825 was potentially more damaging to Boston merchants than steampackets. The Middlesex Canal had diverted traffic from Portsmouth, New Hampshire, to Boston, and the local shippers feared lest similarly the interior trade might go over the Erie to New York. There was talk of constructing waterways from Boston to the West to meet this new competition. Engineers had even decided it might be more practical to tunnel through the Berkshire Hills than to build a series of locks across them. Fortunately, the plan was abandoned as too expensive and unnecessary after the Western Railroad was completed in 1841, connecting Boston with the Erie Canal at Albany. In 1844, the railway transported 300,000 barrels of flour from Albany and Troy to the cities of New England and, 3 years later, 515,000 barrels to Boston alone. Manufacturers responded, sending their products back over the same route. Nevertheless, due to the low water rates, Boston still imported more than half of its flour by schooner, receiving from coastwise shipping more than 1,000,000 barrels in 1847.

Despite the competition of the Erie Canal, Boston's shipowners prospered, devoting their energies principally to the importation of cotton and coal. Massachusetts shoes, Quincy granite, a variety of manufactured goods, rum, and ice for mint juleps were shipped south in exchange for the cotton; this trade increased until nearly one-half the cotton consumed in America came to Boston, where it was distributed by rail to the New England textile centers. While in 1832 Boston received by water 25,000 bales of cotton, only 17 years later, this figure had jumped to the almost incredible total of 270,-000 bales. Due to the extensive use of stoves and furnaces and the growth of industries, the demand for coal was correspondingly on the upgrade; imports of anthracite from Philadelphia increased from 63,000 tons in 1830 to more than a million tons in 1850. Naturally Boston's coastwise shipping kept pace, the total of arrivals and clearances nearly doubling from 5,000 in 1830 to 9,300 in 1848.

South America, California, China

Boston's prosperous coastwise trade was a simple matter compared to the hazards associated with early business ventures in South America. Spain used the death penalty as a threat against any dealings with her colonies; bribes became the sole means of overcoming innumerable restrictions placed in the way of the American merchants. Nevertheless, money-seeking Bostonians persisted with all the skill and ingenuity at their command, and in 1804, William P. White of Pitts-field established a mercantile agency at Buenos Aires. Yet commerce with South America never became as lucrative as some of the older Boston trade routes, largely because of the particularist spirit of Yankee merchants, who preferred their individual ways of making profits to grouping together and forming large companies. Both the importing of such staple products as coffee, rubber, and chocolate and the return ship-ments of manufactured goods were hampered by better organ-ized English competition.

A good share of the South American trade was, however, centralized at Boston. Buenos Aires and Montevideo hides supplied Massachusetts tanneries and shoe factories; River Plate wool, hair, hides, sheepskins, and tallow found a ready market in Boston. Commerce with Buenos Aires was domi-nated by the firm of Samuel B. Hale & Company, established after Hale had visited the River Plate as supercargo aboard a Boston vessel. His agency prospered, and at one time the company operated 46 ships. New England lumber found an excellent market along the River Plate; dilapidated Indiamen, crammed with pine boards, sailed to Buenos Aires, where the timber was sold and the vessels broken up for firewood. The ice sent by energetic Frederick Tudor found a ready sale in South America. Brazilian coffee held an important place in Boston's South American trade; from 1841 to 1850 over 37,000 bags were imported yearly, though shipments at no time approached the imports of New York, New Orleans, or Balti-more, which were averaging between 120,000 and 245,000 bags.

Much of the local South American trade was handled by Augustus Hemenway, an enterprising Boston merchant who controlled the Valparaiso commerce. Like other merchant-princes of the day, he owned both the cargoes and the vessels that plied between Valparaiso and his warehouses in Boston, importing copper ore, nitrates, wool, hides, and goatskins, and exporting soap, lumber, candles, kerosene, refined sugar, boots, lathes, shovels, picks, machines, cotton and woolen cloth, and even organs and pianos. Hemenway was also actively engaged in the West Indies commerce, which pro-

vided stiff competition to South American trade, especially in
the coffee and logwood sent from St. Domingo, Jacmel, and
Laguarra. Sugar and molasses were of course still the principal exports of the islands, and Hemenway, demonstrating his
usual ability to control both ends of a commercial enterprise,
owned both a plantation and a sugar mill. It is said that once,
while traveling on horseback to his estate, he was captured
by Cuban insurgents. Showing no fear, Hemenway sat up all
night bargaining for his ransom, and at daybreak, when the
bandits had agreed to what he considered a just price, he sent
his manager to the bank in Sagua, paid the money, and went
quietly on his way. Thereafter he rode on the sugar train.

The hardy Northwest fur trade, "Boston's high-school of
commerce for forty years," revived in 1815 but flourished for
only a few years thereafter. During the same period, California
saw a brisk trade in furs, but hides became the principal commodity when, in 1822, her ports were thrown open to legitimate commerce by the Mexican Government. Characteris-
tically enough, a Bryant & Sturgis ship was the first to enter
the California hide trade under the new regime; she was
loaded deep with New England knick-knacks which her captain exchanged for hides. With such a beginning, it was not
difficult for Boston firms to maintain a monopoly until the
Mexican War. Trading posts sprang up all along the coast
under the able direction of men who spoke Spanish with a
nasal twang and took California heiresses as their wives.

Honolulu, through the efforts of merchants, whalers, and
missionaries, had become "Yankeefied." Cloth and rum were
in demand, and sandalwood continued to serve as an excellent medium of exchange, until King Liholiho stripped the
islands bare to satisfy his craving for fast vessels, billiard
tables, and good New England rum. In 1820, Bryant & Sturgis
of Boston sent to Honolulu a fleet of five ships, including the
noted *Cleopatra's Barge,* dubbed the Hawaiian royal yacht
after it was sold to King Liholiho for between $50,000 and
$90,000 worth of sandalwood.

Changes also occurred in the China trade. At Canton,
crockeryware, nankeens, crepes, and silks had been crowded
from the market, and teas comprised over 80 percent of the
Boston cargoes. Most of the tea-laden vessels docked at New
York, although, out of 91 such ships entering there between
1838 and 1842, 39 were from Boston. Gradually the importance of the China trade decreased, at least as far as Boston

was concerned, and in 1844 only 2 or 3 Boston firms were actively engaged in it.

After completing one China voyage, Captain John Codman (1814-1900), a Boston sea captain and author of sundry books on the sea, discharged his regular crew in New York. Recruiting a tough gang of down-and-outers along the New York waterfront, he headed his tea ship for Boston. The first morning out, the men refused to holystone the deck, claiming that such work was not in their contract. "Well, what is?" asked the Captain. The men replied, "To make sail, steer the ship, hoist anchor and so forth." "Very good," the Captain murmured cheerfully. "Then you can let go the anchor thirty fathoms and we will keep hauling it in and dropping it again until the gentlemen are satisfied." The decks were promptly holystoned.

Long voyages still attracted sturdy seamen such as Sam Holbrook, a naval shipscarpenter, who in 1817 found the Boston Navy Yard "more like a graveyard than a public naval depot," and promptly got a furlough in order to sail from Boston to India. Three days out a man went overboard, and Holbrook and another seaman, completely disregarding the skipper's vitriolic objections, tossed their drowning companion a wooden skylight cover for a life preserver, nothing else being handy. Then they lowered a boat and finally managed to rescue the man. Months later, in Bombay, a Parsee peddler came aboard, and, as Holbrook relates in his memoirs, *Threescore Years,* sold the seamen vast quantities of "that accursed crazy liquor called arack, made from the cocoa-nut, more maddening in its influence than any other intoxicating drink on earth." The crew mutinied. Two officers, blunderbusses in hand, faced the threatening mob. "If you come any farther aft, we'll fire," warned one of the mates. "Fire and be damned!" came a voice Holbrook recognized as that of the man whom he had helped rescue. There was no shooting, however, for assistance came from other ships in the harbor; the mutiny was squelched, and the men were properly chastened by threat of the rope's end.

Two weeks after Holbrook's departure, 13-year-old Robert Bennet Forbes shipped from Boston. Seven years later, "Mr. Forbes," not quite 20, was bound for Java and China, captain of the 264-ton *Levant.* As a partner in the firm of Russell & Company, he subsequently engaged in the lucrative China trade, leading a life filled with excitement and adventure.

Once, when he was a passenger aboard the *Mary Chilton,* a Chinese pilot hove to and informed the captain that his price for taking the ship into Hong Kong was "hundred dollah, welly cheap!" At this point Forbes approached and was immediately recognized by the Chinese pilot. "Hi-yah, ole Foxe!" the latter exclaimed. "Ten dollah can do, Missee Captain." All told, "Commodore" Forbes, as he was later known, was interested in more than 70 vessels. He founded the Sailors' Snug Harbor in Quincy and, in 1845, built the *Massachusetts,* the first screw-propelled auxiliary steam vessel to cross the Atlantic.

Forbes' most famous exploit, described in his *Personal Reminiscences,* was an errand of mercy. He loaded the *Jamestown* with 800 tons of food supplies for the victims of the Irish famine of 1846-47. Officered by volunteers, the *Jamestown* left the Boston Navy Yard on March 28 with a brisk northwest wind filling her sails. Next morning a terrific storm developed, and driving sleet covered decks and rigging with a glaze of ice; vicious waves snapped at the tossing craft. Thinking of the famine-stricken thousands, Forbes refused to take in sail, forcing her with every ounce of brawn and brain at his command. Just 15 days and 3 hours after clearing Boston, the *Jamestown* dropped anchor in Cork Harbor—one of the fastest runs ever made by a sailing vessel from Boston to Ireland. The supplies were received amid great rejoicing; Irish children were christened "Forbes," "James," and even "Boston"; a silver salver was sent to the shipmaster as a token of gratitude.

The Mediterranean and Fayal

After the Barbary pirates had been forced to cease exacting annual tribute from passing merchant vessels, Boston's Mediterranean trade expanded tremendously. There had been a steady increase in the demand for Oriental fruits, wines, wool, corkwood, and olive oil. Although the Mediterranean peoples lost their taste for New England salt cod, once a staple product, they learned to appreciate the wearing qualities of Lowell cottons and developed a thirst for New England rum. "I find," wrote the American consul at Genoa in 1843, "that a large proportion of our trade . . . has been carried on by Boston and Salem merchants. Some years, more than half the vessels entering this port have been owned by Robert Gould Shaw of Boston."

Although a number of native Bostonians were active at

Smyrna, a considerable percentage of the Mediterranean trade was handled by the Marquis Nicholas Reggio, Genoese resident of Smyrna, and Joseph Iasigi, Smyrnite Armenian, who established themselves as merchant-shipowners in Boston. Their keen understanding of Oriental psychology and their many close connections in Smyrna maintained the city's supremacy in the Eastern Mediterranean down to the close of the sailing-ship era. Iasigi, erector of the statues of Columbus and Aristides in Louisburg Square, and Reggio were financially successful and attained positions of prominence in the Commonwealth. They imported the best Smyrna figs, coarse wool, gum arabic and tragacanth used in the manufacture of cotton prints, sponges, Turkey carpets, and drugs like myrrh and scammony. Other dealers brought in opium for export to China, one-half the entire crop of 1820 being handled by a Boston firm at Canton.

The writers of the 1830's did not often entrust their lives to the sea. Ralph Waldo Emerson, however, ventured to Malta in 1833 aboard the 236-ton brig *Jasper,* along with four other passengers and a cargo of logwood, mahogany, tobacco, sugar, coffee, beeswax, and cheese. He complained of "nausea, darkness, unrest, uncleanliness, harpy appetite and harpy feeding, the ugly 'sound of water in mine ears', anticipations of going to the bottom, and treasures of the memory." In his *Diary,* as quoted by Morison, Emerson wrote:

Out occasionally crawled we from our several holes, but hope and fair weather would not; so there was nothing for it but to wriggle again into the crooks of the transom. Then it seemed strange that the first man who came to sea did not turn round and go straight back again. Strange that because one of my neighbours had some trumpery logs and notions which would sell for a few cents more here than there, he should thrust forth this company of his poor countrymen to the tender mercies of the northwest wind. . . .

The Captain believes in the superiority of the American to every other countryman. "You will see", he says, "when you get out here how they manage in Europe; they do everything by main strength and ignorance. Four truckmen and four stevedores at Long Wharf will load my brig quicker than a hundred men at any port in the Mediterranean." It seems the Sicilians have tried once or twice to bring their fruit to America in their own bottoms, and made the passage, he says, in one hundred and twenty days.

Throughout the nineteenth century the most prominent merchant at the port of Fayal, in the Azores, was always a Dabney of Boston. Outward-bound whalers often stopped there to unload their early oil, which the industrious Dabneys promptly reshipped to Boston, along with such local products as oranges and Pico wine, facetiously christened "Pico Madeira," although of inferior quality. Many pipes of plain Pico were exported from Boston as "Choice old London Particular." The most popular Boston sea captain in the Azores was Edmund Burke, master of the *Azor,* who left in his wake a trail of fast voyages and much affection ashore. Once when the *Azor* was overdue, the local inhabitants offered prayers for the vessel's safety. When on another occasion it became necessary to cut away the *Azor's* masts during a terrific storm, four of the Portuguese sailors were grief-stricken at the necessity of injuring her and wept bitterly as they hacked away.

The Baltic and England

More important than Boston's Mediterranean trade was her commerce with the other European countries. Grain and manufactured goods went all over Europe, France, Germany, Spain, and Holland. On the first leg of their voyage in the Baltic trade, ships resumed their task of carrying New England manufactures, lumber, and fish to Havana or Matazanas, in exchange for sugar, or, as an alternative, sailing to Fayal for whale oil and bones. The vessels then continued to the Baltic where they picked up a return cargo of Swedish steel, which was better than any this country could produce and was used in manufacture of fine tools, and Russian hemp, which was used in local shipyards for bolt rope and stays.

The development of the Russian trade at this period was in large part due to the enterprise of William Ropes, who, while in the Baltic in 1829 as a supercargo, was so impressed with the possibilities of the region that he went back 3 years later and established a trading-post at St. Petersburg. Until this time many Boston ships had put into Kronstadt "dead-freighted" to carry away cargoes of hemp, cordage oakum, iron, and sailcloth. Ropes specialized in shipping cotton direct from the United States to Russia. Ropes' son, William H. Ropes, who took over the Russian end of the business, traveled thousands of miles through Russia each winter creating markets for the goods handled by his house.

Although a New York line inaugurated the first regular passage to Europe, the Boston and Liverpool Packet Company closely followed in 1822. On October 15 of that year, S. Austin, Jr., and J. W. Lewis announced the immediate departure for Liverpool via Charleston, S. C., of the "Boston and Liverpool

Packet Company ship *Emerald,* Philip Fox, master, and of the ship *Herald* for Liverpool direct." Other ships of the line, the *Amethyst* and *Topaz,* also advertised that they would "positively leave on the days stated, if the weather permits." Built by Thatcher Magoun, these four vessels, as well as the *Boston, Lowell, Liverpool,* and *Plymouth,* were known all over the world.

The eastbound Liverpool trade was adversely affected by the lack of suitable export cargo, a handicap that has plagued Boston's operations on many trade routes down to the present. English-owned shipping carried the Liverpool-bound East and West Indian goods, which formed the export staple from Boston on other European routes. Boston had no other cargo to substitute, and the Liverpool packets were forced to go to Charleston for outward ladings of cotton. This extended voyage limited the number of passengers, for many were unwilling to make the extra journey. When the Liverpool Packet Company failed two years later, the only noteworthy achievement of the line was the record-breaking westward passage from Liverpool to Boston of the ship *Emerald.* Leaving the English port at 3 p. m. on February 20, the ship "stayed with an easterly gale" all the way across and hove to off Boston Light just 17 days out. Her owners were amazed at the remarkable passage and scarcely believed Captain Fox until he handed them his Liverpool papers dated February 20, 1824.

The second Boston packet company was equally unsuccessful and for similar reasons. On October 3, 1827, George G. Jones, of No. 41 India Wharf, advertised a list of ships and their proposed departures. By the following spring his agency operated several Magoun-built vessels, such as the *Dover,* some 121 feet in length, with a 45-foot main cabin containing 11 staterooms, a library, a wine and spirit room, a covered deck abaft the mainmast for passenger use, and a "bathing room" with bucket and sea water facilities. Cabin passage, including "matresses, bedding, wines and all other stores," cost $140. A housed-over longboat, securely lashed between the fore and mainmasts, carried pens for pigs and sheep on the bottom, ducks and geese above them, and chickens on top of the geese, while over the main hatch was fastened a cow house, since to take cows along was then the only method of providing milk at sea. By 1834, however, cargoes from Boston had become so scarce that the line was forced to abandon operations.

In 1839, Samuel Cunard, founder of the North American Royal Mail Steam Packet Company, selected Boston as the American terminus of his line. The arrival of the Cunarder *Unicorn* the next year was followed closely by the *Britannia*, which inaugurated a fortnightly schedule of sidewheel steamers. Although the sidewheelers averaged 15 days from Liverpool, they were thought to be dangerous, and could accommodate only a small cargo at a high freight rate. Sailingmasters made a point of running as close as possible to a sidewheeler, when one was encountered at sea, to show the superior speed of sail in a good wind. Passengers generally preferred the dangers of broaching to, shipwreck on a lee shore, and "all hands lost" to those of scalding steam, bursting boilers, and "burning to the water's edge." While the steamer *Sirius* once brought only 7 passengers to New York in 1838, the sailing packets carried 800 to 1,000 immigrants and from 20 to 40 cabin travelers in a single voyage.

The lack of adequate return cargoes effectively prevented the establishment of another Liverpool line until Enoch Train inaugurated his famous Boston to Liverpool clipper packetservice in 1844. Sagaciously noting increased passenger traffic, Train advertised plans for a packet line to Liverpool with his four ships, the *Dorchester* (500 tons), the *Cairo* (600 tons), the *Governor Davis* (800 tons), and the *St. Petersburg* (800 tons)—"all first-class, Medford-built, copper-fastened, coppered, and fast sailing ships." The *Dorchester* sailed for Liverpool on May 27, 1844. Later, Train built expressly for his line the *Joshua Bates, Anglo-Saxon, Anglo-American, Washington Irving, Ocean Monarch* (1,300 tons), and *Parliament*. The Liverpool end of the business was managed by Baring Brothers & Company until Frederick W. Thayer, Train's partner, took it over some years afterward. In 1848 passenger rates were as low as $80 first cabin, $50 second cabin, and $12 steerage, forcing the Cunard Company to reduce their fares from $150 to $120.

Even on Train's packets, passenger travel left much to be desired. The worst sufferers were the people who had to travel steerage; these unfortunates were stowed, together with all their worldly goods, between decks in a space hardly high enough for a tall man to stand upright, and were allowed on deck only in the best of weather. The Irish famine of 1846-47 filled every packet bound for Massachusetts with brawny men who came to work on the railroads and were destined to provide much of the State's political leadership. Since they furnished their own food on the way across, many sailed with only enough for a record trip, facing actual starvation when the vessel was delayed by westerly gales. The suffering in steerage was hardly less than the bitter experience of the Pilgrims.

Boston during the middle of the nineteenth century maintained a dominant position in foreign commerce, through the courage of her sea captains and tough crews who drove her ships and piled on canvas to the limit of the top hamper. The development of the packet lines created a race of seamen described by Charles E. Cartwright in *The Tale of Our Merchant Ships* as the "roughest and toughest class of sailors afloat." Few native Bostonians cared to ship before the mast, and only a scattering of competent British tars and able Scandinavians remained among the motley aggregation of Kanakas from the South Seas, Lascars from India, outcasts, jailbirds, and scum from all the Seven Seas. Easily distinguished by their bell-bottomed trousers and varnished hats, these "packet rats" could thrive on worse weather, poorer food, less sleep, and more rum than any other sailors alive. Only the dread belaying pin wielded by a harsh bucko-mate aboard a Boston "Hell Wagon" could keep them in subjection. Since the packets had to run on schedule, despite the worst kind of weather, the men aboard them were sailing devils, preferring to let canvas blow away rather than take it in. Hard-bitten masters established enviable records for fast runs and brilliant seamanship.

Although the ascendancy of steam should by this time have been obvious to even the most nearsighted of the Boston merchants, the Cunarders were gradually permitted to gain the choicest passenger and freight trade, while Bostonians still remained content with their past achievements. To some extent Enoch Train's line of packets helped to delay the inevitable, although "Commodore" Forbes showed he was not asleep by constructing the *Massachusetts,* with auxiliary steam power and the new Ericsson screw propeller. Most of the Boston shipowners were too busy with the Mediterranean, China, India, California, and South America trades, with the European wave of immigration, and the coastwise commerce to consider what the future held in store for them. In steam navigation, Boston marked time, as if waiting for the white topgallants of the golden clippers to lift above the horizon.

CHAPTER V

THE ROMANCE OF THE CLIPPERS

The Call of Gold

WHEN A California hide-drogher unloaded a cargo of crude leather at the Port of Boston in the autumn of 1848, her skipper lost no time in spreading the exciting news that gold had been discovered in the newly annexed Territory of California. A few months later Captain William Dane Phelps, the first American to carry the Stars and Stripes up the Sacramento River, returned to Boston from California. He brought back a bag of gold that created a wild furore. Boston newspapers printed extravagant accounts about barrels of gold, and hundreds of visitors flocked to Phelps' house, to examine the gold dust and to seek first-hand information about the gold mines of California.

Boston was swept by a "gold fever"; the sight of the yellow metal had given substance to incredible rumors about gold nuggets, as large as eggs, being picked up by the handfuls along the California river-beds. During the "gold rush" that followed, Nantucket lost one-fourth of its voting population, and Boston suffered almost as great a depletion. Lured by the prospect of riches over night, local artisans, merchants, lawyers, and even ministers dropped their work and dashed off to California. True to their seafaring traditions, most of Boston's gold seekers chose the ocean route instead of the Overland Trail. In 1849, 151 ships, barks, brigs, and schooners cleared the Port for San Francisco; the year 1850 saw 166 California-bound vessels depart from Boston and at least an equal number from smaller Massachusetts towns.

All told, about 316 companies of Forty-Niners, ranging from 10 to 150 members, took ship at Boston in 1849 and 1850. The Bunker Hill Mining and Trading Company, for example, consisted of 30 mechanics from Charlestown, Somerville, and Cambridge, each of whom contributed $500 toward their ship. Few groups were as well endowed as the North Western Company, whose members, of the professional class, paid $1,000 each and purchased a luxurious clipper brig.

Since little return cargo was available, only one Boston ship-owner found it expedient to charter his vessels to the emigrants. This was Enoch Train, who felt he could divert several ships from his famous line of Liverpool packets to hurry men and merchandise to the West Coast.

In keeping with lingering Puritan tradition, Boston's gold hunters prefaced their departure by church services and Bible presentations. William H. Thomes, at one time connected with the *Boston Herald* and a member of a company sailing for San Francisco on the *Edward Everett,* wrote *Reminiscences of a Gold Hunter,* a droll account of these sessions and their sequel. Octavius T. Howe, in *The Argonauts of '49,* quotes him at length:

> The Hon. Edward Everett . . . made us a present of 100 volumes as a library and in his letter conveying the gift said, "You are going to a strange country. Take the Bible in one hand and your New England civilization in the other and make your mark on the people and the country". . . . Only a few remembered the excellent advice of the good man, while some of our most promising students of divinity swore like pirates when they lost at monte and had hard luck at the mines; while one day at Sacramento I saw on the counter of a grogshop one of the Bibles which had been presented to us with so much thoughtful care for the welfare of our souls. One of our civilizers had sold his holy book for a drink.

Sponsored by the Boston and California Joint Stock Mining and Trading Company, the first organized Boston prospectors to sail for California embarked on the *Edward Everett* on January 12, 1849. After the landlubbers had found their sea legs, they began to invent diversions to break the monotony of the long voyage around the Horn. Corridors between decks were christened with such familiar names as Dock Square, Beacon Street, and Ringers Row; a weekly newspaper was published; there were Sunday prayer meetings, scientific lectures, and mock trials.

A young man on the *Edward Everett* wrote *A Journal of a Voyage to California,* which is full of pithy comments on events of the passage. In an entry dated February 3, the author comments on the lack of industry among his fellow travelers:

> It is my working day . . . down in the fore hold pickling and stowing port. That Irish stevedore stowed everything just as it happened, so that the barrels that were stowed bung down the pickle run out. About half of the company are regular shirks. Out of the 15 men whose turn it is to work you can't keep more than ten of them where the work is.

The appearance of a passing ship always supplied a welcome interlude for the ocean-weary voyagers. When the

Aurora of Nantucket, bound also for San Francisco, turned up, her crew came aboard and were treated to lemonade. Two days later, February 16, the Swedish brig *Othello,* en route to Rio de Janeiro, was visited by men from the *Edward Everett.* They greatly admired the Brussels carpets, mahogany table, chandelier, and looking-glass of the *Othello.*

During warm starlight nights of February and March while the *Edward Everett* was passing through the southern latitudes, most of the company gathered on deck, spinning yarns and singing songs of home to the accompaniment of a violin and banjo. A stop at Valparaiso was a pleasant change. The passengers hired donkeys and galloped through the streets, attended bull and cock fights, and found relief from the ship's fare in tropical fruits and drinks.

The last month of the voyage saw all hands employed in making tents and boats; mining engines were brought on deck and overhauled, and gold-washing machines were tried out. Evening entertainments followed the day's activities. A band was formed to dispel the gloom of homesickness; parading, dancing, fishing, and target shooting became popular pastimes. On June 22, according to the *Journal,*

We had a great time after supper. About 40 of us dressed ourselves up with our guns, pistols, knapsacks, tin pans, wash bowls, etc., with one of the sailors dressed in regimentals. We marched about decks with a fife and flute at our head.

A special program was arranged in celebration of the Fourth of July. "Hail Columbia" and "Yankee Doodle" were played; "Land of Our Fathers" and "The Star-Spangled Banner" were sung. The Reverend J. A. Benton recited an original poem, Luis Lull delivered an oration, and the Declaration of Independence was read. Dinner included hot biscuits and butter, beef, pork, and applesauce, gingerbread and "fixings," plum cake, tarts, and fruit. In the evening, fireworks and a "grand soiree" by the colored population, some of whom were attired in women's clothes, climaxed the festivities. The holiday spirit still prevailed 2 days later when the *Edward Everett* sailed into San Francisco Harbor, 175 days from Boston. Emigrants and crew alike were sorely disappointed, when they observed that the town was "no place at all. More tents than houses." Shortly after landing the company disbanded.

Thirteen days later another Boston ship, the *Capitol,* docked at San Francisco, after a voyage mainly notable for dissension between the captain and his passengers. The trouble started a few days out of Boston, when the gold seekers demanded better food, more of it, and enough forks and spoons to continue proper table manners. When the captain replied that he was following the shipowner's instructions, the passengers threatened mutiny and drew up a protest. The resolution accomplished its purpose, but ill-feeling never wholly died down. At the order of the captain, the sailors discontinued the practice of hauling water over the side of the vessel for the ablutions of the passengers. An old leather bucket was attached to the monkeyrail, and thereafter every man hauled his own water. At San Francisco the gold-mad sailors promptly deserted, and the harassed captain became insane and took his own life, leaving a lone mate on the vessel.

A few Boston companies took the shorter Panama route and suffered great hardships crossing the fever-infested Isthmus. Sailing vessels or steamers were used to get to Chagres, a port near the Atlantic entrance to the present Panama Canal. Typical of the experiences of travel across the country were those described in letters of the members of the Boston and Newburyport Mining Company, who left Boston on February 24, 1849, and by Samuel Holbrook in *Threescore Years, an Autobiography,* published in 1857. The mining company members hired native guides to take them to Gorgona, about halfway across the Isthmus, for the price of $10 per person. The bargain could not be enforced when, midway of the journey, the guides refused to continue until they were paid an additional $60 for each member. At the end of his first day's journey overland, Holbrook found the only available lodging was a rickety chamber built over a pigsty. Sleep was out of the question, for the hogs sensed his presence and plagued him throughout the dark hours with their grunting and squealing. Nor was his luck any better the next night, when he sought slumber in an old shanty which was nothing more than a few bamboo sticks "stuck in the ground, with others across, and the roof thatched." He had not retired long before he found that "there were others there who claimed a pre-emption right, and had assailed us from the crowns of our head to the soles of our feet." Holbrook and his companions obtained a piece of sperm candle from the old Indian women who owned the hut and by its light cleaned out the rubbish and "made out to live till morning."

Between Gorgona and Panama, the route lay over mountains and was usually traversed by donkeys. The fever-wracked travelers relaxed at Panama if a ship were not immediately available and wasted their money at monte and other gambling devices. Members of the Boston and Newburyport Mining Company had planned to travel from Panama to San Francisco by steamer but found the $400-$600 fare too high for their depleted purses. After several weeks waiting they booked passage on the bark *Circassian* at a fare of $200, having sold part of their stores to obtain that sum. The *Circassian* set sail for the Golden Gate, but head winds drove her back beyond the Equator. Intense heat spoiled the barrels of pork and beef; the vessel's seams began to open. While pumps rattled constantly through scorching days and sultry nights, mutinous looks appeared on the haggard faces of the crew. As the days wore on, the water supply ran low, and the passengers were restricted to a pint a day. So desperate with hunger were the travelers that on one occasion they broke into the storeroom and "found some salt pork which they devoured raw." During the last 3 weeks of the voyage to San Francisco the passengers broke their fast but once a day. At that single meal they ate "two ounces of jerked beef, so wormy that it would crawl, and four ounces of ship bread full of maggots."

For the most part, Bostonians made the hazardous trip to California in the slowest and most decrepit hulks, spending long months at sea and weathering treacherous gales off Cape Horn. Every sort of craft that could float, from whale ship to fragile schooner, was hurriedly pressed into service to carry men and goods to the gold fields. During the 5 to 8 months' voyage, scurvy and ship fever (typhus) took a heavy toll; lacking proper medical care, the less robust died from even simple ailments.

The story of Dr. Samuel Merritt of Boston and Plymouth is illustrative of the fortunes won and lost by emigrating Yankees. While loading his brig at Boston, Dr. Merritt thought of purchasing tacks but was prevented by professional duties from getting to a tack factory, thus losing an opportunity to sell them at San Francisco for $5 a package. During the voyage, he passed up an opportunity to take on potatoes, which were also in great demand at the Californian port. Finding no market for his cargo of general merchandise, Dr. Merritt turned his medical profession to such good account that he received $40,000 in one year. His desire to trade was still strong, however, and he sent a chartered brig to Puget Sound for ice. The captain returned with a load of timber, which happened to be in great demand for the building of wharves. The trip proved so highly profitable that a second one was undertaken for the same purpose. Dr. Merritt next instructed his shipmaster to exchange a load of Puget Sound lumber for Australian coal, but the captain returned instead with a cargo of oranges from the Society Islands. The fruit sold for fabulous prices, and again the venturesome doctor won out.

Boston's waterfront became tense with excitement whenever a gold ship embarked for California. The members of the prospecting society exhibited themselves wearing slouch hats and high boots, in a spirit of reckless daring, and occupied the center of attention as they bade farewell to anxious relatives and envious friends. Arriving in various stages of inebriation, the crew was literally dragged on deck by boarding-house runners. The officers brought well-stocked sea chests; the more provident seamen carried their entire wardrobe in bandanna handkerchiefs. On the quarterdeck stood the mate, to whom the captain had delegated the unpleasant duty of getting the ship out to sea. Nervously mindful that scores of people were studying his every movement, the bucko counted himself lucky if he could muster two-thirds of the seamen in fit condition to cast off hawsers and stand by. According to descriptions furnished by Captain Arthur H. Clark in *The Clipper Ship Era,* once the ship had drifted clear of the wharf, the mate bellowed cheerfully. "Heave on the windlass brakes. Strike a light!" Breaking into a rollicking rhyme that shocked the ladies gathered at the end of the dock, chanteying hands raised the anchor to the rail. The mate cried, " 'Vast heaving!", then to the captain, "The anchor's apeak, Sir." "Very good, Sir. Loose sails fore and aft." "Aye, aye Sir! Aloft, you gentlemen in disguise. You! Up in the tops and crosstrees, and overhaul gear. Royals and topsails! Lay out there, four or five of you, and loose head sails. Bos'n, take some men and look after the main and mizzen. You on the foretops'l! If you cut that gasket, I'll split your . . . thick skull!" Canvas set, sheets hauled to windward, and yards braced, the ship commenced to move. The gold seekers gave a full-throated roar; the crowd on the wharf returned three cheers and watched the Argonaut dwindle to a white speck.

Sighting the sandy coast of California after an ocean voyage of 18,000 miles, the ship-bound Bostonians burst into song:

Jump along, Jonathan, jig along, Jemima,
California's full of gold, we'll all be rich as Lima.

Often a vessel entering the Golden Gate was kept afloat only
by the operation of her pumps and had to be run aground on
the mud flats of Mission Bay. Upon arrival at San Francisco,
passengers and crew rushed off to the "diggin's," the passengers frequently leaving behind their belongings and the crew
neglecting to collect their pay. Many Boston vessels never
again put out to sea; deserted by their crews, they were converted into saloons, hotels, and even prisons. To man outbound vessels at San Francisco captains sometimes found it
necessary to ship jailbirds, regardless of their inexperience.
Crews grew so scarce that the standing joke of the times
depicted seamen requiring letters of recommendation from
pleading sea captains. The *South Carolina,* one of the few
ships to escape from San Francisco in the first year of the
gold fever, returned to Boston with a cargo of Valparaiso
copper.

The passenger register of Boston's gold ships listed a number of courageous and adventurous women. Departing late
in 1849, the *California Packet* carried 12 married and 16
unmarried women as well as 15 children. However, when an
erstwhile matron at Sing Sing, Mrs. Farnham, attempted to
recruit Boston women for a proposed company made up
entirely of the gentler sex, the undertaking failed miserably,
despite the high wages paid on the West Coast, where even
laundresses were earning $1,200 a year. Carrying 15 male pas-
sengers in addition to a maiden lady, two widows, and their
redoubtable leader, Mrs. Farnham's chartered vessel, the
Angelique, finally sailed for San Francisco in May 1849. Early
in the voyage the captain and Mrs. Farnham developed many
differences and aired them all the way to Valparaiso. Here
Mrs. Farnham went ashore to see the sights. Refusing to wait
one minute beyond the scheduled sailing hour, the captain
left the quarrelsome lady behind. Either prompted by Latin
chivalry or dismayed by the prospect of harboring such a formidable person, the Chileans took up a collection and paid
her passage to the Golden Gate. Subsequently, Mrs. Farnham
prosecuted the skipper but lost her $15,000 suit for damages.

Gold ships carried their quota of fugitives from justice, who
employed devious ruses to evade arrest. Holbrook, in *Threescore Years,* described his fellow travelers to Chagres:

On board the steamer there were about three hundred cabin and steerage passengers, among whom were about 40 regular New Orleans gamblers, together with several ladies of doubtful repute. There were also some who had run away from their families, and some who were fleeing from their creditors. . . . One of these worthies was two days and nights stowed away in the coal bunker of the steamer, while two constables were in search of him.

The escape of another lawbreaker, who wished to sail to California on the *Duxbury*, is told by Howe in the *Argonauts of '49*. Upon approaching the vessel, the youthful adventurer noticed the sheriff at the gangplank. Quickly dodging out of sight, the fugitive reflected for a moment. The ship was to leave within 20 minutes, and the obstacle in the way of his boarding her seemed insurmountable. Slipping into a nearby grocery store owned by a friend, he explained his plight. The grocer told him to jump into an empty wooden box, and began to nail on the cover. The inscription "Medicine, this side up with care" was hastily written on the box. A minute before sailing time, under the very nose of the watchful sheriff, the box was rushed up the gangplank and placed in the hold. Unfortunately, the busy freight handlers disregarded the instructions, and the young fugitive spent some time standing on his head before being released.

Boston merchants rushed cargoes of every description around the Horn after reports had reached them that 90,000 emigrants in San Francisco were offering fabulous prices for food, clothing, and every necessity of life. Flour sold for $44 a barrel; potatoes $16 a bushel; eggs $10 a dozen, an unprecedented price for eggs which had aged 160 days without transit refrigeration. Laden with the eagerly sought commodities, no less than 16 Boston vessels entered the Golden Gate between June 26 and July 28, 1850. Overstocked with baby cradles, one enterprising trader sent them around the Horn, to serve as rockers for placer mining. Cargo space on a California-bound ship sold for $1.50 per cubic foot; freight rates soared to such heights that the owners of the Medford-built *Argonaut* cleared their expense before the ship sailed on her maiden voyage. After July 24, 1850, when the New York clipper *Sea Witch* dropped anchor in San Francisco Harbor, completing a record-breaking passage of 97 days, every mercantile agency in San Francisco insisted upon the use of the speedier shipments by clipper. The knell had sounded for the older Pacific carriers, and shipyards, far and wide, responded to the new demand.

Ocean Greyhounds

At first, Boston shipowners had been skeptical of the clipper type of vessel, since, for its size, it had a relatively small cargo capacity and required a large crew to handle its numerous sails. For some time Boston merchants had recognized the need of faster ships for hauling China tea to European markets, but they felt that clipper ships were suitable only if extra money could be collected for greater speed. Added to the requirements of the China trade, the sudden demand for quick passage to San Francisco gave the necessary incentive. There had been "clipper schooners" as far back as 1812— Baltimore clippers, or "opium clippers" as they were called, long low craft with rakish masts and a reputation for speed which made them the darling of pirates, slavers, and opium runners. But not until 1845 did the *Rainbow,* an extreme clipper with square sails on all masts, slide down the ways in New York. Her fine ends and cross-section came from the Baltimore clippers; the concave lines of her bow were taken from a Singapore sampan.

Boston came to play a leading role in the construction of the fleetest and most superbly beautiful clipper ships ever designed. Summoning all the skill gained from nearly two centuries of experience, local shipbuilders fashioned ever larger and speedier ships. Along the East Boston waterfront the clang of hundreds of sledge hammers, topmauls, and caulking mallets rang out in a deafening chorus, as the aroma of boiling Carolina pitch and Stockholm tar mingled with that of fresh-hewn lumber. Close by the shipyards stood the rigging-lofts, sail-lofts, boat-builders' shops, block-and-pump makers' stands, painters', carvers', and gilders' shops, iron, copper, and brass workshops, mast and sparmakers, and ship supply stores, where all that was necessary for the outfitting of a vessel, from sail needle to anchor chain, could be found.

Boston's first clipper, the *Surprise,* was built at Samuel Hall's East Boston yard in 1850. Designed by 23-year-old Samuel Hartt Pook, the "first independent architect of merchant vessels in New England," the vessel registered 1,261 tons, and displayed a narrow beam of 40 feet compared with her 184-foot length. Her launching on October 5, 1850, was an elaborate affair. To provide a place for entertaining the wives and mothers of the craftsmen who had constructed the clipper, Hall's mold-loft, colorfully decorated with bunting, was transformed into a banquet hall, and a ladies' pavilion was set up. Fully rigged, gear-roved, spritsail yard crossed, and pennant flying, the *Surprise* disappointed waterfront critics who had expected her to capsize or stick in the mud. With half of the town cheering, the graceful vessel shot into the water, swayed perilously for a few moments, and then righted herself —haughty as a queen. When she was towed into a loading berth at New York by the Boston steamer *R. B. Forbes,* the *New York Herald* declared the *Surprise* the handsomest ship ever seen in that port. Her maiden voyage under Captain Philip Dumaresq beat the record passage of the *Sea Witch* to San Francisco by one day, even though a capacity cargo of 1,800 tons, worth $200,000, was carried. After a fast voyage from California to Canton, the *Surprise* loaded tea for London at double the freight rates paid to British vessels, and cleared $50,000 net profit, above the cost of construction, for her owners. The ship was one of Boston's most successful clippers.

On December 7, 1850, frostbitten spectators solemnly watched the 1,535-ton *Stag-Hound* speed down the smoking ways of Donald McKay's shipyard. When the shores were knocked out from under the vessel, she fairly leaped into the water, aptly materializing the symbol of her figurehead—a hound straining at the leash. But for the quick-wittedness of the master rigger, who dashed a bottle of rum against her swift-moving hull, the *Stag-Hound* would not have been formally christened. Built like a racer, she measured 215 feet overall, 40 feet in breadth, and 21 feet in depth. Despite sharply rising sides, her mainyard spread out 86 feet and the stump of her mainmast extended 88 feet above deck. Fully clothed, the *Stag-Hound* carried 8,000 square yards of canvas. Frightened by the sharpness of her design and veritable cloud of canvas, the New York underwriters cautiously charged extra premiums.

Although a faster ship than most of her predecessors, the *Stag-Hound* on her maiden voyage broke no records. She lost her upper masts 6 days out of New York, limped around the Horn, and finally put into Valparaiso for repairs. From that port Captain Josiah Richardson wrote to her owners:

Gentlemen—Your ship, the *Staghound,* anchored in this port this day, after a passage of 66 days, the shortest bar one ever made here; and if we had not lost the maintopmast and all three topgallantmasts on February 6, our passage doubtless would have been the shortest ever made. The ship is yet to be built to beat the *Staghound*. Nothing that we have fallen in with yet could hold her in play. I am in love with the ship, a better sea boat or working ship or drier I never sailed in.

Carrying freight at the rate of $1.40 per cubic foot, the *Stag-Hound* anchored at San Francisco 107 days out of New York. On the way to China she beat the famous *Sea Serpent* by 9 days and returned to New York after a fast passage of 94 days, only to learn that the *Swordfish,* which had left Canton at the same time, had already been in port for 5 days. Financially the maiden voyage of the *Stag-Hound* was a huge success; she earned $80,000 above her construction costs.

The *Witchcraft,* first clipper of another East Boston builder, Paul O. Curtis, was also launched in 1850. One of the few sailing vessels to make the San Francisco run in less than 100 days, her speed ranked with that of the *Surprise* and the *Stag-Hound*. In appearance she was a handsome, beautifully finished vessel, bearing on her masthead the carved figure of a Salem witch astride a broomstick. Ill fate dogged the *Witch-craft* on her maiden voyage. She lost her spars during the first stage of the trip and, like the *Stag-Hound,* was forced into Valparaiso for repairs. On the way to China a typhoon partially dismasted her.

The gold rush to California keyed up every shipyard in Massachusetts to a peak of efficiency. Wild, speculative years of shipbuilding followed the successful launching of Boston's first clippers. Nine clippers were built at Boston in 1851; during the next year 19 more were completed, while New York constructed only 8. Clipper building reached its zenith in 1853, when 48 huge ships were added to the California fleet, 21 being launched from Boston. The enormous cost of construction caused Boston shipowners to finance clippers by the public sale of stock. Every Boston citizen with money to spare, and some who could not spare the funds, proudly purchased one or more shares in the ocean greyhounds; both the pride of ownership and the hope of fabulous profits prompted their investments. But most of Boston's clippers flew the ensign of New York or British firms and operated out of New York. It was with mixed feelings of joy and sadness that Bostonians watched their splendid vessels glide down the harbor under the flag of another port, perhaps never again to return.

Boston shipbuilders vied with each other in turning out handsome clippers. There was no tinsel or veneer about these vessels; no expense or detail which might increase their speed was spared. The best material and the most painstaking care went into their making—solid oak beams and southern pine planks, sheathed and fastened without stint of the best copper. Contractors often spent large sums for such rare woods as India teak and Spanish mahogany. Many Boston clippers boasted pretentious staterooms and bathrooms for passengers; stanchions, fife railings, and deck houses fairly shone with brass, rosewood, and mahogany. If a Boston builder had dared skimp, his craftsmen would have deserted him. Larger in size, sharper at the bow, longer in relation to its beam, more heavily sparred, more gracefully designed, with inclined waterline and V-shaped sides, the clipper differed as much from its bluff-bowed predecessor as the modern streamlined engine from the old-fashioned steam locomotive.

In the spring of 1851 Donald McKay launched the *Flying Cloud,* one of the fastest sailing vessels ever built. Designed for his friend and former partner, Enoch Train, the clipper was sold, while still in the stocks, to a New York firm for twice the contract price. The 1,783-ton vessel supported a mainmast 88 feet high and featured a full poop deck which provided cabin accommodations described by Morison as "most elegant and tastefully wainscoted with satinwood, mahogany, and rosewood, set off by gilded pilasters." Command of the *Flying Cloud* was awarded to Josiah Perkins Cressy, a Marblehead captain who had established a noteworthy record in the East Indian trade as a master of the *Oneida.* On June 3, 1851, the glorious craft left New York for her record-breaking maiden voyage around the Horn to California. Entries in her log quoted by Lubbock in *China Clippers,* indicate the desperate doggedness of her skipper, who established a new mark for the hazardous passage.

June   6.—Lost main-topsail yard, and main and mizen topgallantmasts.
June   7.—Sent up topgallantmasts and yards.
June   8.—Sent up main-topsail yard and set all possible sail.
June   14.—Discovered mainmast badly sprung about a foot from the hounds and fished it.
June   24.—Crossed the Equator, 21 days out.
July   11.—Very severe thunder and lightning. Double-reefed topsails—latter part blowing a hard gale, close reefed topsails, split fore and main topmast staysails. At 1 p. m. discovered mainmast had sprung. Sent down royal and topgallant yards and studding sail booms off lower and topsail yards to relieve the mast. Heavy sea running and shipping large quantities of water over lee rail.
July   12.—Heavy south-west gales and sea. Distance 40 miles.

July   13.—Let men out of irons in consequence of wanting their services,
          with the understanding that they would be taken care of
          on arriving at San Francisco. At 6 p. m. carried away main-
          topsail tye and truss band round mainmast. Single reefed
          topsails.
July   19.—Crossed latitude 50 south.
July   20.—At 4 a. m. close-reefed topsails and furled courses. Hard
          gale with thick weather and snow.
July   23.—Passed through the Straits of Le Maire. At 8 a. m. Cape
          Horn north 5 miles distant, the whole coast covered with
          snow.
July   26.—Crossed latitude 50 south in the Pacific, 7 days from same
          latitude in Atlantic. (This was a record passage of the Horn.)
July   31.—Fresh breezes and fine weather. All sail set. At 2 p. m. wind
          south-east. At 6 squally, in lower and topgallant studding
          sails. 7 p. m., in royals. 2 a. m., in foretopmast studding sail.
          Latter part strong gales and high sea running, ship very wet
          fore and aft. Distance run this day by observation 374 miles.
          During the squalls 18 knots of line were not sufficient to
          measure the rate of speed. Topgallant sails set.
August   1.—Strong gales and squally. At 6 p. m., in topgallant sails,
          double reefed fore and mizen topsails. Heavy sea running.
          At 4 a. m. made sail again. Distance 334 miles.
August   3.—Suspended first officer from duty, in consequence of his
          arrogating to himself the privilege of cutting up rigging
          contrary to my orders and long-continued neglect of duty.
August 25.—Spoke barque *Amelia Pacquet* 180 days out from London
          bound to San Francisco.
August 29.—Lost fore-topgallant mast.
August 30.—Sent up fore-topgallant mast. Night strong and squally—
          Anchored in San Francisco Harbour at 11:30 a. m. after
          a passage of 89 days 21 hours.

Sandy Hook to Equator.....................................21 days
Equator to 50° South......................................25   "
50° Atlantic to 50° South Pacific......................... 7   "
50° South Pacific to Equator..............................17   "
Equator to San Francisco..................................19   "
                                                         _____
                                                          89 days

Distance Run ....17,597 statute miles
Daily Average 222   "   "

A wave of enthusiasm swept San Francisco when the *Flying
Cloud* entered the Golden Gate on August 30, 1851. After
being given a public reception, Captain Cressy was lavishly
entertained at a succession of private banquets. Old salts
gazed in admiration at the fishings and extra-rackings on the
spars of the *Flying Cloud,* and noted her chain frappings, mast
doublings, and splintered topmast fids, which bore mute
evidence of the noble craft's strenuous endeavors in the teeth
of Cape Horn storms and gales. Cressy lost no time in discharging his refractory first mate, who immediately hired a
lawyer and brought suit, but later dropped his charges upon

reading a false story of the captain's death on the second day out to China. After loading tea at Macao, a Portuguese port on the Canton River, the *Flying Cloud* sailed for New York on January 6, 1852. Halfway across the Indian Ocean, Cressy exchanged Anjer's fruit for newspapers, only to read his own obituary notices. His vessel arrived at New York 96 days out from China, but 10 days behind the *N. B. Palmer*, a New York-built clipper. On his next voyage to California, Captain Cressy left New York 8 days before the *N. B. Palmer*, which overtook the *Flying Cloud* when the latter was becalmed off the coast of Brazil. From there the *Flying Cloud* had the better of the race, and Cressy brought his ship into the Golden Gate 113 days out and 3 weeks ahead of his rival.

In five voyages between New York and San Francisco, Donald McKay's *Flying Cloud* averaged 101 days, 7 hours—a record which has never been beaten by a sailing vessel. In describing this marvelous vessel, Morison noted that "for perfection and beauty of design, weatherliness and consistent speed under every condition, neither he (McKay) nor any one else surpassed the *Flying Cloud*. She was the fastest vessel on long voyages that ever sailed under the American flag."

In front of the old Merchant's Exchange on State Street, Boston's shipping fraternity supported their favorite clippers with wagers ranging from the customary beaver hat to thousands of dollars. Shipowners lavished almost as much affection on their vessels as they did on their own flesh and blood. Proud of the speed records of their clippers, the American Navigation Club, of which Daniel C. Bacon of Boston was president, challenged British shipowners and merchants to a stake race in 1852, stipulating that

two ships should be modelled, commanded, and officered entirely by citizens of the United States and Great Britain respectively, and that they should sail with cargo on board from a port in England to a port in China and back to the English port, the prize for the winning vessel to be £10,000.

When no English shipowner dared to accept the challenge, the stake was doubled, and the British entry was even offered a two weeks' start. Despite the exhortations of London newspapers, no British merchant could be persuaded to make the race. If it had ever taken place, Captain Philip Dumaresq would have commanded the American ship.

The outstanding clipper of 1852, and naturally a product of McKay's unequalled shipyard, was the *Sovereign of the Seas*.

Sparing no cost, Donald McKay had supervised every aspect of the vessel's construction down to the minutest detail. Directly after her launching, she was turned over to McKay's younger brother, Captain Lauchlan McKay, who superintended the rigging and sail-fitting. Measuring 265 feet overall, registering 2,421 tons, running 6,000 square yards of canvas, and carrying a crew of 105 men and boys, the *Sovereign of the Seas* was by far the largest clipper yet built in America. Flying the ensign of Grinnell & Minturn's Swallow Tail Line, with Captain Lauchlan McKay in command, the handsome vessel sailed with $84,000 worth of freight for San Francisco on August 4. Although it was a bad season of the year for the run down the Atlantic, the new clipper crossed the Equator in the remarkably good time of 25 days. Negotiating the difficult passage around the Horn in only 9 more days, Captain McKay set his vessel on a northerly course, only to see her main topmast, mizzen topgallantmast, and foretopsail yard go by the board. Although this accident would have impelled the ordinary skipper to put into a Chilean port, Captain McKay lost no time in refitting the stricken ship at sea. While the vessel was kept moving, the crew rerigged her by working day and night under extraordinary danger. Her hard-driving captain did not leave the deck once during these 14 days.

When the *Sovereign of the Seas* sailed past the Golden Gate, after a record passage for that time of the year, 103 days, her arrival was the occasion of an impressive popular reception. Crowds assembled on nearby wharves gazed in admiration at the carved figurehead of a marine deity blowing a conch. While her extra large crew warped the handsome clipper into her berth, they sang in chorus:

> Oh! Susannah, darling, take your ease,
> For we have beat the clipper fleet—
> The Sovereign of the Seas.

Despite Captain McKay's humane treatment, many of his vessel's company "skipped" to the diggings, reducing her complement to a modest 34. The clipper sailed to the Hawaiian Islands, where the prospect of a homeward cargo of sperm oil seemed more promising than China tea. Loaded with liquid cargo and favored by strong quartering winds, the *Sovereign of the Seas* fairly ran over the South Pacific to the Horn, and astonished her crew as well as her captain by logging 19 knots, covering 3,144 miles in 10 days, with a single day's run of 411 nautical miles. Undermanned and handicapped by a badly sprung foretopmast, the clipper reached New York in 82 days. Within a year the glorious craft had earned her unprecedented sale price of $150,000.

Boston's fleet of majestic clippers catapulted past Boston Light and whipped around the Horn to California, thence squared away for Canton, where they loaded tea for London as well as Boston. Rounding the world on nearly every voyage, many of these clippers—like the *Sovereign of the Seas*—paid for themselves within a year of their launching. Laden down as they were with excessive cargoes, the great ships nevertheless moved through the water faster than any sailing yacht or racing craft ever invented. Eight knots is considered a good average for a modern "American Cup" yacht course of 30 or 40 miles, yet the *Red Jacket* logged 14.7 knots for 6 successive days, while the *Lightning* logged 15.5 knots for 10 days. More than anything else, the clipper ships strove for speed. Every passage became a contest on which depended the reputation of the master, the builder, and the vessel.

The most notable race ever staged by American clippers took place between several Boston and New York clipper ships. Owned by the Boston firm of Sampson & Tappan, the *Flying Fish* entered the competition against such fast vessels as the newer *Westward Ho!*, the *John Gilpin*—pride of Samuel Hall's yard—and the New York clippers, *Wild Pigeon* and *Trade Wind*. The *Wild Pigeon* had departed from New York on October 12, 1852; the *Westward Ho!* left Boston on the twentieth; the *John Gilpin* sailed on the twenty-ninth; the *Flying Fish* followed 2 days later. Favored by an early start, but delayed by calms and head winds, the *Wild Pigeon* did not cross the Equator until her thirty-second day out, and even then, too far to the westward, in violation of Maury's *Sailing Directions*. Meanwhile, driven forward by strong winds, the *Flying Fish* and the *John Gilpin* gained rapidly on the leader. However, Captain Edward G. Nickels of the *Flying Fish* had also paid scant heed to Maury's instructions, and lost 3 days working eastward to clear Cape San Roque. When the *John Gilpin* overtook the becalmed *Flying Fish* off the Horn, Nickels invited Captain Doane of the *John Gilpin* to come aboard for dinner. But Captain Doane expected the wind at any moment and noted in his log, "I was reluctantly obliged to decline the invitation." Despite westerly gales in the Pacific, the *Flying Fish* moved 4 days ahead of her rival, caught up with the *Wild Pigeon*, and reached the Equator 25 miles in the lead. The *Westward Ho!* crossed the Line at the same time, and both McKay-built clippers raced it to a tie into San Francisco Harbor on February 1, 1853. The *Flying Fish* won the laurels with an elapsed time of 92 days, 4 hours. The *John Gilpin* took 93 days, 20 hours, the *Trade Wind*, 102 days, the *Westward Ho!*, 103 days, and the *Wild Pigeon*, 118 days.

This poor performance of Donald McKay's *Westward Ho!* on her maiden passage was explained later in a letter from one of her passengers, which was quoted by Lubbock in *China Clippers*.

> *Westward Ho* ought to have done the run in 90 days. The captain was a drunken beast and remained in his cabin for nearly the whole passage, boosing on his own liquor and that of the passengers from whom he could beg, and at last broke out the forehold in search of liquor, and found some champagne cider on which he boosed the remainder of the passage. We were off the River Plate with a fair strong wind, headed east and north for several days, until there was nearly a mutiny among the passengers. I finally told the mate to put her on her course and we would back him up in any trouble. The captain never knew of any change; we lost at least 10 days by such delays. At one time after passing Cape Horn we were running about N. by W., wind S.S.W., long easy sea and wind strong under topgallant sails, and she was going like a scared dog, her starboard plank sheer even with the water, two men at the wheel and they had all they could do to hold her on her course. One day she ran over 400 knots —17 knots per hour—another day she ran 388 knots. The drunken captain was at once displaced in Frisco, and the mate, who had navigated from Boston, placed in charge. He made the run to Manila in 31 days.

In June 1853, with Donald McKay as a passenger, the *Sovereign of the Seas* crossed the Atlantic. Her builder spent much of his time on deck, noting the behavior of the vessel and gaining ideas which he incorporated into his later masterpieces. The first trans-Atlantic passage of the *Sovereign of the Seas* began very unfavorably. Leaving Sandy Hook on June 18, she was becalmed for 8 days off the Banks. After the wind was caught, however, her time for the deep-sea passage to Liverpool was only 5 days and 17 hours, which is still regarded as the finest performance by any wooden sailing vessel. Dropping anchor in the Mersey 13 days, 22 hours out from New York, the *Sovereign of the Seas* was immediately chartered for the booming emigrant trade by the Australian Black Ball Line of James Baines & Co. Her fast passage across the Atlantic enabled the lessees to charge the unheard-of rate of £7 sterling a ton for freight to Melbourne, with a guaranty of a rebate of £2 a ton, if passage were beaten. It was not.

Boston's waterfront presented an extraordinary sight during

the heyday of the clippers. Towering masts, acres of gleaming white canvas, and handsomely decorated bows revealed clippers in various stages of construction. From Jeffries Point to Chelsea Creek uncompleted hulls were ranked on the stocks. On an April morning in 1854, looking through his counting-room window on Central Wharf, F. O. Dabney observed no less than 6 new clippers in the process of being rigged. In East Boston, near McKay's busy workshop, spread the shipyard of Robert E. Jackson, who built such famous clippers as the *Blue Jacket,* the *John Bertram,* and the *Winged Racer.* Other outstanding East Boston builders were Samuel Hall, Paul Curtis, A. & G. T. Sampson, and Jackson & Ewell. In South Boston sprawled the shipyard of Edward and Henry C. Briggs, whose clipper ships were noted for their carefully molded waterline and small displacement, which frequently produced remarkable speed. The creations of the Briggs brothers included the *Northern Light,* holder of the all-time record of 76 days, 5 hours from San Francisco to Boston, and the ill-fated *Golden Light,* which was struck by lightning when only 10 days out on her maiden voyage. Many beauties were launched into the Mystic from the yards of S. Lapham, Hayden & Cudworth, and J. O. Curtis.

The huge cost of clipper construction had brought new faces into the ranks of the Boston shipowners. Prominent were John Ellerton Lodge, whose large fleet engaged in the China trade; R. C. Mackay and J. S. Coolidge, leaders in the East Indian commerce; Osborn Howes, whose ships plied to California and Australia; George B. Upton, who sent many McKay-built clippers to every part of the world under Captain Philip Dumaresq; and Daniel C. Bacon, president of the American Navigation Club and owner of the *Gamecock,* an extremely fast clipper built by Samuel Hall. In recognition of the financial investments of noted Boston citizens, local clippers bore such names as *Thomas H. Perkins, Russell Sturgis, Enoch Train, R. B. Forbes, Rufus Choate, Starr King, John E. Thayer, George Peabody, Samuel Appleton, Robert C. Winthrop,* and *Amos Lawrence.*

Meanwhile the queen of all clippers, and one of the largest sailing vessels ever constructed, was taking shape in Donald McKay's yard. Amid the boom of artillery and the blare of bands, the *Great Republic* slid into Boston Harbor on the afternoon of October 4, 1853.

> She starts,—she moves,—she seems to feel
> The thrill of life along her keel,
> And, spurning with her foot the ground,
> With one exulting, joyous bound,
> She leaps into the ocean's arms!
> —Longfellow, "The Building of the Ship"

It was a gala day in Boston. Business was suspended, schools were closed, and all industry was at a standstill, so that everyone might have an opportunity to witness the launching of the vessel. More than 30,000 people were present at East Boston. The ship was solemnly christened with a bottle of Cochituate water, in deference to the Temperance Movement, which had the support of numerous shareholders. In the afternoon she was towed to the Navy Yard across the harbor to receive above-deck fittings under the personal supervision of Captain Lauchlan McKay. The *Great Republic* measured 335 feet in length, registered 4,555 tons, supported 4 masts with a mainyard 120 feet long, displaced 4 decks, and carried a 15 horsepower engine for hoisting and working the pumps.

Intended for the new Australian trade in competition with British-built clippers, the *Great Republic* was towed to New York, where she was loaded with cargo for Liverpool. Again the magnificent vessel drew throngs of visitors and inspectors; Government officials from neighboring States came to view her size and beauty. Never had such enormous spars, towering masts, and expansive sails been seen in New York Harbor. But her glory was brief. On December 26, 1853, when she was almost ready to embark on her maiden voyage, a fire broke out one block from her wharf and spread so rapidly that sparks ignited the ship and burned her to the water's edge. Although McKay built several distinguished clippers for the Australian trade, the loss of the *Great Republic* was a severe disappointment to him—a loss from which he never fully recovered. Later, lowered (or in terms of naval architecture, razeed), the hull of the scuttled vessel was refloated, and her superstructure was rebuilt. Reduced to 3,357 tons, yet retaining much of her former beauty, the razeed clipper was still the largest vessel on the seas. Finally departing on February 21, 1855, the *Great Republic* made a fast maiden voyage to England. Upon arrival at London, the ship was obliged to anchor in the Thames, since no dock was large enough to receive her.

Donald McKay built his last and fastest extreme clippers for the Australian Black Ball Line in 1854. In the market for the largest and swiftest vessels afloat, James Baines contracted with the American master builder for the construction of the *Lightning,* the *James Baines,* the *Champion of the Seas,* and the *Donald McKay.* On her maiden voyage across the Atlantic, the *Lightning* logged the astonishing distance of 436 miles on March 1, 1854, achieving a record speed of 18.2 knots for 24 consecutive hours. When the 2,096-ton vessel arrived at Liverpool, Baines added a moonsail and a host of ringtails to the 6,500 square yards of canvas. On her first homeward passage from Australia, the *Lightning* was put through her paces and established a mark of 64 days, 3 hours, from Melbourne to Liverpool, after numerous sails, spars, and masts, blown away in the tempestuous weather, had been replaced en route.

The *James Baines* was judged by the shipping experts of Liverpool to be the finest of all Donald McKay's clippers. Modeled after the *Lightning* but larger in size, the *James Baines* was the greater masterpiece, since McKay had corrected several minor imperfections that had been noticed in the design of the *Lightning.* On her maiden voyage, the *James Baines* completed the trans-Atlantic passage from Boston Light to Rock Light in 12 days and 6 hours, and was clocked off the Irish coast doing 20 knots. Anchoring at Liverpool, the clipper was pronounced the most perfect sailing ship that had ever entered the Mersey. When Queen Victoria inspected the costly interior fittings, she expressed great surprise that her merchant marine possessed so fine a ship. Leaving for Melbourne on December 9, 1854, the *James Baines* reached Port Phillip's Head 63 days, 18 hours out from Rock Light, beating the *Lightning's* mark, but showing a best day's run of only 423 miles. Later she attained an epoch-making speed of 21 knots on her voyage to Australia, practically encircling the globe in the unbeaten time of 132 days. On October 30, 1856, the *James Baines* was overtaken by the *Lightning,* which had sailed from Melbourne three weeks behind her. For the next 6 days, the two great rivals were together, pitting every square inch of canvas against light head winds. But the smaller ship had the advantage, and the *Lightning* arrived at the Mersey 24 hours before the long overdue *James Baines,* which completed the passage in the unusually slow time of 101 days, resulting in a tenfold increase in the insurance rates on the 174,000 ounces of gold carried by the clipper.

In a long and famous career Donald McKay completed 21 clippers, 16 ocean packets, several schooners, 2 sloops-of-war, and 4 steam vessels—not one of which was a failure. For his sailing ships, Donald McKay chose poetic and appropriate names such as *Stag-Hound, Mastiff, Flying Cloud, Flying Fish, Westward Ho!, Romance of the Seas, Sovereign of the Seas, Glory of the Seas, Champion of the Seas,* and *Republic.* Because six vessels already carried the name of Daniel Webster, McKay decided to name two sister clippers the *Expounder* and the *Defender,* in recognition of Webster's understanding and defense of the Constitution. In Donald McKay were fused the qualities of scientist, artist, idealist, and man of business. Although several decades of adversity and ingratitude followed his early years of success and prosperity, his calm, thoughtful temperament remained unchanged. In 1877 he retired to his farm at Hamilton, Massachusetts, and died 3 years later. Half a century passed before a new generation erected a 52-foot granite obelisk to his memory on the grassy slope of Castle Island. Adorned with the shipbuilder's classic face against a model of the *Flying Cloud,* the marker overlooks the main harbor channel, symbolizing the exalted position of Donald McKay in the maritime story of the Port. Today, visitors may read at the base of the shaft an imposing inscription.

Master builder whose genius produced ships of a beauty and speed before unknown, which swept the seven seas, made the American clipper famous the world over, and brought renown and prosperity to the city of Boston.

Iron Men on Wooden Ships

Boston's clipper captains rivaled the builders of her ships in skill and energy. While many a foreign vessel wallowed under double-reefed topsails, the powerful clippers carried royals and studdingsails. They were driven by their captains around the Horn with their sheets chained and padlocked to prevent weak-kneed sailors from tampering with the gear. When a strong wind whipped the mountainous waves, and heavy seas sent the spray flying masthead high, the top-hampered vessels fairly leaped through the crests, skidded down the troughs, and then straightened with the poise of a terrier, ready to spring forward once more. Although voyages often ended with topmasts "broomed" and splintered from hard driving, the exploits of these gallant vessels spoke well for the daring navigation of the Boston sea captains. They testified with certainty to the shipbuilders' judgment of the terrific strain on wooden spars and hemp rigging, which was tested only when the prow sliced the storm-driven billows.

Most of Boston's clipper captains came from New England stock. Few others could manage these wild clippers against Horn howlers, where the slightest error resulted in the loss of canvas, the loss of precious minutes, possibly the loss of the ship. Recruited from the quarterdecks of roaring Liverpool packets, stately East Indiamen, swift privateers and opium runners, the men who commanded these untamed beauties had followed the sea from early boyhood. Philip Dumaresq, first commander of the *Surprise* had been bred from generations of sea captains. Like "Nat" Palmer of Stonington, and "Perk" Cressy of Marblehead, he was a follower of the stern and rigid traditions of the quarterdeck. The shipmasters lived in dignified seclusion, gave all orders through their first officers, and were never spoken to unless they spoke first. They were paid $3,000 for an outward passage to California; if they made the trip in less than 100 days, they received a bonus of $2,000.

Occasionally the clipper captains took their wives along, and in China and India merchants vied with one another in offering them costly gifts and lavish entertainment. One of these seafaring women, Mrs. Patten, 19-year-old wife of a Boston skipper, proved herself a heroine off Cape Horn during the cold and stormy winter of 1856. With the first mate under suspension for neglect of duty, her husband stricken with brain fever, and the second officer unable to navigate, she commanded the 1,600-ton clipper during the remaining 52-day passage to San Francisco, at the same time nursing her husband back to health.

Although Yankees captained the Boston clippers, a motley gang gathered at the forecastle when the crew was mustered. They were British and Scandinavian for the most part, with a sprinkling of Spaniards, Portuguese, and Italians. Discipline was severe, brutality more than common, and redress before the law difficult. Low wages kept Americans off the clippers. In an age when ship caulkers and carpenters received $3 a day, and longshoremen $2 per tide, ordinary and able seamen earned only $8 to $12 a month. As applicants for clipper berths grew scarce, masters were forced to resort to shipping agencies and boarding-house keepers. While the majority of the shanghaied crews were taken from the merchant marine, some were not sailors at all, but habitual drunkards and loafers. Once at sea, however, mates, bo'sun, and captain put belaying pins, capstan bars, heavers, fists, and boots to good use, and in short order so stimulated a spirit of honest toil that by the time the Equator was crossed, the harassed seamen leaped up instantly upon command and scurried up the rigging as though blown there by the bellow from the mate's bull-like throat. In general, the clipper sailors had the reputation of being indefatigable workers. It was said of them that they "worked like horses at sea, and behaved like asses ashore."

The Vanishing Clipper

Although the California trade lasted until 1860, the year 1854 ended the construction of fast sailing vessels for the Pacific Coast service. In that year only 20 clippers were built throughout the United States, 10 of them in Boston yards. By 1855 San Francisco had become flooded with merchandise, and freight rates had dropped to a level which was barely remunerative. Even in shorter coastwise and trans-Atlantic voyages the clippers had proved too costly to operate. When David Snow of Boston ventured his *Reporter* on the Boston-New Orleans-Liverpool route, he found her "a thousand ton ship in capacity and a two thousand ton ship to keep in repair." Hard-pressed by steamships and "medium" clippers, the extreme clipper type began to vanish from the seas. Some were destroyed by fire, some foundered off the China coast; others were sold into foreign service and hurried off to the Australian gold fields, where their rigging was cut and their identity lost.

After a glorious career in the California and China runs, several Boston clippers, water-soaked and strained, spent their declining years in the most depraved business then known, the smuggling of Chinese coolies. Clippers in this trade carried coolies imprisoned in their holds, like former ships' cargoes of "black ivory"; the Chinese almost starved during the passage.

The *Sovereign of the Seas* finished her ocean days in the service of a Hamburg firm. Although her German captain claimed that she made a 24-hour run of 410 miles, her last owners expected too much from her. Having lost her topmasts, she arrived at Sydney after a slow passage of 84 days. On her homeward voyage, cholera brought about the death of nearly half her crew. The end of the handsome clipper came in 1859, when she ran aground on Pyramid Shoal in Malacca Straits. In 1857 the *James Baines,* the *Lightning,* the *Champion of the Seas,* and several other famous Boston-built clippers were chartered by the British Government to transport troops to far-off India, where the Sepoy Mutiny had broken out. Upon her return to Liverpool the *James Baines* was destroyed by fire. The *Lightning* entered the Australian wool trade and continued in active service until 1869, when fire finished her also.

Boston's lament over the passing of the clipper is aptly expressed in verses found in *Some Merchants and Sea Captains of Old Boston:*

The old Clipper days are over, and the white-winged fleets no more,
With their snowy sails unfolded, fly along the ocean floor;
Where their house-flags used to flutter in the ocean winds unfurled,
Now the kettle-bellied cargo tubs go reeling around the world.

But 'twas jolly while it lasted, and the sailor was a man;
And it's good-by to the Lascar and the tar with face of tan;
And its good-by mother, once for all, and good-by girls on shore;
And it's good-by brave old Clipper-ship that sails the seas no more!

CHAPTER VI

THE TRIUMPH OF STEAM

Prelude to the Civil War

AT THE END of the clipper ship era, Boston was a metropolis of refinement and wealth, the richest city for her size in the world. Her per capita assessment averaged $1,804 in comparison with New York's $1,004. Brownstone mansions fronted broad Commonwealth Avenue and exclusive Beacon Street; the *élite* summered at Beverly or along the Maine coast. Successive generations of bold traders, hardy sea captains, and shrewd investors had finally given birth to a Boston aristocracy. But in reality these evidences of financial well-being were relics of the Port's earlier prosperity rather than symbols of current enterprise. By 1855 New York's imports surpassed Boston's fivefold, and local business houses had established branch offices in the rival city. Furthermore, the Government-subsidized Collins Steamship Line from New York to England not only deprived Boston of her share of the European trade, but drew many of her sons and much of her capital to the nation's first port.

Worse still, when New York inaugurated steamship lines to the far South during the 1830's and 1840's, Boston even lost her former domination over southern commerce. It is true that tons of cotton continued to arrive at the Port of Boston from New Orleans, which also sent flour, pork, corn, rice, and tobacco for the New England millhands, as well as reshipments of South American, West Indian, and Azorean commodities. The largest share of Boston's outbound southern trade was also directed to the Louisiana port, 175 vessels clearing Boston for New Orleans in 1855. In this southward traffic, Boston packets carried great cargoes of ice, fish, apples, rum, lumber, sheetings, furniture, carriages, boots, shoes, and saddles. By 1857, however, this upward movement in southern shipping had ceased and, as a financial writer observed, "for ten years there can not be said to be a general increase in any leading articles except in cotton, wool, and oats. The receipts of corn, flour, and wheat have rather declined."

For this decline Boston merchants found partial compensation in the growth of trade with the Maritime Provinces. Canadian imports and exports more than doubled between 1850 and 1855, accelerating markedly after the signing of the Reciprocity Treaty with Canada in 1854. Awkward Canadian "Geordies" or "Johnny-wood-boats", as they were dubbed, carried lumber, fish, coal, grain, spirits, provisions, and dairy products to Boston, and returned with their holds filled with hides, whale oil, Yankee manufactures, and imported goods. No less than 63 Boston firms handled Canadian lumber, a business which annually yielded about $2,500,-000. Unfortunately, treaty provisions did not favor American manufactures, and Canada soon doubled the tariff on boots, shoes, ironware, and textile fabrics, though it remained a ready market for other New England products.

Boston received spruce, hemlock, pine, and fish from nearby Maine and New Hampshire; in 1856 these receipts were valued at $1,000,000. Maine schooners also brought into the Port large quantities of hay, stacked on deck in piles so high that the helmsman had to be directed by a lookout stationed forward. Since this cargo could be loaded or unloaded only during dry weather, the arrival of a "hay barge" presaged rain to superstitious Boston mariners. In some it revived grisly memories of the *Royal George,* whose deckload of hay was so thoroughly drenched after a gale had blown off the tarpaulin cover that the schooner became top-heavy and turned turtle.

Notwithstanding the gradual falling off of commerce with the South, Boston's shipping enjoyed a most prosperous decade between 1850 and 1860, except for the temporary check which came as a sequel to the financial panic of 1857. The reexport of foreign commodities dwindled to some extent, but the loss was offset by the expanding shipments of domestic goods. Local manufacturing had increased, and a large volume of the output was sent to Europe and to the markets of the Orient, to South America, and to Australia. At no time during the 1850's, however, did Boston's total exports amount to as much as one-half of her imports, which continued to arrive over the established trade routes from China, Manila, the East Indies, Africa, South America, and Europe.

Boston merchants generally relied on the regular sailing packet lines rather than on steam craft; in 1857 the total tonnage of steamers that made Boston their home port was only 8,100 as compared to New York's 84,662 tons. Boston remained content with her Cunard Line in foreign commerce, with the "Down East" steamers and the Merchants and Miners Line to Norfolk and Baltimore in domestic coastal services and with local steamers to Gloucester, Nahant, Hingham, and Cape Cod. But this was a minor factor in the Port's future evolution compared with the nearsighted stubbornness of her shipbuilders who, because of the scarcity of coal and iron, continued to send sailing vessels down the ways, when they should have been devoting money and energy to the construction of iron screw steamers. The complaint that there was no steam communication between Boston and any port south of Norfolk was not answered until 1860 and 1861, when Bostonians built four iron screw steamers for service to Charleston and New Orleans. Actually, steam was in the ascendency on land and sea, and the Civil War served to emphasize this fact in a manner most distressing to the pocketbooks of Boston shipowners.

Bostonians had made several abortive attempts in the 1850's to build steamships and capture their full share of ocean commerce. The Ocean Steamship Company had taken advantage of the "Railroad Jubilee," in 1851, to announce ambitious plans for the construction of four ocean-going steamships. On October 4, the flagship of the new fleet, the 1,104-ton screw-propelled *Lewis,* sailed from Boston to Liverpool on her maiden voyage, but the enterprise was doomed to almost immediate financial failure. Undaunted, the Boston and European Steamship Company was incorporated 4 years later and advanced as far as the experimental stage, with Donald McKay exhibiting the model of a steamer which he predicted would cross the Atlantic in 6 days. But, like its ill-fated predecessor, the proposed venture came to nothing in the face of powerful British competition. Up to 1860 the active and successful operation of the *Persia* and other Cunard steamers definitely controlled local steamship relations with Great Britain.

Civil War Years

The Civil War hastened the crumbling of Boston's commercial prestige. Her large trade with the South was disrupted. The loss of export cotton, an important item in the European trade, retarded trans-Atlantic traffic. Increased rates, forced high by the presence of Confederate raiders on shipping lanes, made voyages unprofitable and led to the sale of ships to foreign companies. In addition to these immediately effective conditions, Boston was a victim of a vast and extended economic movement which, while it had been underway for a decade or more, was accelerated by the Civil War. Railroads boomed, and the westward course of the nation advanced at an amazing rate. Fortunes wrested from the ocean by energetic Bostonians were turned more and more to the development of the prairie lands.

Unlike preceding wars, the Civil War gave Boston no opportunity to add to her maritime glory. Privateersmen were not used by the North, and locally built naval ships, formerly followed with great interest, became merged with the large Federal fleet. Boston played a novel quiescent role on the sea; while Confederate raiders snatched at her commerce, she did nothing save withdraw or try to outwit the enemy by sailing new routes. The Southern seamen were bold and even raided in New England waters. The *Florida* visited the fishing grounds and some of her men attempted a raid on Portland, Maine.

The Confederate cruiser most feared by Boston shippers was the *Alabama,* British-built, which sent about 100 Northern ships to the bottom between July 1862 and June 1864. At least 13 Boston ships were among those destroyed. The first was the *Starlight,* bound from Fayal to Flores. Then followed in 1862 the bark *Lamplighter,* from New York to Gibraltar with tobacco, the *Lauretta,* also bound for Gibraltar, and the *Parker Cook,* for Haiti. Most of the captures were burned after the crews were taken off. A favorite trick of the *Alabama* was to approach the Northern vessels under the flag of a neutral nation or even that of the United States itself. During 1863 and 1864, the successful career of the raider continued, and several Boston vessels became her prey. Two contained English-owned cargo and were ransomed; another, the *Martha Wenzell,* was captured in English waters and promptly released. The rest were burned. The sinking of the *Alabama* in 1864 by the U.S.S. *Kearsarge* brought an end to the major threat to Yankee shipping, and Boston ships were again free to roam the seas.

Expansion Along the Waterfront

During the decades preceding and following the Civil War extensive improvements, dredging the channel, removing shoals and rocks, and corseting the crumbling islands, were undertaken in Boston Harbor. Mayor Frederick W. Lincoln succeeded in persuading the United States War Department to cooperate in the preservation of the Port's channels and anchorage basins, and in 1859 the Federal Government renovated Boston Light, elevating the tower to permit installation of the Frennel illuminating apparatus. The 14 lamps were replaced by a single central beacon, whose French lens radiated the light in a horizontal direction. Pilots disliked the change and actually petitioned the Lighthouse Board to reinstall the "old reflectors", but the authorities ignored their protests.

Seven years later a board of commissioners considered the possibilities of reclaiming some 916 acres of South Boston flats, filling them in and protecting them by an outer wall, erecting wharves, and dredging Fort Point Channel to the required depth. The estimated cost was $19,219,000, exclusive of $418,000 required for an exterior wall to hold the filling. But objections were so numerous that the ambitious plans of the commissioners were later modified.

Between 1867 and 1892 the Narrows Channel was dredged to a depth of 27 feet and a width of 1,000. Although the Broad Sound South Channel was then unnavigable at low water for large ships, it had remained the logical entrance to the harbor from Europe, and between 1892 and 1905 it was deepened to 30 feet and widened to 1,200 feet by United States Army engineers. The North Channel, the present main ship channel, was dredged between 1902 and 1916. A considerable part of the cost of these improvements was borne by Federal appropriations made after the visit of the Congressional Committee on Rivers and Harbors in March 1896. Channels were constantly being deepened, and every effort was made to keep the Port abreast of shipping developments. In 1878 the steamer *Hooper,* next to the *Great Eastern* the largest ship in the world, and drawing 29 feet of water, chose Boston as a port-of-call in preference to all other Atlantic ports. By 1894 a lightship was in place at the harbor entrance, and a year later range lights were installed to mark the ship channels.

Terminal facilities on the Boston waterfront were greatly enhanced when the railroads extended their lines to the more important docks. As early as 1851, the Grand Junction Railroad, a waterfront "trunk" line 6.6 miles long, had connected the Eastern, Boston and Maine, and Fitchburg and Lowell tracks with the steamship wharves at East Boston. But this important link soon fell into disuse. The Boston & Albany

A view of the harbor in the direction of Commercial Wharf, *circa* 1870. *Courtesy of the Peabody Museum of Salem.*

The *Wabash*, a steam frigate serving as a receiving ship at Charlestown Navy Yard, *circa* 1875. In the background is the steeple of the Old North Church. *Courtesy of the Peabody Museum of Salem.*

Railroad repaired the Grand Junction in 1868 to run trains which picked up passengers at the Cunard and neighboring docks. A track had been laid by the Marginal Freight Company connecting the railroads at the north of the city with the wharves on Commercial Street; the construction of Atlantic Avenue in the sixties was considered an important aid. Finally in 1872, the answer to the businessmen's need came with the opening of the Union Freight Railway, uniting the tracks of all the principal railroad lines terminating in Boston, and affording direct access to the principal wharves of the city.

Gradually wharves, warehouses, and large grain elevators equipped with belt conveyors were erected by the railroad companies to handle the increasing volume of merchandise. By the last decade of the century, the Boston and Lowell, the Fitchburg, and the Hoosac Tunnel Lines had well-established terminal facilities in Charlestown; in East Boston the Boston and Albany owned some 6 docks, 7 piers, 17 warehouses, and a million-bushel grain elevator, capable of discharging 120 cars of grain a day and 20,000 bushels an hour to a vessel. In 1868 the Boston, Hartford, and Erie Railroad bought from the Boston Wharf Company over two and a half million feet of South Boston flats and solid land, and within 10 years a million dollars had been expended in improving the area. By 1883 this road had completed new warehouses, a 520,000-bushel grain elevator with belt conveyor, a new 1000-by-200-foot pier, and had enlarged an old pier to 850 feet. Of the 8,000 feet of water frontage on the main ship channel and on the Fort Point Channel owned by the railroad, 3,879 feet were available for wharfage. The establishment of these rail and terminal facilities at East Boston, Charlestown, and South Boston drew most of the foreign commerce in the latter half of the century and the old waterfront was used mainly by coastwise steamers, towboats, excursion steamers, and fishing smacks. In all, 42 steamships could be accommodated on the entire Boston waterfront.

The Great Fire of 1872 brought about many waterfront improvements, including the erection of "six magnificent blocks of business structures" on Atlantic Avenue from Congress Street down to the Railway Depot, 5 of which were promptly occupied by wool firms. The conflagration had swept the rich wholesale and financial section of Boston, destroying 776 buildings and causing damage estimated at more than $75,000,000. Vast quantities of hides, leather, shoes, drygoods, domestic and foreign wool, ready-made clothing, hardware, and other wares were completely ruined. Reconstruction was so rapid, however, that 3 years later a writer remarked:

Whole forests from the State of Maine, and vast quarries of granite, and hills of country gravel have been put to service in fringing the water margins, constructing wharves, piers and causeways, redeeming the flats, and furnishing piling and solid foundations for the stately edifices, private houses, halls, churches and railroad stations, principally between the Charles River and the old Dorchester flats.

Ever since Boston merchant-shipowners began meeting "on 'change'," attempts had been made to develop business associations for the common good. Few, however, lasted any great length of time. In 1854 the Boston Board of Trade had been formed to re-arrange the credit system, settle disputes, and promote local cooperation and good feeling. But the board could not, as had been hoped, restore the former maritime prosperity of the city, and in 1873 the association amalgamated with the Merchant's Exchange. Eventually this organization and the Commercial and Produce Exchanges were all consolidated into the Chamber of Commerce. Meanwhile various groups were chosen to supervise the filling-in of flats and bays; Port Wardens were appointed; a Pilot Commission was established; a police division was organized to guard the harbors and the islands; and a Marine Hospital was erected at Chelsea.

Gales, Shipwreck, and Murder

To protect Boston shipping, many new lifesaving stations were erected and dangerous portions of the Massachusetts shoreline were regularly patrolled. By 1897 Massachusetts had 25 such stations along the seaboard, involving a yearly payroll of $125,000, yet vessels continued to be driven ashore at distressingly frequent intervals. Tragedy and heroism marked the great gale and snowstorm of November 25 and 26, 1888. Early in the afternoon of the twenty-fifth, ships in the harbor began dragging anchors, and Captain Joshua James, head of the famous volunteer lifesavers of Hull, prepared a crew and lifeboat for instant action. When the schooner *Cox and Green* smashed against Toddy Rocks, the crew was safely brought ashore by a breeches-buoy. Hardly was this rescue completed, when the coal-laden, three-masted schooner *Gertrude Abbott* struck the eastern edge of Toddy Rocks and hoisted distress signals. The vessel lay too far offshore to be reached by the beach apparatus, and the high tide and tremendous surf made it impossible to launch a boat until between 8 and 9 o'clock that night. Efforts were then successful, and the 8 members of the crew were saved. At 3 the next morning, the *Bertha F. Walker* was discovered ashore half a mile northwest of the *Abbott,* and her crew was brought to land in a lifeboat obtained in Hingham Bay, the regular boat having been damaged in the *Abbott* rescue. Next the *H. C. Higginson* and the *Mattie E. Eaton* were wrecked at Atlantic Hill, 5 miles distant. The surviving members of the *Higginson's* crew had to be rescued but the *Eaton's* men were able to walk on to dry land, the vessel being driven high ashore. All told, the Hull volunteers saved 29 lives in less than 24 hours, and were awarded gold medals by an act of Congress.

Even more disastrous was the "Portland Storm" of November 26 and 27, 1898, beginning with a deceptively quiet fall of snow and then changing to thunderous icy winds, impenetrable clouds of snow, and mountainous seas. More than a score of vessels were wrecked between midnight and the next afternoon. Among them were the four-masted Boston schooner *Abel E. Babcock,* which pounded to pieces on Toddy Rocks with the loss of all on board, and the *Coal Barge #4* from which only 2 were saved. Terrific losses during this storm were in part responsible for driving at least one Boston firm out of business. The J. J. Baker Company, founded in 1844, and interested in some 90 vessels engaged in the coasting trade in 1881, lost 17 of them on the night of the *Portland* disaster. When in 1898 the Baker Company sold out to Harrington & King, there were only 12 vessels left in the fleet.

Outside the harbor this same night occurred one of the most horrible sea tragedies in New England history. At exactly 7 o'clock Saturday evening the handsome side-wheel steamer *Portland* sailed for Maine under command of Captain Hollis Blanchard, with 108 passengers and a crew of 68. In service for only 8 years, she was equipped with adequate lifesaving devices, including 758 life preservers, 8 metallic lifeboats and 4 metallic life rafts. Snow was softly blanketing the water as the *Portland* sailed out of the island-dotted harbor and turned northward to fight her way into a raging blizzard. At 9:30 p. m. she was seen by a schooner about 4 miles off Thatcher Island, making little headway. The increasing wind apparently kept driving the *Portland* offshore, for when next sighted, by the captain of the schooner *Grayling* at 11 o'clock, she was 12 miles south by east of the island but still headed into the wind. Shortly after that another schooner passed her. At 11:45 p.m. a large paddle-wheel steamer, believed to be the *Portland,* was sighted by a fourth schooner. This time the effect of the gale was evident. Lights were out and the super-structure showed signs of damage. Exactly what happened aboard the *Portland* is not known. The engines may have failed or the force of the gale been greater than their power. Whatever the reason, she was pushed across the 40-mile wide mouth of Massachusetts Bay to a position off Cape Cod. The keeper of the Race Point Lifesaving Station heard 4 distress signals on a steamer's whistle at 10 o'clock Sunday morning and at about the same time the crew of the schooner *Ruth M. Martin* sighted the *Portland* and another steamer, the *Pentagost,* about 4 miles off Peaked Hill Bar. The first wreckage drifted to land at 7 o'clock Sunday night at Race Point. Bodies began coming ashore all along the Cape from Highland Light to Chatham, and during the course of the next 2 weeks 35 bodies were recovered. The steamer undoubtedly sank off the tip of the Cape, but no one lived to tell the tale.

Sea captains faced more than the danger of ships lost in storms; occasionally fire and mutiny added to their hardships and distress. When this happened there was little chance for escape, as was tragically emphasized aboard the 1,600-ton Boston vessel, *Frank N. Thayer,* on the night of January 2, 1886. She was 700 miles off St. Helena when two seamen taken aboard at Manila ran amuck, fatally stabbing the first and second mates and wounding Captain Clark as he came up the companionway to learn the cause of the hubbub on deck. Nine members of the crew attempted to overpower the crazed mutineers and only gave up after four of their number had been knifed. Robert Sonnberg escaped aloft and, from the crossjack yard, witnessed the brutal murders of the helms-man, the shipscarpenter, and another seaman. Meanwhile the injured captain crawled back to his cabin, locked himself in, and repulsed an attack through the skylight with his revolver. By daybreak, Sunday, the two Manila men were complete masters of the ship, having barricaded the forecastle door from the outside, thus preventing the captain and the crew from communicating with each other. The madmen forced the Chinese cook, Ah Say, to prepare meals for them; other-wise Sunday passed uneventfully. The terror of the crew gave way to desperation, when on Monday morning Sonnberg looked down from his perch in the rigging and made the horrifying discovery that the murderers were about to set the ship on fire. Ah Say, who was more or less at liberty, also saw what was going on, and managed to pass an ax through one of the forecastle ports to the captive sailors within.

In the interim Captain Clark, partially recovered after the able ministrations of his wife, made a sortie long enough to learn that the two Manila men were the only mutineers, rather than the entire ship's company. Sounds of another attack sent him rushing back to the cabin, where he shot one of the murderers in the chest as he attempted to get in through the skylight. The wounded desperado dashed forward as the crew broke from the forecastle, recognized the hopelessness of his plight, and leaped overboard. His companion scurried between decks and set afire the inflammable cargo of jute. Thick clouds of smoke shielded the man's movements for a while. Finally a well-directed bullet struck him in the shoulder, and he, too, leaped into the water. Both murderers clung to a spar until a fusillade of shots from the captain and the crew killed them. Immediately all aboard the *Frank N. Thayer* turned their attention to the menacing flames, but it was too late, and they were forced to take to the boats. After a crowded and dangerous trip, using blankets sewn together as sails, the survivors reached Jamestown, St. Helena. Following this terrible experience, Captain Clark retired from the sea.

One of the most gruesome stories concerning Boston ships is the tale of the barkentine *Herbert Fuller,* which sailed from Boston on July 2, 1896, with lumber for Buenos Aires. Charles P. Nash was captain, and the first mate was Thomas M. Bram, a native of St. Kitts. Also aboard were the captain's wife and a passenger, Lester H. Monks. Ten days out, Monks was suddenly shocked into wakefulness at midnight by a woman's scream. He jumped from bed, revolver in hand, and found that the captain, his wife, and the second mate had been murdered with an ax as they slept. Suspicion fastened on Bram, and he was put in irons. The vessel made its way to Halifax, and the crew was brought to Boston.

On December 15, the famous Bram murder trial opened in Boston, and almost a month later the jury brought a verdict of guilty against Bram. The storm of protest which followed was raised to a furious pitch the next day when Harry J. Booth, one of the jurymen, told the press that he and three others had voted against their better judgment, that they did not believe the evidence proved Bram's guilt beyond a reasonable doubt. In a new trial, Bram was again convicted and sent to Atlanta for life. Some years later, President Woodrow Wilson, while reading a mystery story, *The After House,* which Mary Roberts Rinehart had written on the *Herbert Fuller* murders, had his interest so aroused that he requested the Attorney General to examine the case. And as a result Bram was paroled. He carved a new life for himself in Atlanta. Starting as a vendor of hot-dogs and peanuts, he gradually became the builder and manager of the Bramwell Apartments and the owner of a schooner.

The Boston Fishing Fleet

The new method of packing fresh-caught fish in ice developed a greatly expanded market and caused the Boston fishing fleet to grow rapidly after 1860. Frequently, the supply was not equal to the demand, and dealers stood sentinel along the fish wharves night after night, anxiously watching for the sight of a sail, ready and eager to bid for the cargo of the first arrival. Occasionally, even before a schooner eased into her berth, the captain accepted offers shouted to him by jostling dealers. More often he went ashore and investigated the state of the market before selling any of his hard-earned fish. In winter, stout-timbered fishing craft plowed up the harbor to Commercial Wharf, bearing the scars of savage encounters with Arctic gales and tremendous seas on the Banks, "a flag at half-mast for lost men; with spars or dories or rails gone . . . or with bowsprit, decks, dories, masts and rigging so thickly caked with snow and ice that the vessel looked like a fantastic iceberg." The Gloucester short-story writer, James B. Connolly, has vividly described the Boston fishermen:

The T Wharf fleet was an all-sail fleet, handsome, able vessels which shared with the great Gloucester fleet the admiration of the world. The annual race between the Boston and Gloucester men was the classic sailing race of the North Atlantic; perhaps it would be fair to call it the classic of all the seas of the world, because here were no freak boats, fit only for light air and smooth water, but able schooners fit to battle, as out on the fishing banks they did battle regularly, with the strongest of gales and the roughest of seas.

The produce of the deep was brought into Boston with profitable regularity. In season, codfish was received from Swampscott to Ipswich Bay, from the Newfoundland Banks and the back of Cape Cod. Halibut came from Greenland,

Iceland, and, beginning about 1900, from the Pacific coast; haddock was caught principally north of Cape Cod; salmon in Maine and Canadian waters; mackerel off the New England coast as far north as Halifax and as far south as Cape Henry; herring abounded in local waters during October and November. Lobsters were obtained from Maine and oysters from Cape Cod, Rhode Island, Connecticut, and Virginia. Pollock were netted in Boston Bay by means of seines stretched from one vessel to another; at times the ships were so close together on the half-mile-square pollock fishing grounds that they had to be held apart by oars. Warm weather found T Wharf most attractive to the comfort-loving landlubber, who watched wind-burnt men hoisting baskets of glistening fish from holds, their hoarse voices echoing between the boats like the strange cries of the circling sea birds. During the noon hour the tangled mass of spars, tarry rigging, and the pungent nets, stretched out for drying and mending, even attracted stoop-shouldered clerks, who gorged their starved senses on the sounds and odors of the sea, before hurrying back to their litanies of debits and credits.

An idea of the size and foraging habits of the Boston fishing fleet may be obtained by examining a typical year such as 1879, when 76 vessels and 119 sailboats and rowboats were trying to earn a living from the sea. Of the 76 boats, 5 were idle, 60 were employed in the food-fish industries, 1 went out for lobsters, 4 for menhadens, and 6 for sperm whales. The 60 engaged in catching food fish made only short trips, one-third of them following mackerel from April to November and bringing in their wares fresh or cured on board. In 1885 the personnel of the fleet numbered 876 men, 636 of whom were American, 142 Irish, 56 from Canada and the British Provinces, 50 from Portugal, and 2 from England. They fished on shares, one-fifth of the proceeds going to the owner; the remainder, after deducting the cost of bait, tackle, and other items, was divided equally among the men, including the cook. One thousand dollars was considered a top share for the crew.

Since Boston served more as a marketing place than as a fishing center, her annual catch represented only one-fifth of the total fish products received by the local dealers. All told, one-half of the fish arriving in Boston was distributed throughout New England, one-fifth throughout New York State; the remaining three-tenths were consumed by Baltimore, Philadelphia, Washington, and cities and States as far west as Chicago and as far south as Texas. Once the catch was brought ashore, it was either dried, pickled, frozen, or canned, before being shipped to distant points. Dried fish took the form of "boneless," "minced fish," and "fish balls"; pickled fish included mackerel, herring, alewives, salmon, salmon-trout, and shad; seasonal frozen fish consisted of salmon, shad, blue-fish, and mackerel, charged with ice and salt and piled in ice chambers "like billets of wood"; lobsters, salt mackerel, fresh mackerel, smelts, fish chowder, fish balls, and clam chowder were sealed in cans. Fresh fish was packed, well iced, in covered boxes and barrels. Some lobsters, in canned form, were even shipped to Europe.

Outstanding among the men who played prominent parts in the development of the Boston fishing industry between 1860 and 1900 was Orson W. Arnold, a former mackerel seiner, who became associated with C. C. Richards on Commercial Wharf in 1878 and, 3 years later, organized the firm of Arnold and Winsor. Arnold became president of the New England Fish Company in 1906. Two other men whose energies quickened the trade were Albert F. Rich, secretary-treasurer and director of the New England Fish Company, and Franklin Snow, who was largely responsible for the organization of the Boston Fish Bureau in 1875. Commercial Wharf served as headquarters for fish dealers until 1884, when they moved to T Wharf. In 1897 several Boston firms became interested in the possibilities of halibut fishing on the West Coast, and the New England Fish Company sent a $50,000 steamer, the *New England,* around the Horn and up to Seattle to investigate. The century closed with local fishermen unaware of the competition this Pacific venture was later to offer the Boston industry.

Excursions in Massachusetts Bay

Like Boston fishermen, local shipowners recognized and developed the commercial possibilities of Massachusetts Bay. Excursion boats and commuters' services operated regular lines out of Boston to neighboring cities. In 1880 the Nantasket Beach Steamboat Company, now the oldest existing steamboat line in the bay, celebrated its 50th season. By 1884 the side-wheel steamers *Nantasket, Twilight, Rose Standish,* and *William Harrison* were all in the service of the Company.

The *Twilight* had a licensed carrying capacity of 1,500 passengers. Sailings were advertised as at "Nearly every hour of the Day and Evening," fare 25 cents each way. In summertime, Rowes Wharf presented a scene of merry, bustling activity, as hundreds of Bostonians sought relief from the city's sultry heat. Basket-laden Nantasket excursionists descended from the horse cars of Atlantic Avenue; others came from the various railroad depots on horse-drawn versions of the modern bus; still others arrived in cabs and carriages. A pamphlet issued by the line modestly described the attractions of Nantasket:

There is no monopoly on the sea and the air and the magnificent surf bathing is open to all. Almost as exhilarating as actual indulgence is the near view to be obtained of the hundreds, and sometimes thousands, of bathers, from the piazzas of the hotels which line the beach. It is impossible not to catch the spirit of fun which prevails. . . . Fish stories of any size can be manufactured to order, and warranted to fit. If you are over-pressed with care, take a rowboat, go out, throw care overboard with a splash, and row back.

Other Boston steamships appeared in Massachusetts Bay between 1880 and 1890. Captain J. N. Phillips sent the *Empire State*, self-styled the largest, staunchest, and most magnificent excursion steamer in our waters, to Provincetown three times a week, devoting the remaining days to trips along the South Shore, Cape Ann, and the Isle of Shoals. A few years later the business-minded captain substituted moonlight sails down the harbor for the beauties of Cape Cod. About this time Captain E. S. Young ran three daily excursions among the islands and fortifications of Boston Harbor aboard the *William Harrison,* with single fare 15 cents, two fares for a quarter. The Boston and Gloucester Steamboat Company inaugurated a schedule of two daily boats to Gloucester during July and August, weather permitting; they charged 50 cents for a one-way passage when the company added a new steel ship, the *Cape Ann,* to its run in 1895. The Morrison Steamboat Company advertised 45 miles for 45 cents on the journey to Salem Willows. A newcomer, the *Frederick de Barry,* carried excursionists to Nahant. Right up to the twentieth century, however, the steamer business in Massachusetts Bay remained almost exclusively in the summer-excursion domain, with the railroads monopolizing the freight and express business during the winter, when steamship lines were forced to operate on greatly curtailed schedules.

Domestic Commerce and the Heyday of the Schooner

Although slow to adopt steam, Boston experienced a gradual increase in the number and importance of her coastwise steamship facilities. In 1849 the Sanford brothers began sending their new 220-foot side-wheeler *Ocean* over the Boston-to-Bath run, and for 5 years maintained steady summer service on that route. On November 24, 1854, the *Ocean* collided with the inbound Cunarder *Canada* in Broad Sound, Boston Harbor; the impact upset the *Ocean's* kerosene lamps and stores, and the ship sank in flames. Five passengers leaped to death, and 100 others were saved by rescuing steamers.

The experience of the *Ocean's* successor, the *Governor,* was illustrative of the keen competition that developed among the "Down East" steamship lines which sailed out of Boston. The *Governor* was sold to another company when the Sanford's new steamer *Eastern Queen* was put into service in 1857 on the Bath run. The *Governor* became a rival of the *Eastern Queen,* sailing from Boston to Gardiner. At once the rivalry caused heavy cuts in freight and passenger rates, and the price war continued during 1857 and 1858. Successive slashes brought the fare to Boston on the *Governor* down to 25 cents, and the *Eastern Queen* countered with a 50-cent round trip rate for a 300-mile voyage. It was estimated that while these prices prevailed, nearly every resident of the Kennebec Valley went to Boston by boat. One day, placards appeared in Gardiner announcing that passengers would be carried to Boston on the *Governor* for 12½ cents—the lowest rate ever charged for passage on the run. When the Sanford Line met even this challenge, the *Governor* was taken off the route. Thereafter passenger rates resumed their normal level of $1 to Portland and $2 to Bath.

The cut-throat quarrel between sail and steam is shown by a story told in George Wasson's recent book, *Sailing Days on the Penobscot.* A Bangor business man, financially interested in steamships, was traveling to Boston by steamer. When his breakfast was interrupted by a severe shudder along the length of the craft, he rushed on deck to learn the cause of the disturbance. "We've run down another schooner, sir," was the laconic explanation. "She undertook to tack ship right under our bow." The steamship stockholder spied the wreckage, chortled, "Good! That's the talk! Cut 'em plumb in two while you're about it," and calmly returned to his breakfast. His delight was short-lived, however, for he soon learned that the schooner had been laden with coal badly needed by his own steamers in Bangor.

The wooden side-wheel steamers often had a difficult time in plying between Boston and "Down East" points. They traveled in the trough of heavy seas that pounded up under the guards and sought to tear the deck-house from the hull. On account of their enormous paddle-wheel boxes, they were wider than was justified by their shallow hulls, built to ascend rivers. As the captain of one steamer put it, "once let a sea strike with full force under those infernal sponsons and it would start off the whole top hamper." The successor of this skipper had that experience a few years later. A huge wave hit the ship off Portsmouth, shattered her top structure, and flooded her coal bunkers. Listing badly, the crippled steamer headed for Portsmouth; while every combustible piece of freight was tossed into her firebox to maintain steam. The ship finally crawled into port with a load of terrified passengers and 7 feet of water in her hold.

Shortly after the Civil War, the Boston and Philadelphia Steamship Line had been inaugurated, seriously cutting into the profits previously realized by clipper packets operating between the two ports. Joseph Whitney and William B. Spooner founded a steamer line from Boston to Baltimore. In 1864 the Metropolitan Line to New York was organized and for many years continued to be successful. The first steamer of the line was the *Jersey Blue,* followed by the *City of Bath, Ceres, Salvor, Wyandotte, Mary Sanford, E. B. Hale,* and *Miami,* all operating on regular schedules from T Wharf and, later, from Hittinger's Wharf in Charlestown. Before the end of the century, steamship lines were maintaining regular schedules from Boston to Philadelphia, Baltimore, Savannah, Charleston, Jacksonville, and Galveston. There was no waiting for wind and weather, and the steamers provided quicker and safer methods of travel than did the sailing vessels. In the year 1900, of 10,436 ships entering the Port of Boston, exclusive of fishing vessels, only 2,686 depended on sail for navigation.

A share of the business between Boston and the South was, nevertheless, still conducted by means of coastwise sailing craft. Squat, sturdily built Boston schooners, without either the beauty or the speed of the earlier clippers, plied along the Atlantic Coast laden deep with cumbersome cargoes of coal, ice, granite, lumber, sand, and cement. The schooner, distinguished by its fore-and-aft rig, was born in Gloucester in 1713, though it was not fully developed until 1833; and its heyday was not reached until the period from 1870 to the World War of 1914-1918. There was need for coasting vessels to carry coal from the black-diamond regions to the hungry boilers of New England manufacturing plants and railroads, and the schooner was a practical vessel for the purpose, since it could be handled easily and economically by a small crew. The famous McKay clipper, *Sovereign of the Seas,* required a crew of 105; a schooner of the same size, carrying about 3,000 tons, as the clipper did, could be handled by 10 men. The ease and economy of schooner operation was increased after 1879, when the *Charles A. Briggs* introduced the steam donkey engine to hoist sail and anchor, man the windlass and pumps, and perform much of the heavy work that formerly had to be done by human brawn. Furthermore, because of its rig, the schooner could sail close to the wind, and its shoal draft allowed entrance to bays and rivers perilous to the great square-riggers. At the same time, the schooner was sturdy enough for the most turbulent transoceanic lanes, as many of them proved through years of service.

Boston played a significant role in the financing and use of schooners. Among the large operators here were William F. Palmer, who owned and operated a fleet of 13 five-masters and two-masters; the Thomas family, large investors in the Thomaston fleet of schooners, named after members of the family and managed by the Washburn Brothers; and John S. Emery and Company of Boston. Crowell and Thurlow, who proudly listed their crack vessels on their stationery, managed about 60 large schooners in addition to 13 steamships. They were at one time so successful that $100 shares in their company were selling for $1,400. Another great Boston fleet was owned and operated by John G. Crowley under the name of the Coastwise Transportation Company.

This company operated the only seven-masted schooner, and the largest sailing vessel, ever built—the *Thomas W. Lawson,* designed by B. B. Crowninshield of Boston, constructed at the Fore River Shipyard in 1902 and named after a prominent local financier. The steel vessel of 5,218 tons had 3 decks, was 395 feet long, 50 feet in beam, with molded depth of 34 feet, 5 inches and a dead-weight cargo capacity of 7,500 tons.

Space between her double bottoms allowed for 1,000 tons of water ballast. Mainmasts 135 feet tall, with topmasts 58 feet tall, raked the sky. It took 40,617 square feet of canvas to dress her, and 19 men plus a double cylinder ship engine and 5 hoisting engines to operate her. The total cost of the vessel was $250,000. The *Thomas W. Lawson* carried coal on the coast for 3 years and then was converted into a tanker. In 1907 she was to carry a cargo of oil in bulk from Philadelphia to London. Broad Sound, Scilly Islands, was reached safely, a pilot taken aboard, and preparations made to have the vessel towed to London on the next day. During the night a gale arose which drove the magnificent schooner onto the rocks and left her a total loss. One old Boston salt, relating the story, concluded significantly, "the name *Thomas W. Lawson* contained thirteen letters and she was wrecked on Friday, December 13."

Not only individual vessels, but whole fleets of schooners one by one met violent ends—witness the fate of the Palmer fleet. On December 24, 1909, the *Davis Palmer,* her holds weighted down with coal, nosed her way around Cape Cod and anchored in Broad Sound under the watchful eye of Graves Lighthouse. All hands looked forward eagerly to an early morning tow into Boston and Christmas at home. But that night a roaring southeaster swooped down out of the icy skies and screamed through the rigging. Huge seas battered the vessel. Dawn added to the danger by bringing a northwest blow and an ebb tide that swung the schooner into the trough of the sea. In a short time the vessel's hatches were splintered and all hands drowned. Exactly 7 years later, on Christmas Eve, 1916, the second *Fanny Palmer* went to the bottom while en route to Spain with a cargo of coal. Four of the Palmer vessels were lost in 1915: the *Paul Palmer* burned off Cape Cod; the *Maud Palmer* went down with all hands in a Carribean hurricane while bound from Trinidad to Mobile with asphalt; the *Baker Palmer* foundered while carrying coal to South America; and the *Elizabeth Palmer* crashed with the American-Hawaiian sugar steamer, *Washingtonian,* off the Delaware coast.

Most of the other Palmer vessels met similar violent fates. The *Marie Palmer* ran ashore on Frying Pan Shoals, North Carolina, in 1911; the *Prescott Palmer* and *Fuller Palmer* both sank off Georges Bank in 1914. Sold to the France and Canada Steamship Company during the World War—the prices rang-

ing from $300,000 to $400,000 each—the remnant of the
Palmer fleet was subjected to further hazards, but only one
vessel met a martial end. That was the *Harwood Palmer,*
shelled by a submarine and beached off St. Nazaire, France, in
1917. The *Rebecca Palmer,* sold to Greece during the war,
was scrapped in 1923. The *Jane Palmer* was abandoned off
Bermuda in 1920, after 16 years of service; the *Singleton
Palmer* sank in a collision off Delaware in 1921; and the
Dorothy Palmer, last survivor of the line, was abandoned off
Nantucket in 1923.

Methods of financing and operating schooners changed as
their use and size increased. In the day of the small schooner,
the resources of the captain and a few friends were sufficient
to finance the expense of construction, the investors taking
shares of sixty-fourths in the vessel. Once the schooner was
launched, the captain took full charge of the financial management, paying all dividends and making all disbursements.
Generally he sailed the vessel on half-shares, that is, the net
proceeds of a trip, after pilotage, towage, and stevedoring bills
were paid, were divided into two portions. Out of one portion, the paint, sails, and chandlery, excepting provisions, were
paid, and the residue went to the holders of shares in the
vessel. From the other portion, the captain paid the provision
bill and the crew's wages and kept the rest for himself. After
1880, when the operation of schooners became a big business,
and the number of shareholders increased, the proprietary
interest of the captain diminished, especially in the case of
the large schooners, and captains were then generally hired by
the schooner operators at $45 or $50 a month, plus primage,
usually five percent of the gross return from a trip.

The itinerary of the schooners varied with the business they
found, but there were a number of well-marked sea paths
which almost all of them followed. The 3-year Odyssey of one
Boston vessel was probably typical: the schooner started out
for Martinique with a general cargo, sailed thence to Port de
Paix in Haiti and loaded logwood for Boston; from Boston it
took Bibles and rum to the African Gold Coast, where it
loaded palm oil and returned to Boston. After a few days the
vessel started in ballast for Norfolk, where it took coal for
Savannah, Georgia. There it loaded lumber for Gardiner,
Maine. At nearby Portland it picked up a cargo of barrel
staves for the molasses and rum trade in Puerto Rico; from
Puerto Rico it beat its way to Jamaica, where it loaded log-

wood for Boston and, having deposited its cargo here, again set sail for the African jungles with Bibles and rum and returned with palm oil.

Although life on board a schooner was not luxurious, there were usually decent living quarters and working conditions, and no bucko mates or mutinous crews. The natural pride seamen have always taken in the vessel on which they ship was heightened. On the large schooners quarters for both officers and crew were always clean and well-ventilated, and the captain, housed in a comfortable suite of rooms, lived as handsomely as he would in an apartment ashore. The salt pork and hardtack of an earlier day had given place by this time to more varied and appetizing menus, and ice boxes kept the food fresh. The tradition of spotless "shipkeeping" was rigidly observed. Schooners came into port with spars and rigging gleaming and decks scrubbed white. Even the least among the crew would feel disturbed at the most trifling disorder. Captain Harold Foss remarks:

I have seen a poor, ignorant sailor when leaving my schooner throw on the dock his clothes-bag containing his entire worldly possessions—a few cheap, patched rags—and stoop to pick up a rope and coil it on a belaying pin. He never glanced at me as I stood on the quarter-deck. He hated all the officers of the ship and they despised him. Yet he could not leave the schooner without coiling the rope. It made me feel somewhat ashamed of some of the harsh things I had said to him on the voyage. Yet my next thought was that if I never saw him again it would be too soon.

The Decline of Shipbuilding

The shift from sail to steam had a marked effect upon the Boston shipbuilding industry. Already the Civil War years had exhausted the financial resources of the local builders, and the changing conditions that followed retarded their recovery. Construction figures emphasize this fact clearly. During the year closing June 30, 1860, Boston built 23 ships, 15 schooners, 2 sloops, and 7 steamers, with an aggregate tonnage of 21,147. In place of the great, proud clippers, harbors along the Atlantic seaboard were visited more and more by iron-hulled shipantines, or four-masted barks, as they were sometimes called. So long and narrow that they might well have split their own backs had they been made out wood, these iron boats were equipped with donkey engines for hoisting sail and pumping and with derrick booms and cargo side ports for loading and unloading. Such a craft could carry 2,000 tons, and unload as fast as a 1,000-ton wooden ship operated by hand winches and man power. Since many American merchant-owners preferred them to the older types of vessel, local shipyards, which did not build their kind, suffered.

Between 1867 and 1900, Boston built 58 three-masted schooners. In the eighties the first great four-masters appeared, in sizes ranging from 1,000 to 1,700 tons, and the decade following saw the five-masters of from 1,800 to 2,500 tons. The turn of the century brought the six-masters of from 2,800 to 3,800 tons. Four hundred and forty-two four-masted schooners were built on the Atlantic Coast between 1888 and 1920; of these, 7 were built in Boston, 1 in Somerville, and 1 in Chelsea. The tonnage of these vessels ranged from the 718-ton *Howard Smith,* the first of the Boston four-masters, to the 1,467-ton *Richard T. Green,* which was built at the Green Shipyard in Chelsea. The last Hub four-master was the *Isabella B. Parmenter,* later named the *Tremont,* a 979-ton vessel constructed at Somerville in 1920, and lost off Cape Henry on October 21, 1925. In addition, in 1879 a Boston yard converted the 598-ton steamer, *Weybosset,* built at Mystic, Connecticut, in 1863, into a four-masted schooner. Thereafter the *Weybosset* carried coal in the coastwise trade for many years, until she foundered in the Pollock Rip slue near the Cape after striking the submerged wreck of Cornelius Vanderbilt's yacht, *Alva.* Only 1 five-masted schooner was a product of Boston shipyards, the *Jane Palmer,* a 3138-ton vessel constructed in 1904.

Shipyards were still active in East Boston, South Boston, Boston, Medford, Charlestown, Quincy, Dorchester, and Neponset, and in the 1880's several hundred Boston-built schooners and brigs were carrying cargoes along the shipping lanes to foreign ports. The East Boston yards were especially busy. Curiously enough, one of the first Boston-built steamships, *Le Voyageur de la Mer,* was launched there February 25, 1857, as a result of an Egyptian pasha's interest in iron vessels. George A. Stone, a native Bostonian who had business contacts with the pasha, heard so much about the advantages of iron ships from the Egyptian that he eventually ordered Samuel H. Pook to construct such a craft.

During the latter part of his career, Samuel Hall built many fast fishing schooners of about 100 tons, his first two schooners being the *Express* and the *Telegraph.* The *Marion F. Sprague,* a handsome three-masted schooner, was designed by John Frisbee, who divided his time between designing boats and teaching ship-drafting in Charlestown and South Boston schools, thereby laying the foundations of the modern drafting system. Several of the Frisbee creations ranked with the best coasters launched during these decades.

A number of larger vessels were turned out by the Boston shipyards, among them the *N. Boynton*, tonnage 1,065, in 1866; the *Sea Witch* in 1872; and the *Sachem*, 1,380 tons, in 1876. Iron steamships for Russia, China, and the East Indies were produced by the Atlantic Works. This firm built two monitors, the *Nantucket* and *Casco*, as well as fleets of ferry-boats and tugs, marine and land engines, turrets and other parts of ironclads, giving employment to several hundred machinists. Active also were the Lockwood Manufacturing Company on Summer Street, Webb and Watson on Border Street, makers of marine engines and propellers, the Robinson Boiler Works on Liverpool Street, and the Boston Forge Company on Maverick Street, builders of steel shafts, anchors, and other ship accessories. Nearby, seven drydocks and marine railways steadily employed a large group of shipwrights and caulkers doing repair work. In Charlestown, F. J. Baldwin was one of the more important builders of iron and steel vessels.

South Boston combined the launching of commercial craft with the creation of graceful yachts for wealthy sportsmen. Here could be realized the most extravagant nautical ideas, and many magnificent sloops and schooners were designed for men who desired a gentle taste of sea life. Smaller yachts were also produced, including steam launches and tiny catboats noted for their speed. The *Burgess*, named after her designer, Edward Burgess, was among the many famous racing yachts constructed at City Point. In the same vicinity was the City Point Iron Works, founded in 1847, and owned by Harrison Loring. This firm was employed by the Government in the construction of naval cruisers and tugs. In 1860 South Boston and East Boston together employed about 60 shipwrights and caulkers, yet, by the end of the century, changing business conditions had reduced the number to a scant half-dozen. Shipbuilders decreased from 12 to less than 6 over the same period.

Similarly Medford and Quincy felt the effects of the shifting maritime scene. Medford, in particular, was forced to watch changing fashions pass her by, leaving vacant shipyards and empty purses. From 1853 to 1862, 70 ships, with an aggregate tonnage of 57,815, were launched in Medford, yet in the next decade only 14 vessels, with a tonnage total of 12,049, came off the ways. The Mystic River was too shallow to float the larger schooners and steamers then coming into vogue. Quincy was not so handicapped. At East Braintree the Fore River Engine Company began building marine engines in 1883, and the work increased so rapidly that the factory was forced to move to Quincy in 1900. Other concerns were also active in Quincy; one of the best known was a yard owned and operated by Deacon Thomas from 1854 to 1870. He constructed vessels of all sizes, from tiny cockleshells hardly large enough to weather a bathtub storm to craft of more than 2,000 tons burden. Between 1870 and 1880 other Quincy yards launched such famous ships as the *Triumphant* and the *Modoc*.

Close by, Neponset gradually grew into one of the leading yacht-building centers of the country. During normal years the business averaged about $5,000,000 annually, garnered from the construction of knockabouts, sloops, schooners, private steam yachts, racing ships, combined wood and steel craft; in fact anything that touched the fancy of owners or designers. Before the close of the century a number of beautiful racing vessels were built by George Lawley and Sons, makers of such exceptionally fine boats as the sloop *Puritan*, successful defender of the America's Cup against the British cutter *Genesta*, and the *Mayflower*, cup defender against the *Galatea*. Other sections of Dorchester, Quincy, and Medford also produced yachts of varying sizes and abilities.

Inevitably associated with a shipbuilding center or a great port are ship chandlers, provisioners in the broadest sense, supplying vessels, not only with food, but with all nautical necessities. "Rope, duck, oakum, and paints, beef, pork, flour, molasses and canned goods," read the signs on one ship chandler's store of the late nineteenth century. The business of the few genuine ship chandlers that remain is limited today; whereas once the captain of a vessel brought his requisition directly to the chandler who filled the order, no questions asked on price or quality, the modern skipper places his supply requisitions into the hands of the ship company's purchasing agent or marine superintendent, and he in turn places his orders according to the type and quality of the merchandise required.

The chandler had other functions besides that of provisioner. He often acted as a banker, lending anywhere from one to three thousand dollars to a captain to defray the expenses of a trip. No interest was charged on these loans, nor were the debts set forth in writing—an eloquent testimony to the confidence these business men had in one another's honesty. The chandler was also a large investor in newly built vessels, taking shares in them with the implied understanding that the vessels would patronize his establishment when they came to port for provisioning. James Bliss and Company at one time had shares in all the vessels of the Crowell and Thurlow Company, the Rogers and Webb Line, and the Palmer fleet.

Few of the old ship chandlers are now in existence, although 50 years ago there were 18 or 20 of these tradesmen in Boston. Most prominent were George Billings (known as "Honest George"), Hinkley Brothers and Company, Timothy L. Mayo, Peter McIntyre and Company, Harrington and King, J. H. Flitner and Company, which later became Flitner Atwood Company, Googan and Stodder, Snow and Higgins, S. P. Blackburn and Company, French Brothers, Walter W. Hodder, Inc., and the Bliss Company. The last two firms are still in existence and, together with the Boston Provision and Ship Supply Company, successor to French Brothers, and the Crowell Supply Company, they are the only real ship chandlers in Boston today.

The Bliss Company deserves particular mention, for it is probably the oldest active ship chandlery concern on the Atlantic coast. It was founded in 1832 by James Bliss, and its first order was delivered in a wheelbarrow to a vessel at Long Wharf. The Company was then located at 328 Atlantic Avenue, where it had one floor or "loft," as the ship chandler would say, and a cellar. In 1876, when Bliss died his adopted son, James F. Bliss, and Israel Emerson Decrow of Camden, Maine, took over the business as equal partners. On the death of James F. Bliss in 1923, the business went to the surviving partner, and in 1925, the firm became James Bliss and Company, Incorporated. In 1931, Israel Decrow died and for a time it looked as though the old firm, which had just passed the century mark, would have to close its doors. But Israel Decrow's daughter, Miss Marion L. Decrow, assisted by experienced employees of her father, piloted the firm successfully through the worst of the economic blow. The new management added to the steamship supply department a marine hardware department, which carries equipment for small boats, and a ship model department where completed models of vessels, including famous McKay clippers, and blueprints for the construction of model ships are on sale. Associated with the Bliss Company is the Crowell Supply Company, operated by J. Edgar Crowell, who left the Blackburn Company in 1888 and is probably the oldest living man in the chandlering business in Boston. Through his London agent, Mr. Crowell holds yearly contracts with about 40 British steamship companies to supply their vessels when they put into the Port of Boston.

Around the World Again

Despite various trade fluctuations, Boston experienced a gradual and general commercial advance between 1860 and 1900. The development of great textile centers in eastern Massachusetts made Boston after 1880 the second largest wool market in the world, surpassed only by London. Improved rail connections with the West brought a flood of grain and livestock which, supplemented by locally manufactured products, boosted Boston's exports to a high 5-year average of $111,000,000 from 1896-1900, a 77 percent increase over the corresponding period of the preceding decade. During the same years, exports were 62 percent greater than imports, an unusual trend at Boston. As the century drew to a close, Boston was strongly entrenched as the second United States port in foreign trade. Its $180,000,000 overseas commerce was over 50 percent larger than that of its nearest rival, Baltimore.

Boston's commerce with South America had developed far less rapidly than trade with Europe and Asia, since the Old World offered better markets for raw products. The steady growth of manufacturing had tended to change this situation, however, and by 1860 commercial relations with South America ran into many millions of dollars. Principal imports from South America in that year were coffee, copper, hides, nitrates, petroleum, and rubber; while exports largely consisted of finished manufactured goods, semi-finished products, and manufactured foodstuffs. Boston merchants purchased $3,000,-000 worth of goods from South American countries in 1870, or 6.4 percent of the city's total imports, and in return shipped merchandise valued at $1,800,000, or 15.3 percent of the city's export business. Imports from South America continued to increase and passed the $6,000,000 mark in 1880. By 1890, however, the trade had dropped to $4,000,000, although the proportion to total imports remained about the same as in

1870. Exports showed a greater fluctuation, dropping in 1890 to $1,340,000, which equalled only 2 percent of the total exports from Boston in that year. Imports from the Argentine exceeded those from all other South American countries combined, and exports to Chile led the list for South America.

From neighboring Central America, mahogany logs furnished a profitable supplement to bananas in the trade of the eighties and nineties. The George D. Emery Company imported mahogany from its concession in Nicaragua to its mill in Chelsea. The timber was cut in the dry season, floated down river during floods, towed offshore by tugs, and loaded on chartered British schooners. Two logs of Spanish cedar were lashed to each log of mahogany to keep it afloat. This cedar was also brought to Boston where it was used to make cigar boxes and other light cartons. The mahogany trade was carried on until Emery's plant was destroyed by fire and the firm moved to New York.

Local merchants found trade with the Far East a precarious business at best during the changing decades between 1850 and 1900. Imports from and exports to China and Japan were greatly curtailed, dropping 75 percent in some cases. By 1857 New York had definitely supplanted Boston as the terminus of the China trade, and in that year could boast of 41 arrivals to Boston's 6. The transition had been under way since 1824, when the Massachusetts Legislature laid a tax of one percent *ad valorem* on all merchandise brought from beyond the Cape of Good Hope and auctioned in Boston. Although the tax was reduced in 1849 and repealed in 1852, it was then too late to stop the trend to New York. More contemporary reasons for the loss of the China trade were such general conditions as the changing demands of local markets, the transfer of clipper ships to other routes, and the concentration of sail and steamship lines at the Port of New York. The dropping off of the China trade was noted as early as the 1840's, and it was hoped that the arrival in Boston in 1848 of the sensational Chinese junk *Keying* would halt the decline. Bizarre in decoration, with elaborate saloons, cabins, and a josshouse containing the 18-handed idol "Chin-Tee," the teakwood junk registered about 800 tons, was shaped like a Spanish galleon, and displayed wooden anchors and thatched mat sails. Thousands of Bostonians visited the Oriental craft and marvelled that she had proved seaworthy during a voyage half-way around the world. The display of this strange craft failed to produce the desired effect, and, with the exception of one or two periods of unusual activity near the end of the century, trade with China remained at a low level.

Similar conditions marked Boston's trade with India and Africa. Business continued good through 1857; in that year no less than 96 of the 122 ships loaded in India sailed to Boston. Cargoes included Java coffee, Singapore rubber, Philippine sugar, and an assortment of jute, indigo, linseed, shellac, and gunny-cloth. In turn, Western corn growers purchased the gunny-bags from Boston merchants, while the uncut cloth was sent to the South to bale cotton. Linseed oil and jute factories near Salem and in Charlestown prepared these East Indian products for the American market. Typical of the uncertainties of the trade was the barter in gunny-sacks and gunny-cloth. While less than 5,000 bales came to Boston in 1840, the number had increased to 86,000 bales in 1867. Ten years later, however, the importation of this commodity had completely ceased. African trade also fell off between 1860 and 1890. Importations of wool, goatskins, ostrich feathers, and diamonds, which amounted to $3,779,000 in 1860, dropped to less than $500,000 by 1890. Exports were equally weak.

Meanwhile Boston's export trade to Australia had gradually advanced. For some 20 years after 1860, diversified New England manufactures, "from cradles and teething rings to coffins and tombstones," were dumped into waiting holds and shipped half around the world. In return Australia sent great loads of wool and hides. In 1880, Boston's imports from Australia and Asiatic British possessions amounted to $1,703,000, while exports to these countries were valued at $1,130,000.

One of the important firms in the Boston-Australian trade was the Henry W. Peabody & Company. Peabody, who learned the business from Samuel Stevens, operator of the Australasian Line in the fifties and sixties, sent out the packetship *Nellie Chapin* to Melbourne in 1867 and followed with the *Surprise, Sarah, Richard Bustead, Franklin,* and *A. W. Stevens.* Vessels for this line were chartered. Their sailings were advertised on a colorful card, surmounted by the house insignia, which gave the destination of the vessels, the type, name, tonnage, and captain, and sometimes the vessel that preceded on the voyage. The loading berth named was most frequently Lewis Wharf, although one or two cards mention Constitution Wharf. The cards announced that "carload lots of freight are delivered

A Leyland cargo liner, probably the *Istrian* (built in 1867), photographed from the Boston and Albany Railroad's Grand Junction grain elevator. *Courtesy of the Peabody Museum of Salem.*

A southwesterly view towards Roxbury taken in 1877. *Courtesy of the Mariners' Museum, Newport News, Virginia.*

direct to vessel's tackles, thus saving rehandling, and no charges except actual disbursements are made on goods consigned to our care." The rating of the vessel either by Lloyd's or Bureau Veritas was given, and, if the vessel had been chartered before by Peabody, that fact was solemnly stated with a line to the effect that goods were received previously in good condition. Many of these cards are kept in the offices of the company today.

By 1890 much of the traffic on the Atlantic seaboard was clearing from New York, and Peabody established the headquarters of his commission business there. The Boston office took over the importation of the hard fibers, sisal and hemp, and today handles more of these products than any other firm in the country. The demand for sisal as a binder of wheat interested the Peabody Company in the eighties and by 1890 an office had been established at Merida, capital of Yucatan and center of great sisal plantations. Cultivation of the fiber spread to other countries, and Peabody now gets it from East Africa, Java, and Haiti, as well as Yucatan. In 1890, Henry W. Peabody & Company also opened an office in Manila to facilitate the importation of hemp and later added sugar, copra, and cocoanut oil to products handled in Boston. Sisal was first brought by schooners, hemp by clippers. Most of the latter were chartered for a full cargo from John G. Hall, Charles Hunt, or John S. Emery. They came by way of the Cape of Good Hope and, from the time the ship left Manila until it was sighted off Highland Light, probably 5 months later, it was rarely heard from. Sisal is now handled by chartered steamers; Manila hemp is brought in as part of the cargo of steamers on regular Far Eastern runs.

Although sailing vessels could not match the smokestack in the widening area of world trade, Boston sail was not completely outmoded in the second half of the century. The largest merchant fleet in the United States, more than 50 square-rigged vessels proudly flying the "Black Horse Flag," was still owned by William F. Weld & Company of Boston. Weld ships saw every principal port in the world and continued to traverse trade routes almost up to the turn of the century. On the Atlantic seaboard, "Black Horse" ships regularly put into New York, Philadelphia, and Baltimore. Sometimes they called at Halifax, Charleston, New Orleans, and Rio de Janeiro, while Pacific stops included San Francisco, New Tacoma, and Vancouver. Often returning by Cape Horn, these vessels would cross the Atlantic and anchor at the mouth of the Thames or dock at Dublin and Liverpool.

Famous sailing ships belonging at one time or another to the Weld firm included the *William Sturgis,* lost in 1865 just outside Iloilo in the Philippines; the brig *Laurillia,* which disappeared without a trace; and the ship *Meridian,* abandoned at sea after being swept by a hurricane. But the three Weld ships that stand out in American sailing history are the *Enoch Train,* the *Golden Fleece,* and the *Great Admiral.* Misfortune dogged the *Enoch Train* from the moment the 1787-ton ship left the ways of Paul Curtis' East Boston shipyard in 1854. Once she sprung her whole port bow; another time, with 33 inches of water in her pumps, and making only 1 knot an hour, she put into Norfolk, where her entire crew deserted. After carrying rails from England to the United States without mishap, the *Enoch Train* strained herself so badly on a trip to Rio that she had to put back into port for recaulking. On that single passage her deficit was over $5,000.

In 1872 the *Enoch Train* was sent to Hong Kong. Believing that the vessel was accursed, her captain thought on several occasions that all was lost. His log reports that near the China coast he ran into "Hard squalls, weather looking wild and dirty. Corposants (St. Elmo's fire) at all mast-heads and topgallant yard-arms. Heavy north-west gales, and a bad sea running." The squalls increased to hurricane violence, and by the next day the vessel was almost totally dismasted. By noon, unable to ride the heavy seas, she had shipped so much water that her best boat was stove in, the bulwarks and monkey rail from poop to forecastle had been torn out, and everything movable on deck, including the water casks, had been washed overboard. When the seas abated somewhat, the vessel was in such disorder that the captain wrote in his log, "A stinking, miserable mess." A steamer passed the *Enoch Train,* paying no regard to her distress signals. The crew managed to clean up the ship and finally drifted in close to the coast, where they got out an anchor. A Chinese gunboat came within hail, but the current was so strong that no headway could be made when it tried to tow the stricken vessel. So the gunboat took the mail into Hong Kong, and left behind arms for the *Enoch Train* to use, if necessary, against the Chinese pirates that infested the waters. Then another typhoon struck, and the ship rolled helplessly until a steamer came out from Hong Kong and towed her in. The hawser broke in the wild sea but was made fast again; the *Enoch Train* finally got into port after a passage of 146 days.

Proudest and ablest of all the Weld fleet was the *Great Admiral*, built in 1869 at the Boston shipyard of E. R. Jackson. Among skippers and sailors, competition was keen for a place on the *Admiral*, and insurance agents vied for her coverage. The ship passed through three terrific typhoons, suffering nothing more serious than a sprung rudder post. Last of the Weld fleet, she was sold in 1897, and sank 9 years later, while carrying a cargo of lumber from Puget Sound to San Pedro, California.

European Trade, Travel, and Immigration

The commercial life of Boston still hinged on trans-Atlantic service and trade with England and the Continent. In 1868, however, Boston merchants had been forced to sit back despairingly and watch the Cunard Line shift its steamer service from Boston to New York. The reasons for this change were a reduction in the English mail subsidy and the inability of Boston merchants to supply full return cargoes to Liverpool. Although Cunard freighters occasionally did put into the Port on the way from Halifax to New York to complete their cargoes, not a single steamer sailed direct from Boston to Liverpool for nearly 3 years.

Individual sailing packets sought to recapture segments of the trade lost by the departure of the Cunarders, and when these efforts were in some measure successful the Cunard Line made an abrupt about-face and re-established connections with the Port of Boston. Accordingly, on September 22, 1870, the Cunard cargo steamer *Palmyra*, sailed directly from Boston for Liverpool, and Boston maritime interests took on a new lease of life. The railroads cooperated, the Boston and Albany even joining with the Cunard Line in purchasing large quantities of grain to assure the company full cargoes. Other vessels followed the *Palmyra* at varying intervals until April 8, 1871, when the departure of the *Siberia* marked the inauguration of a regular schedule.

A number of steamship lines followed the wake of the Cunarders into the Port of Boston. In 1871, the Warren Line, successors to the old Enoch Train Line of sailing packets, established a route between Boston and Liverpool. Some months later, the British Inman Company sent the steamer *City of Boston* to Boston and New York as the pioneer vessel of their new line. On her return voyage to Liverpool, the *City of Boston* touched at Halifax and then was never heard from. Her tragic loss changed the plans of the Inman Company, which withdrew from the Boston trade. Five years later, trans-Atlantic sailings received a fresh impetus when the Leyland Line inaugurated a series of fortnightly departures, followed by Boston sailings of vessels of the Anchor, Allan, Wilson, and White Cross Line. In 1880, Bostonians waved bon voyage to no less than 322 steamers carrying merchandise to European ports. Of these, 196 were for Liverpool, 47 for Glasgow, 42 for London, and 37 for West Hartlepool and Hull.

The Port continued to hold a dominant position in dealings with the Mediterranean. Arrivals from Bordeaux, Marseilles, Malaga, Messina, Palermo, and Smyrna were exceeded only by those from the West Indies. From Smyrna alone, several hundred thousand drums of figs were imported annually, besides wool, gums, drugs, and dyes. The Dabney family continued to dominate trade with the Azores; S. W. Dabney served there as consul from 1871 to 1892. A Bostonian named Nichols brought the first steamship to the islands, causing great excitement among the inhabitants. When it departed, the natives saw clouds of steam rising from the smokestack and decided the vessel was on fire. Frantically they rushed down to the water, pushed off in their boats, and hastened toward the steamer to save the unfortunate crew.

Closely integrated with Boston's commercial expansion was the varying volume of immigration entering the Port through the decades. Following the great wave of Irish immigration in the 1840's and early 1850's, the entrants at Boston dropped steadily until after the Civil War. The Massachusetts Legislature in 1870 repealed the State head tax on immigrants entering through Boston and going on to interior States, and in that year some 30,000 immigrants entered the Port. Hoping to attract a greater number, since other States retained the head tax, the legislature in 1872 exempted also immigrants intending to remain in the Commonwealth. Any advantage that might have been gained was blocked by the depression of 1873 and by an edict of the Supreme Court 3 years later, which declared all State head taxes unconstitutional. Boston remained second to New York as an immigrant port, although its entries were very small in comparison to those of the great metropolis. A rapid increase in the eighties, caused by the flow of southern Europeans, sent Boston entrants soaring to over 58,000 in 1882. From then until the close of the century, the figure fluctuated considerably, reaching a low of 12,271 in 1898.

War and the Close of the Century

The influx of immigrants into Boston lagged in 1898, when war was declared between Spain and the United States. Rumors of a Spanish attack along the New England coast had turned the attention of Boston's citizens to their harbor defenses. Four guns were installed on Long Island; Fort Warren was inspected and strengthened; cannon were set up at Winthrop; and a concerted plan of battle was drawn up. Already the sinking of the *Maine* had thoroughly aroused the local citizenry, and a committee, headed by Mayor Quincy, had launched a city-wide subscription for the erection of a monument to the victims. Within a few months, hundreds of Boston's sons had joined the Sixth Massachusetts Regiment and departed for Cuba.

After anxiously following the course of the war throughout the summer, Boston greeted with gay enthusiasm the news of the cessation of hostilities. Returning from San Juan, the Sixth Massachusetts steamed up the harbor on the transport *Mississippi* with colors flying, while whistles and sirens screamed from every boat along the waterfront. The transport was met by a tug, which brought a supply of heavy clothing and overcoats to the men. Sailing under the white flag of the Commonwealth, the *Vigilant* carried Governor Wolcott along the starboard side of the *Mississippi* and gave three long whistles as his salute to the returning boys. To the tune of "Stars and Stripes Forever," the troops paraded up Congress, Milk, Broad, State, Washington, School, and Beacon Streets to Charles, where the regiment was dismissed.

The close of the Spanish-American War found Boston merchants and shipowners busily engaged in sending schooners up and down the coast, directing steamers across the Atlantic and to distant ports, and generally handling commercial activities with more efficient methods and with their eyes wider open than had been the case since the golden era of the clipper ships. Prosperity was not a myth to be idly dreamt about; it was ripe and ready for the picking, and Bostonians were not slow in harvesting the profitable crop. With extraordinary consistency, Boston had remained second only to New York in the volume of shipping; jumping from $54,535,000 in 1860 to $192,609,000 in 1900, while New York showed an improvement from $371,839,000 to $1,068,700,000 for the corresponding years. All told, Boston handled approximately one-fifth of the aggregate foreign tonnage of the country, and her commercial activities were still accelerating as the century ended.

CHAPTER VII

A TWENTIETH CENTURY PORT

Expansion to Meet New Demands

AT THE OPENING of the twentieth century Boston was the second most important port in the United States and the only Massachusetts city that still upheld the maritime traditions of the bold Yankee skippers. Steel-hulled, steam-powered ocean "leviathans" of 10,000 tons or more ploughed up the main ship channel, and then were pushed by squat, smoke-belching tugs to their berths in Charlestown and East Boston. Smelly, storm-battered fishing vessels crowded about T Wharf and sailed in and out of the harbor. Along the wharves, steam winches shrilled into life, hoisting cargo from unbattened holds, and brawny longshoremen moved ant-like up and down the gangplanks. While passengers streamed aboard or moved gingerly about, trying to accustom "sea-legs" to the solidity of land, coastwise steamers and excursion boats cluttered the old piers off Atlantic Avenue, which had remained the center of much port activity. Receiving shipments from the ancient brick and stone warehouses in the vicinity, the steamships and sailing vessels of 18 companies berthed at Long, Lewis, India, and Central Wharves.

The natural advantages of Boston Harbor were being enhanced by important alterations and improvements. In 1902 the United States Government began dredging a channel 35 feet deep at mean low water, 1,200 feet wide from Charlestown, Chelsea North, Meridian Street, and Charles River Bridges to President Roads and 1,500 feet wide through Broad Sound to the sea. Three years later the largest stone and concrete drydock then in the world was completed at the Boston Navy Yard and immediately put into use. The armored cruiser *Maryland* was the first ship to enter its tremendous steel caisson.

The Commonwealth undertook a series of extensive improvements planned to care for the increased tonnage expected to be attracted to the Port by the enlarged channels. Under the direction of the Board of Directors of the Port, established in 1911, the large and excellently equipped Commonwealth Pier No. 5 was completed in South Boston in 1913. Some 1,200 feet in length, with a 400-foot frontage on the main ship channel and a 35-foot depth at mean low water, the pier was equipped with three two-story fireproof sheds, six railroad tracks, and electric winches for handling freight, and could accommodate five steamships at once. The Boston Fish Pier nearby was opened a short while later, the most modern and largest plant of its kind in the world. Practically all the fishing fleet moved to the new location, leaving T Wharf to the mercy of a few small Italian and Portuguese vessels, various "atmospheric" tearooms, and groups of literary folk. At the new pier, the industry soon reached a point where 750,000 pounds of fish were being processed daily. Across the harbor, adjoining the Boston & Albany piers, the Commonwealth Pier No. 1 was completed in 1919, to supplement the excellent facilities that were already attracting much of the trans-Atlantic trade to East Boston.

Throughout these years of remarkable waterfront improvements, the Honorable John F. Fitzgerald played an outstanding rôle in the progress of the Port of Boston. During his entire career in public office, the energetic Fitzgerald spared no effort, left no stone unturned to make Boston the greatest seaport of the nation. In Congress he demanded a deeper channel for Boston Harbor and a lighthouse and fog signal on State Ledge; he introduced a bill for the construction of drydocks in Charlestown and urged changes in the law requiring the installation of life-saving apparatus on ships. Reading a newspaper statement that the beloved Boston frigate *Constitution* was in danger of sinking in Portsmouth Harbor, Fitzgerald made a stirring speech on the floor of the House on January 14, 1897, and, as a result, the famous vessel was repaired and then towed to the Charlestown Navy Yard, where a solemn celebration was held. In and out of New England, "John F." advocated the bringing of new steamship lines to Boston and enthusiastically furthered Boston's trade relations with the South American countries. In 1905 a prophetic note had appeared in an address delivered by Fitzgerald in favor of port development.

Perhaps . . . airships may be invented to sail from this country to other parts of the world (laughter). Unless something of that kind happens there must be improvements in order to provide for the cheaper transportation which follows the increased carrying capacity of ships.

Mr. Fitzgerald has continued his deep interest in the Port and, since 1934, has served as an active member of the Boston Port Authority.

The opening of the Cape Cod Canal in the summer of 1914 cut the running time and increased the safety of the "outside" line of boats between Boston and New York and facilitated coastwise traffic to the south. From the earliest days, settlers at Plymouth had realized the possibilities of a cut across the Cape's neck, a fact noted by Samuel Sewall in 1676 and officially recognized by the General Court of Massachusetts in 1697. But the matter was dropped for nearly a century until the General Court in 1776 appointed a committee to determine the practicability of a canal. Thomas Machin, an engineer, surveyed the proposed route and recommended a canal 14 feet deep with two double locks at each end and two bridges, all at an estimated cost of £32,146. Nothing came of this, however, and the matter again hung fire. The Federal Government considered the canal question in 1818, and in 1824 Congress authorized the President to cause "necessary surveys, plans and estimates to be made." But no action was taken.

Finally in 1860 the Massachusetts General Court decided to take a firmer stand on the subject of the canal and appointed a committee, which reported favorably on the project. The committee supported its opinion by calling attention to the fact that 10,000 ships annually sailed around the Cape and that in 17 years there had been 827 marine disasters in that region, with an annual loss of $600,000. In 1883 the recommendation for a canal without locks attracted private capital and the Cape Cod Ship Canal Company was incorporated. Before difficulties terminated the work, a canal 1 mile long, 15 feet deep, and 100 feet wide was actually excavated across the marshes of the Scusset River. Later a charter was given to the Boston, Cape Cod, and New York Canal Company; building was resumed in June 1909, and the waters of Buzzards and Cape Cod Bays met on July 4, 1914. On the thirtieth of the same month, the canal was opened to navigation, but only for vessels drawing less than 15 feet. The need of enlargement was recognized from the beginning, and by 1916 the minimum bottom width of the canal extended 100 feet, with a depth of 25 feet at mean low water. Even these improvements did not attract sufficient tonnage to make the operation of the canal profitable to a private company. During the World War it was taken over by the United States and afterward it was purchased by the Government.

Storm and Shipwreck

Even the completion of the canal did not do away with adventure on the high seas off the New England coast, and often Boston ships ran into difficulties reminiscent of former days. The tragic loss of the *Portland* was still fresh in the minds of Boston mariners, and available weather reports were carefully scrutinized for storm warnings, resulting in a considerable decrease in the number of local shipwrecks. Yet there was still justification for the likening of Cape Cod to a mailed fist warning vessels to keep their distance or take the consequences. Many a stout sailing vessel or ably built steamship met disaster in the "ocean graveyard" of Massachusetts Bay.

In December 1902, two heavily laden coal schooners, the five-master *Louise B. Crary* and the four-master *Frank A. Palmer*, collided while maneuvering against headwinds no more than 5 hours' sail from Long Wharf. The terrific crash stove in the side of the *Palmer* and demolished the bow of the *Crary*. Within 10 minutes both vessels were at the bottom, carrying down 6 men. The remaining 15 were picked up by the lifeboat of the *Palmer* and began a terrible battle against intense cold, thirst, hunger, and the savage sea. For 3 days the men rowed as best they could, while frigid water lapped over the gunwales, transforming hands into icy claws. Five of the suffering crew died. In desperation a pair of trousers from one of the frozen victims was hoisted on an oar in an effort to attract attention. Finally, late on the third day, this distress signal was sighted by the fishing schooner *Manhassett*, and the survivors were rescued and brought to Boston. That same month a large steel barge, *Number 48*, owned by the Standard Oil Company and probably laden with gasoline, was sighted in a leaking condition and minus its crew, off Highland Light, by the fishing schooner *Blanche*. It was immediately taken in tow and a salvage crew put aboard. About 10 miles from Gloucester, George Riley, one of the salvage crew on the barge went below to look for a chain. He struck a match to penetrate the gloom, and an instant explosion tore him to pieces and set the barge on fire. Undeterred, the men on the Blanche lengthened the hawser and towed the flaming vessel into the harbor.

Due to better navigation and the able efforts of lifesaving

crews, disastrous shipwrecks occurred less frequently in Massachusetts Bay. In January 1909, the three-masted schooner *Myra W. Spear* sprang a leak while carrying a cargo of railroad ties across Massachusetts Bay, became water-logged and rolled over on her side. George Loveland, the cook, was washed overboard and drowned. When the hulk unexpectedly righted itself a short time later, Mate Peterson and a sailor known as "Dan" lost their holds and went down. Captain E. T. Rogers and a member of the crew clung to the wreck until the fishing schooner *Manhassett* rescued them. Early on the morning of July 30, 1912, in a dense fog off Thatcher Island the Eastern Steamship Company's *City of Rockland*, carrying some 400 passengers, collided with the steam collier *William I. Chisholm*, and the impact sheared the *Rockland's* bow as cleanly as if it had been clipped off by gigantic scissors. The stricken liner sounded shrill blasts for help, and with an appearance of magic the steamship *Belfast*, of the same company, loomed out of the fog and stood by to give assistance. Two lifeboats overturned as they were being launched, but nobody drowned and eventually all the passengers were removed to the *Belfast* and taken to Boston. The rammed ship *Chisholm* was not seriously damaged and, aided by the tugs *Mercury* and *Juno*, successfully beached the *Rockland* stern first in the shoal water off Deer Island.

Five years later the busy movement of war vessels in and out of Boston Harbor accounted for several accidents that just avoided tragic consequences. On the afternoon of August 11, 1917, the Nantasket-bound *Mayflower*, carrying 1,164 passengers, was rammed by the U. S. submarine L-10 in a dense fog between Spectacle and Castle Islands. The submersible literally gored the steamer, burying her steel prow 20 feet into its side. While the panic-stricken passengers were being quieted, the *Rose Standish* arrived and all on board were saved. The following year the U. S. destroyer *Reid*, then on neutrality duty at quarantine, collided with the coal barge *Mauch Chunk* from New York, crushing the stem of the barge and damaging her own bow. Another crash occurred the same season during a dense fog, when a British freighter with a full cargo of munitions collided off Boston Light with a steamship owned by the same company. Fortunately there was no explosion, and the pumps kept both vessels afloat until they were able to put into port.

More Fish

But events of wider scope were also taking shape at the Port. The fishing industry underwent a series of changes during the first decade of this century. A number of immigrants from the Azores, Italy, and the Maritime Provinces had gradually replaced the old New England stock on the Boston fishing boats. As early as 1902, small dories with gasoline or naphtha engines were "put-putting" off the Massachusetts shore, forming the nucleus of what was later dubbed the "kicker fleet." That same year Thomas B. McManus designed a new type of sailing schooner, minus bowsprit and with changed rig, while 3 auxiliary schooners made their debuts, averaging more than 100 feet in length and capable of making 7 or 8 knots under power. A new steamer, the *Kingfisher*, was added to the halibut fleet, and another steamer was fitted out for mackerel fishing. Following the lead of European concerns, the Bay State Fishing Company introduced the first of a fleet of steam trawlers in 1905. Typical was the *Foam*, steel-built, about 126 feet overall, with a capacity of 120,000 pounds of iced fish and a 140-foot wide, winch-operated trawl which swept the sea floor, garnering sunken refuse, marine plants, and vast quantities of fish. Such a craft carried a crew of 19 or more men who worked in shifts and harvested large cargoes on voyages of a week's duration to the Grand Banks.

Decisive changes were also made in every branch of Boston's fish-marketing system. The organization of the New England Fish Exchange in 1908, under the direction of William K. Beardsley, eliminated much of the chaotic hubbub of the past and provided a comfortable place where bidding could be done within specified hours. Relations between wholesalers and retailers were placed on a similarly efficient basis a few years later, when Mr. Beardsley organized the Boston Wholesale Fish Dealers' Credit Association. Other improvements included an attempt to remedy unsanitary conditions in retail markets and to emphasize the quality rather than the quantity of fish sold. Unfortunately, dishonest dealers began to misrepresent their wares; the humble pollock became the "Boston Bay Blues," or even "Bluefish," and the lowly catfish was sold as Great Lakes' "Whitefish." This situation was not corrected until 1919, when the State Legislature appointed Arthur Millett as Inspector of Fish, and he introduced regulations forbidding falsification in advertising and governing

A lumber schooner, *circa* 1885. *Courtesy of the Society for the
Preservation of New England Antiquities.*

The crew of a fishing trawler, *circa* 1900. *Courtesy of the Peabody Museum of Salem.*

the grading, sale, and marketing of fresh and cold-storage fish.

At the beginning of the twentieth century, it became evident that the rapidly growing Boston fishing fleet had expanded beyond the confines of T Wharf. In 1906 the Massachusetts Commissioners of Fisheries and Game branded the facilities as "grossly inadequate," unsanitary, and uneconomical, and the Boston Board of Health also raised its voice in protest. On March 17, 1909, a total of 61 vessels put in at T Wharf, the largest number to arrive in a single day that season. Masts spiked the sky; husky seamen moved about the dock with the roll of the boat still in their walk. The ships were so close together that

it would have been possible to explore the entire district comprised by T, Commercial, and Long Wharves without setting foot on the piers, simply by stepping from the rail of one vessel to the rail of the next. When the fish exchange opened at 7 a.m., there was not room for a dory to push its nose in anywhere in the solid mass of hulls.

Such conditions were intolerable and the very next year work was started on the new Fish Pier in South Boston.

The pier was constructed by the Commonwealth on State-owned land at a cost of $1,017,000. The Boston Fish Market Corporation leased the pier for 15 years at a rental of $35,000 per year, with provisions for further rental at 15-year periods to 1973, and erected buildings at a cost of slightly more than $1,035,000. By April 1914, nearly all the firms had moved to the new location, anxious to take advantage of its 1,200-foot length, 300-foot width, and accommodations for discharging 80 vessels at one time. On the water end stood the Administration Building, headquarters for exchange and commission dealers; up the pier extended two parallel rows of three-story brick wholesale fishstores with the latest sanitary equipment; in the middle was a broad avenue for teams; the outside space between stores and caplogs was utilized for unloading. At the head of the dock loomed the tremendous plant of the Commonwealth Ice and Cold Storage Company, with a capacity of 15,000,000 pounds, the largest of its kind in the world. By 1920, the new center was distributing 150,000,000 to 175,000,000 pounds of fish yearly.

Although Boston led all other cities in the United States in the value of her fresh-fish trade and next to Grimsby, England, was the largest fresh-fish market in the world, the city had a great rival in Gloucester, which was not only first in the saltfish field, but even threatened Boston's supremacy in

the fresh-fish business. Competition was so keen between the
two cities that biased financial experts were able to pick various figures and claim that either Boston or Gloucester was
in the lead, whichever they preferred. Thus in 1905 there
were 77 Boston firms engaged in the wholesale fresh-fish business; in Gloucester there were 53. Boston firms employed 887
persons, Gloucester, 1552. The cash capital invested in the
Boston trade was $888,000; in Gloucester, $780,000. The wages
paid in Boston amounted to $498,000; in Gloucester, $727,000.
Except for the first 2 years of the century, the annual pound-
age of fresh fish received in Boston direct from the fishing
fleet was well over the 77,000,000 pound mark, and went above
the 100,000,000 mark six times. There was no falling off of
returns during the war years, and the 1920 receipts were the
highest of the period—118,559,000 pounds.

Long before the introduction of mechanized fishing methods
Boston vessels were bringing in record catches. For 6 months'
work in 1902, the 18 sharesmen in the crew of 23 aboard the
steamer *Alice M. Jacobs* made $862 each. The year previous
the steamer *New England* plunged heavily back to port 7 days
after departure, weighted to the deckline with 125,000 pounds
of halibut, and the two top men on this vessel earned $2,000
apiece in the season of 1901. But these returns were excep-
tional, and most Boston fishermen earned a great deal less
than the crews of the *Alice M. Jacobs* and the *New England,*
although the industry as a whole grossed over $1,000,000 a
year.

A wide gap existed between the price paid to the Boston
fishermen for their catch and that charged the ultimate con-
sumer. According to the report of the special committee of
the General Court which investigated the fishing industry in
1918-19, haddock sold on the Exchange for 1 to 2 cents per
pound retailed for 6 to 7 cents. The report also revealed Boston as a high-priced fishmarket in which little or no attempt
was made to sell fish according to grade. The prevailing price
was usually that for the highest grade. In one particular instance, it was found that codfish, shipped from Boston and
assessed a duty of one cent a pound, could be bought in
Toronto at 11 cents a pound on the same day that codfish
was selling in Boston at 15 cents. Throughout the State, the
average cost price to the retailer was found to be greater than
in 22 other States, although the expense of handling was
presumably less.

A disproportion between labor expended and wages received resulted in various labor disputes. Mutinies of ships' crews due to lack of bait were frequent in 1903 and numerous voyages were interrupted. In 1917 the Fishermen's Union of the Atlantic called a strike at Boston and Gloucester with the object of effecting changes in the apportionment of certain operating costs of vessels, part of which were borne by the crews. The walk-out tied up practically the entire industry and lasted 8 weeks, ending only after Governor McCall intervened and effected a settlement for the duration of the war. The terms included concessions by the operators on towing charges and the cost of oil and food. Again in 1919, on the eve of Independence Day, the Fishermen's Union called a strike which involved the Boston, Gloucester, and Provincetown fleets of about 175 steam trawlers and schooners and between 3,000 and 4,000 men. The fishermen demanded a fixed minimum price for fish, on which their wages could be based. After the State Attorney-General ruled that price fixing was illegal, the fishermen shifted their demands to a wage based on an agreed minimum value for the fish, irrespective of the price actually brought. On August 14, the union and the owners agreed to this principle as a basis for arbitration and the fleet went back to work.

Unions and Strikes

Other labor organizations were also active on the Boston waterfront. The longshoremen developed sufficient strength to make demands on employers and in a number of cases saw these demands granted. Playing an important part in the organizational struggles of the longshoremen for more than 30 years, until his death in 1936, was John P. Mullen, president of Local 800 of the International Longshoremen's Association as well as of the Longshoremen's District Council. Although his activities were more outstanding in the postwar period, he participated in the longshoremen's strike of 1909, about which a Boston newspaper report furnishes a few details.

The foreign steamship agents and the stevedores have been in conference at the chamber of commerce to consider the latest demands of the longshoremen. Nearly every line was represented and the demands of the men were carefully considered. They ask an increase in pay for handling bulk cargo, besides other concessions. While the consensus of opinion seems to be that the request of the men was ill-timed in that the steamship people are facing one of the worst periods of depression they have known for years, still a committee was appointed to confer with a committee of the longshoremen and report at a subsequent meeting of the agents.

Along with the numerical growth of the longshoremen's union, there came a decided change in the nature of their work. Whereas at the opening of the century waterfront huskies were given such elementary tasks as the unloading of lumber from Maine and New Hampshire, by 1919 their jobs included not only the loading and unloading of ships, but also grain-elevator operating, dock and marine engineering, and stationary dock hoisting, requiring a wide variety of specialized ability. This emphasis on craftsmanship as well as strength resulted in a higher wage scale. In 1914 Boston longshoremen operating deep-water shipping received 33 cents an hour, in 1916 it was 40 cents, and by December 1918, the figure jumped to a 65-cent per hour level. During April 1918, the old Boston Marine Engineers Association secured from the local adjustment commission a wage of $24 a week for engineers on lighters and $22 a week for engineers on wharves.

The International Seamen's Union of America, affiliated with the American Federation of Labor, was represented in Boston by a local of the Marine Firemen, Oilers, and Watertenders as early as 1902 or 1903, and by the Marine Cooks and Stewards Association in 1903 or 1904. The actual number of members for any given year during the first decade of the century would be hard to determine; that they were organized, however, they made evident. On June 30, 1911, the United Fruit Company's steamer *Limon*, finally sailed for Costa Rica after having been delayed nearly 2 hours waiting for 2 men to complete her crew, following a strike among the firemen. The day before, a detail of police was assigned to the company's terminal on Long Wharf, and the *Limon* was moved from the dock to an anchorage in the harbor. That night the ingenious firemen's union chartered a steam launch and picketed the United Fruiter, moving in circles about the ship to prevent the taking on of nonunion firemen. These tactics failed to hold the steamer at the Port, for on the morning of the thirtieth the 10 passengers and their baggage were taken to the *Limon* by the tug *Neponset*. When the steamer finally weighed anchor, only 5 of her crew were visible on deck, and the persistent union-chartered launch followed her halfway down the harbor, displaying large signs which read, "Where are your men?"

The Boston seaman fared less fortunately than the longshoreman, at least so far as union organization was concerned. Aboard ship he had to accept hard work, long hours, and small pay. Ashore he was frequently "broke," and his local had no widely known general headquarters available for a meeting place. Members of the I. W. W., which was taboo in Boston, were constantly seeking him out, and the seaman was thus placed between "the devil and the deep blue sea." Furthermore, by 1917 every man had to have a "Seaman's Employment Book" containing his record before he could obtain work aboard a vessel, thereby enabling the Employers' Association to check the individual's past. The adoption of the Military Defense Act the same year suspended various beneficial labor laws, thus depriving labor, under the stress of war, of part of its hard-won gains. The ordinary and able-bodied seaman worked on deck or stood watch 4 hours "on" and 4 "off" for from $30 to $60 a month, with bed and board furnished. Salaried ship's officers no longer received a share of the profits over and above their regular pay.

Schooners and Steamers

During the first two decades of the twentieth century more than 200 schooners, as well as many square-riggers and barks, operated from the Port of Boston. The fleet of Crowell & Thurlow, a firm founded in 1900, comprised about 100 sailing vessels and included the largest schooners on the Atlantic coast, which were engaged in African, European, South American, West Indian, and Atlantic coastal trade. Sending schooners to Gulf ports and to the West Indies, C. S. Glidden & Company did not buy any vessels outright, but purchased a sufficient number of shares to gain control. Hundreds of similarly operated schooners were jointly owned by the builders, riggers, sailmakers, chandlers, shipbrokers, and merchants of Boston. Like most operators, Glidden & Company also leased privately owned schooners and loaded them with freight for Europe and South America. The firm went bankrupt in 1913, seeming to confirm an oft-repeated saying among captains and traders that Glidden was too honest in business to succeed. Until bought out by C. H. Sprague & Son, the William F. Palmer & Company maintained vessels in the coastwise trade and owned many five-masted schooners with a deadweight of about 5,000 tons. J. S. Winslow & Company, one of the more important Boston firms, had 40 vessels and ships in service at one time, including barks, schooners, brigs, and steamships. Carrying heavy cargoes of Chilean nitrate, Winslow's vessels, known as deep-water ships, sailed all over the world.

Coastal arrivals came to the city from Maine and the Maritime Provinces, from the Gulf of Mexico and many Atlantic ports. In 1908, 2,500 steamers, 1,100 schooners, 3,300 barges, and 2,000 tugs arrived at Boston, and the actual number of coastwise craft entering the Port exceeded the arrivals at both New York and Philadelphia, Boston boasting 9,115 arrivals as compared to New York's 5,470 and Philadelphia's 4,280. The principal inbound cargo included coal, raw cotton, petroleum products, sugar, molasses, fish, sand, lumber, and wool. Raw cotton proved to be a large and commercially profitable item in the coastal trade, although the World War caused a decrease from 530,000 bales in 1913 to 278,000 bales in 1918. Vast quantities of domestic wool continued to pour in to supply one of New England's largest industries. The receipts doubled between 1900 and 1907 and reached 205,000,000 pounds in 1916. However, lumber sent by water declined from 158,000,000 board feet in 1910 to a mere 20,000,000 board feet in 1918.

The bulk of this merchandise was carried by over a score of steamship lines, which called at Boston on regular schedules. The Clyde Steamship Company had two steamers offering a weekly freight service on the Boston-Charleston-Jacksonville run, southbound with burlap bagging, meat products, paper stock, fertilizer, boots and shoes, and northbound with cotton, lumber, and naval stores.

After operating clipper ships between Boston, New York, and San Francisco for almost half a century, the American-Hawaiian Line inaugurated a steamship service over the same route on October 30, 1900, reducing the sailing time to 56 days. By establishing a rail transshipment line across the Isthmus of Tehuantepec, sailing time to San Francisco was further cut to 26 days in 1907. The United American Lines, the C. & T. Intercoastal Line, the Luckenbach Line, the Nawsco Line, the W. R. Grace & Company, the Tri-National Steamship Corporation, and the Panama Pacific Line of the International Mercantile Marine had weekly or fortnightly sailings from Boston to various West Coast ports and offered various freight and passenger-freight services. By 1915 a new type of "steam schooner" was developed for the lumber trade with the Pacific coast. Slightly more than 200 feet in length, with a

40-foot beam, such a schooner could carry 1,500,000 feet of lumber below hatches and on deck, and could sail in a fair breeze or buck rough weather under steam power.

Coal was the most important tonnage commodity in the coastal trade, and over 100 schooners were engaged in carrying it between the Chesapeake region and Boston. Many of these vessels were built along the Maine coast, at Kennebunkport, Bath, and Hancock, and many were owned by Bath citizens, who operated them out of Boston. Costing about $250,000 each, such sturdy "four-masters" as the *Wyoming*, the *Edward J. Lawrence*, and the *Winslow* were engaged in the coal-carrying business. The average schooner was manned by a crew of 12 and completed 15 voyages a year to the Chesapeake Bay, transporting on each trip its own weight in "black dirt." Surpassing the average, the *Sarah W. Lawrence* landed 26 cargoes of coal at Boston in a single year.

The Coastwise Transportation Company, founded by John Crowley and later bought out by the C. H. Sprague Company, was the first Boston steamship line to enter the coal trade. During the years 1905-06 Crowley operated six steamers, two of which were appropriately enough called the *Norfolk* and the *Suffolk*. Six years later, eight new steam colliers were introduced into the Boston fleet, leading to a marked decline in the number of coal schooners. With 3 tons of bituminous being carried for every single ton of anthracite, receipts of coal at the Port jumped from 3,000,000 tons in 1902 to twice that figure in 1916.

Berthing its ships on the Atlantic Avenue waterfront, the Eastern Steamship Lines was engaged exclusively in the coastwise traffic. This organization was the successor to several of the oldest steamship companies in New England, including the Portland Steam Packet Company, which had never recovered from the loss of the ill-fated *Portland*, the International Steamship Company, which maintained a service between Portland and St. John, New Brunswick, and Yarmouth, Nova Scotia, and the Boston and Bangor Steamship Company. Following the consolidation of all these lines into the Eastern Steamship Company of Maine in 1901, the *Governor Cobb* and the *Calvin Austin* were built for the International Line, the *R. B. Fuller* for the Kennebec Line, the *City of Rockland*, *City of Bangor*, and the *Belfast and Camden* for the Boston and Bangor Line. A year later the Eastern absorbed the Kennebec Steamboat Company, which had already driven all competitors from the Boston-Bath-Gardiner run. After operating the combination freight and passenger steamers *Harvard* and *Yale* between Boston and New York, and then the *Massachusetts, Old Colony,* and *Bunker Hill,* the Metropolitan Line joined with the Eastern in 1912, the latter being reorganized as the Eastern Steamship Corporation with a capital of $6,150,000. The new corporation also included the Maine Steamship Company and the Marine Department of the Dominion Atlantic Railway, which had developed a passenger service from Boston to Yarmouth. In January 1917, the Eastern Steamship Corporation went into bankruptcy and was sold at auction. In March of the same year the Eastern Steamship Lines was reorganized and incorporated under the Maine laws. During the World War, the United States Government took over some of the Eastern's ships; the remainder maintained the company's regular service.

Between 1900 and 1920 Boston underwent a serious dislocation of its trade, losing ground along all commercial lanes of the world and only maintaining her position as the center of transportation for New England. In 1902 the formation of the International Mercantile Marine Company transferred to New York the independent management of many of Boston's steamship lines, and a year later Canada became sea-conscious, discontinuing much of the business that had previously passed through Boston. The remaining foreign commerce was constantly changing to meet new conditions. Vast quantities of raw materials from the East Indies, Australia, Egypt, and Argentina were included among the imports from more than 40 different countries. The city held her position as the second largest importing center of the country, with aggregate imports mounting from $61,452,000 in 1901 to $160,109,000 in 1914. Boston had become the leading wool market in the United States, importing $36,772,000 worth in 1914; she sent thousands of tons of hides and leather to such prosperous tanning communities as Peabody, Salem, and Woburn. Unfortunately adverse rail rates from the interior of the country diverted much of Boston's export business, and the volume of foodstuffs available for shipment out of the Port diminished between 1905 and 1920. Exports of grain dropped from $25,000,000 in 1900 to $2,361,000 in 1914, and the export of livestock decreased from $9,697,000 to $20,600 during the same period. The rapid industrial expansion in the State, nevertheless, had led to a marked advance in the shipment of tools and machinery; the export of articles manufactured in Massachusetts more than tripled between 1890 and 1925. Though Boston's total overseas commerce improved from $192,600,000 in 1900 to $584,632,000 in 1920, this development did not match similar advances in competing shipping centers. Boston rapidly lost ground, descending from second to fourth place in the total volume of her foreign trade as early as 1908 and to the sixth position among American ports in 1920.

The most important single factor affecting the Port's commerce was the fight over freight rates. The struggle reached its first peak in 1877. After several years of disastrous rate wars, the trunk-line railroads established freight rates, arrived at by use of agreed port differentials on export-import commerce between points located west of their western terminals (Buffalo, Pittsburgh, etc.) and North Atlantic seaports. These port differentials, which are still adhered to, resulted in rates that bore some relation to relative distance and relative cost of service, and gave Philadelphia and Baltimore rates less 2 and 3 cents per hundred pounds, respectively, than those to Boston and New York on east-bound traffic. West-bound differentials were even more unfavorable to Boston. Between 1877 and 1912 Boston made a number of unsuccessful efforts to maintain import rates on the same level as those in effect from Baltimore to these western destinations, and tried to maintain rates on ex-lake grain for export which were lower than the ex-lake rates to New York. In 1912 the Interstate Commerce Commission ruled that Boston must go on the same basis as New York, and this ruling has not been changed. The differentials set up during these controversial years were partially offset by the fact that ocean rates were maintained on the "distance principle"; and Boston, being nearer to European, African, and many South American ports, really had through rates equal to those of other ports. In 1916, however, the North Atlantic Conference, composed of steamship lines operating in the foreign trade, equalized ocean rates to all ports on the North Atlantic range, from Portland to Norfolk. In 1920, the United States Shipping Board extended these equalized ocean rates to all Gulf ports. This destroyed any advantage Boston had had with respect to through rail-ocean rates and theoretically placed her on equality with New York. In actuality, the practice of absorbing charges for lighterage and other accessorial services rendered by the railroads serving New York gave that port an advantage over Boston that attracted to it a large portion of the commerce to and from the interior which might otherwise have passed through Boston.

After long sharing in the growth of the Port's foreign business, the Furness Withy Company, Ltd., experienced the same difficulty as other steamship lines which called at Boston—a dearth of export cargoes. The Port situation had changed radically since December 1884, when Christopher Furness, a member of the English shipping family of that name, had come to Boston and established the firm of C. Furness & Company, which acted as agents for the Warren Line to Liverpool and the Furness Line to London. At that time Boston stood second to none as an Atlantic port for sailings to England, and shippers had no trouble in finding capacity cargoes for their vessels. Averaging two sailings a month, the Furness Company operated five steamships, the *Boston City*, the *Durham City*, the *Stockholm City*, the *Gothenburg City*, and the *Carlyle City*, each of which registered from 3,000 to 4,000 tons dead-weight and was capable of about 9½ knots. Boston then provided such export cargo as cotton, leather, lumber, meats, and provisions, as well as large shipments of grain and flour, which originated in the Central Freight Association territory and Canada. This heavy movement of freight had encouraged the expansion of its steamship services, and from 1885 to 1903 the Furness Company represented the Puritan and Wilson Lines operating between Boston and Antwerp. Its Liverpool and London services were maintained until 1914, when all the company's regular schedules were discontinued, because every ship flying the British flag then sailed under orders from the British Government. During the World War the Furness Withy Company acted as Boston agents for the British Ministry of Shipping, and sent to Europe large quantities of freight, including grain, foodstuffs, frozen meats, forgings, and munitions.

During the early 1900's the Warren, Cunard, Leyland, and Dominion Lines operated between Boston, Liverpool, Bristol, Hull, Copenhagen, and Rotterdam. The Dominion Line put into service two 12,000-ton ships, with accommodations for 300 cabin and 1,500 steerage passengers, and the Red Star Line to Antwerp and the Leyland service to Manchester maintained biweekly sailings from Boston. The North German Lloyd Line established a freight and a passenger service between Boston, Bremen, and New Orleans, with winter sailings every 3 weeks.

The advent of many European steamship lines led to the establishment of local shipping agencies. Among them A. C. Lombard's Sons, founded in 1825, has held a leading place for decades. Before the World War, the Lombards acted as agents for 13 prominent steamship lines which offered services to England, France, Germany, the Scandinavian countries, and Greece.

Although primarily a ship-owning concern, John G. Hall & Company also conducted a ship-agent's business, handling freight cargoes for the Elder-Dempster Line, which ran from Boston to Hull and Avonmouth. As early as 1847 the Hall Company had sent small sailing packets to the Canadian Maritime Provinces, exchanging flour, beef, and anthracite coal for smoked and salted fish, timber, piling, ships' knees, and the produce of the Provinces. Setting up a storage basin for piling in South Boston, Hall became the leader among New Englanders supplying spruce piling and hackmatack ships' knees to local builders and shipwrights. At the time of the rapid development of the steamship, the company secured an interest in several steamers, though it continued to operate a fleet of sailing vessels. Among them was the last Boston square-rigger, the bark *Belmont*, which was used as a freighter until 2 or 3 years after the World War. For decades the sturdy vessel had sailed to Australia for wool and to South America for linseed, following sea trails wherever a cargo could be found and carrying the American flag to all parts of the world.

Passenger traffic played a prominent part in the development of Boston's steamship lines, accounting to a considerable degree for the continued growth of trans-Atlantic services. While in 1900 ocean liners carried a total of 40,905 persons, 3 years later the number of inbound passengers alone had advanced to 101,700, and it remained well above the 100,000 mark until 1915; a pre-war record of 138,000 was established in 1913. About two-thirds of this prosperous passenger movement was composed of immigrants. In 1907, 85,580 aliens came into the United States through Boston, and in 1913, when immigration was at its height, the Port had 101,700 foreign-born entrants. By 1915, however, the immigration figure had dropped to 11,250, the non-immigrant traffic to 8,687; from that year until 1920 the number of people entering and leaving the Port diminished annually.

In contrast to export losses abroad, Boston's trade made definite gains in the countries ceded to the United States at the end of the Spanish-American War, since the added territory was not bound by the tariff barriers of the past. Between 1900 and 1920 most of Boston's trade with Cuba, Porto Rico, and the Philippines was one-way trade, consisting almost entirely of imports. Cuba, rather than Porto Rico or the Philippines, accounted mainly for the large increase in trade with the islands. In 1900, trade with Cuba, Porto Rico, the Philippines, and the Virgin Islands amounted to approximately 2.6 percent of Boston's total foreign commerce. Two decades later Cuba, the Philippines, and the Virgin Islands contributed 15.2 percent and this might have been even greater if Porto Rico had been included in the 1920 figures.

Bananas, Wool, and Lumber

The largest American trader in the Caribbean area was the United Fruit Company, incorporated in 1899, which had its offices and warehouses on Long Wharf. This corporation immediately bought the Boston Fruit Company and its seven subsidiaries, headed by Andrew W. Preston and Captain Lorenzo D. Baker, which had interests in the West Indies; at almost the same moment it acquired the four companies under the control of Minor C. Keith and his associates, which operated steamers to the Central and South American banana fields. About 1910 local business men were attempting to boom the Port, and the United Fruit did its share by shifting several crack liners to the Boston service. In 1913 a weekly passenger-freight sailing to the West Indies and Panama was inaugurated, and the Great White Fleet of the United Fruit Company became a familiar sight in Boston. During several succeeding years, the company was successful in maintaining Boston's position as the "mart town of the West Indies."

Boston still played an important role in South American trade. Carrying general cargo both ways, 2 British firms, R. P. Huston and Lamport & Holt, ran steamers out of Boston to South American ports. N. W. Rice operated a fleet of iron sailing-vessels to the River Plate, and chartered them to the Boston wool traders. Frequently John G. Hall sent a Nova Scotian vessel to South America, and sometimes C. H. Sprague loaded a schooner with lumber for the Argentine.

By 1912 the Furness Withy Company had 3 or 4 steamers plying between Boston and Rio de Janeiro; the opening of the Panama Canal further facilitated commerce to the west coast of South America. The inauguration of the Huston and Barber lines increased Boston's trade with the River Plate region and Buenos Aires at an amazing rate. In 1915 the 2 lines sent 32 ships from the Argentine to Boston, and local imports leaped to over $30,000,000 in that year.

Prominent in the South American trade was the Boston firm of John S. Emery, established in 1852. Between 1880 and 1928 the company owned all together about 350 barks, brigs, schooners, and steamers and did a lucrative business carrying cotton, coal, lumber, machinery, and manufactured goods along the Atlantic coast and loading cargoes of sugar, rum, and asphalt in the West Indies, oil and wool in Australia, and mahogany and palm oil in Africa. The largest part of Emery's fleet sailed to the Argentine, Brazil, Venezuela, Chile, Mexico, and the Honduras, bringing back bones and guano for fertilizer, quebracho for tanning, wool, hides, mahogany logs, oil, and Spanish cedar. The trading activities of the company were not always tied to a specific schedule, vessels being sent wherever a cargo could be picked up, much as in the old days. Profits were high, sometimes running to 35 percent a year. When the further decline of sail set in at the Port in the 1920's, Emery operated only 6 vessels in the South American trade, the last run for sail from Boston.

Another Boston firm outstanding in South American commerce was the Charles Hunt Company, which has had a ship-brokerage business since 1871. Ranging from 2,100 to 2,800 tons cargo capacity, a dozen square-riggers and schooners belonging to the company carried lumber to Buenos Aires and returned with wool and hides. If no return cargo was available, the vessels loaded molasses and salt at some West Indian port or pitch at Trinidad, and marketed the commodities in ports north of Cape Hatteras. Before the entrance of the United States into the World War, the Hunt vessel *Brynhilda* took on hay at Buenos Aires and carried it to a German military reservation at Swakopmunde, in German South West Africa, and, after landing the cargo there, came back in ballast to the West Indies. During the war this trade ceased, and another change took place in the company's route. Vessels were sent in ballast from the River Plate to Calcutta, where they loaded jute for Boston.

The Hunt fleet did not escape unscathed the hazards of the sea and the destruction of the World War. In 1914, on her maiden voyage in the Hunt service, a large schooner capsized and plunged to the ocean bottom; Irish deities, so it was said, vented their wrath on the vessel because her name had been changed from *Gael* to *Pilgrim*. Fortunately all hands were saved; less lucky was the *Timandra's* crew, and their captain, Richard Lee, and his wife, all of whom went down with their craft and a cargo of coal on a voyage to Buenos Aires. The *Avon* met a similar fate in 1918, when it sank with all hands. The cause of these disasters was never known, but they occurred during the war, and it is thought a sea-raider operating along the Atlantic seaboard might have caused their tragic end. In fact, one of the most famous German raiders of the World War was a vessel formerly belonging to the Hunt Company, the *Pass of Balmaha*. It was stopped by the British off the Norwegian coast. The vessel was captured from them by the Germans, equipped with Diesel engines and guns, and was renamed the *Seeadler*. Commanded by the daring Count von Lückner, the raider passed through the British blockade on January 9, 1917, and destroyed about 10 Allied ships before being wrecked on a reef off the Society Islands.

Rum and Bibles

Although less adventurous than in the past, Boston's rum trade with the Gold Coast of Africa flourished until the Volstead Act closed down the local distilleries in 1919. Medford rum had remained a medium of exchange among the natives throughout the nineteenth century, and Massachusetts distilleries had never stopped shipping the potent liquid, despite the abolition of slavery. The Chase distilleries of Somerville manufactured a large share of the rum, and such shipping firms as John G. Hall, Charles Hunt & Company, Crowell & Thurlow, and the John S. Emery Company carried it, as well as missionary supplies, flour, and lumber, to the West Coast of Africa. Several staid Bostonians, staunch supporters of the temperance movement, participated in this trade, and often a teetotaler Boston sea captain hedged his barrels of rum with boxes of Bibles. Instead of "black ivory," more than a score of Boston schooners brought back mahogany for a Kentucky manufacturer and palm oil for Lever Brothers of Cambridge.

A remnant of the old Yankee sea-faring tradition clung to these Boston rum schooners. Manned by a crew of seven and captained by 19-year-old Harold Foss, the three-masted *John Paul* sailed from Boston on March 13, 1901, carrying 650 tons of cargo insured for $150,000. After an uneventful passage of 45 days, the schooner arrived at Accra on the Gold Coast, where part of its cargo of supplies, oil, rum, Bibles, and lumber was unloaded. The supplies and Bibles were for the missionaries, and the lumber was purchased by the natives, who had religiously adopted the Christian custom of fashioning coffins for their dead. The *John Paul* spent 40 days on the African coast stopping at the Secondi, Axim, Cape Coast Castle, and Adda trading stations to discharge cargo and receive palm oil, palm kernels, and cocoa beans. Since there were no harbors or docking places, the schooner anchored offshore, and small boats were used to load and unload the vessel. On her homeward voyage the *John Paul* completed a fast passage of 45 days, reaching Boston Harbor on September 13, 1901.

Ships of War and Peace

Although schooners and sailing vessels were still being used extensively, Boston shipbuilding had entered a period of swift change at the opening of the twentieth century. Steel had supplanted wood and iron in the construction of larger vessels, and there was no steel in New England, a fact which materially increased building costs. A number of Boston shipyards were forced to curtail ambitious plans and devote most of their time and money to doing repair work and turning out fishing boats and pleasure craft, especially yachts. Among the active shipbuilders and repairers were the Atlantic Works in East Boston; Fore River Shipbuilding Company, Quincy; Richard T. Greene Company, Chelsea; Lockwood Manufacturing Company, William McKie, and Story and Wardwell of East Boston. Leading yacht builders and repairers included George Lawley & Son, Neponset; Ambrose A. Martin, East Boston; Murray & Tregurtha Company, South Boston. The great majority of these concerns failed to develop shipbuilding on an impressive scale.

The exception was the Fore River Shipbuilding Company. The plant sprang from a marine engine shop built at East Braintree in 1883. The organization began to produce hulls for its own engines, and on September 29, 1898, the Navy Department awarded the Fore River Ship and Engine Company, as it was then called, contracts to build two destroyers, the *Lawrence* and the *MacDonough*. Other contracts followed, and it became necessary to increase the facilities of the plant. A deep-water site was selected 2 miles downstream on the Quincy side of Fore River, which was 30 feet deep and wide enough to float four battleships abreast, and in April 1900, work commenced at the new location. In the "City of the Presidents," one of the great industries fast being lost to Massachusetts returned to its own, as riveters' hammers, the clang of steel, and the thud of presses echoed across acres of land formerly used for residential and farming purposes. In 1901, contracts were awarded for the battleships *Rhode Island* and *New Jersey*, of 14,948 tons each, and 3 years later the name of the concern was changed to the Fore River Shipbuilding Company.

There followed a period of rapid growth for the organization, and ships of many different classifications were launched in almost continuous succession. In 1908 the company set a new record when it won 18 contracts, an achievement not bettered for 8 years. The Bethlehem Steel Corporation purchased the Fore River Shipbuilding Company in 1913 and reorganized it as the Fore River Shipbuilding Corporation. The construction of warships required improved equipment, for these mammoth fighters were the most complete and complex of all marine accomplishments, being in themselves both forts and floating hotels with refrigeration, electric light and power stations, telephones, large kitchens, and powerful and perfect engines. Many new buildings were erected in the yard, and others were enlarged until there remained hardly a structure less than 100 feet in length; a number were more than 400 feet, and some were so constructed that they could be joined with other buildings. The forge shop contained 2,200 square feet of floor space; the interior was lighted by the red eyes of flaming furnaces, while giant hammers and huge traveling cranes loomed through the half gloom. Near the door stood the second-largest anvil in existence, with a steam-driven arm that could strike a 250-ton blow, yet under such perfect control that it was said to be capable of cracking a walnut shell without breaking the kernel. There were others of lesser size, the equipment graduating down to small machines necessary for the formation of nuts and bolts.

The year 1916 saw an even greater boom than in the past, with contracts signed for the construction of 19 vessels at Fore River, including 8 submarines and 8 destroyers for the United

Mr. J. M. Brooks in the doorway of his office in East Boston, *circa* 1900. *Courtesy of the Peabody Museum of Salem.*

The harbor viewed from the Atlantic Avenue waterfront in 1906. *Courtesy of the Library of Congress.*

States Government, the freighter *Katrina Luckenbach,* and the tankers *George W. Darnes* and *W. L. Steed.* Back in 1900 the destroyer *MacDonough* was 47 months in the building; the 8 new destroyers were built in less than 12 months from the time the contract was signed. Entrance of the United States into the conflict precipitated a flood of orders, among them requests for a total of 63 destroyers, a battle cruiser, 15 submarines, and the merchant vessels *Andrew F. Luckenbach* and *Lewis Luckenbach.* The ever-increasing demand for destroyers led to a contract with the Government calling for the construction of 83 destroyers, and 3 new plants in which to produce them. By far the largest was the Squantum establishment, which was almost immediately named the Victory Plant. Soil had been broken October 7, 1917, and work had progressed so rapidly despite the exceedingly severe winter that by the spring of 1918 it was possible to lay the keels of 5 vessels. The plant cost approximately $16,000,000, occupied 70 acres of land, and included 10 covered building slips, 6 wet slips, and all the miscellaneous equipment requisite in an up-to-the-minute shipbuilding yard.

The success of the Victory Plant depended on capable mechanics as well as machinery, and skilled men were hard to find during the war years. The result was the formation of classes for instruction in many special lines of work, such as shipfitting, welding, and coppersmithing, and the eventual development of a large number of trained workers. By the close of 1918, eighteen keels had been laid, 8 ships launched, and 1 delivered. In June 1919, four destroyers were launched and 2 delivered; in July, 2 were launched and 5 delivered; in September, 6 were launched and 4 delivered. During the last month the Victory Plant made a record drive of 422,591 rivets in 5½ working days. Another record was established when the destroyer *Reid* was completed in 45½ days.

The year 1919 saw the delivery of a total of 69 ships from the 2 plants, including 29 destroyers from Squantum, and 19 destroyers, 8 merchantmen, and 13 submarines from Fore River. One of the notable feats accomplished at Fore River during this period was the launching of the S. S. *Hadnot,* a 13,500-ton tanker, 430 feet in length. She slid into the water 99 and 9/10 percent complete, with steam up and ready to sail. All told, the Quincy plant built 36 destroyers in 27 months and 5 days, and 16 of these destroyers went into active service abroad. The Fore River Yard had expanded to meet the rush of war orders. Beginning in 1916 a series of new buildings and shops had been erected, among them a steel fabricating shop 770 feet long and 186 feet wide, with 75 machines served by 8 cranes, and capable of fabricating 250 tons of steel in a single day. In 1919 a 10,000-ton floating dock was built, 4 new slips were constructed, and another office building was added. Besides the main activity of shipbuilding, the yard also did engine and machine work, tank construction galvanizing, wood finishing, and locomotive reconditioning, and made brass castings. When the war ended the Fore River Yard and its subsidiary plants at Squantum, Buffalo, and Providence, employed more than 26,000 men.

In the meantime the Charlestown Navy Yard had sprung into renewed activity under the driving influence of the international conflict. The Navy Yard produced four vessels between 1902 and 1919, although none had been built there between 1874 and 1902. Actually this construction program represented only a fragment of the war work carried on at the Navy Yard, since it also fitted out many of the war vessels built at Quincy and Squantum.

This tremendous emergency shipbuilding rapidly increased the number of American vessels engaged in Boston's foreign commerce. In 1900 only 12 or 13 per cent of the foreign trade was being carried in American bottoms; of the 1,109 steamships entering the Port, 973 were foreign craft and of the 496 schooners sailing into the harbor just 58 were under American registry. But the tumultuous war years of 1917 and 1918 completely changed this picture and resulted in the building up of an American Merchant Marine consisting of 4,889 vessels registering almost 14,000,000 gross tons, thereby placing the United States second only to Great Britain as a shipping nation. By 1920 more than 40 percent of Boston's foreign trade was being carried in American vessels.

War Activity

When the World War broke out in 1914, the Boston Stock Exchange, following the example of New York, closed down, and local shipping firms, alarmed about the future, curtailed operations. Scores of Boston's European travelers, caught unawares, were later repatriated with much difficulty. The withdrawal of European steamship lines sharply reduced the foreign shipping of the Port, since the American Merchant Marine was too small at the time to compensate for the loss.

But foreign ships gradually became available again as the Allies' need for our products increased.

A lively demand for foodstuffs and other commodities was felt throughout 1915. Exports of flour rose from 556,000 barrels in 1914 to 738,000 in 1915; about 150,000 quarters of beef were shipped in 1915 whereas none had gone out of the Port in 1914. Fifty-three thousand horses and 2,300 head of cattle were also sent abroad in 1915, an increase of 100 percent over the preceding year. Freight rates increased as the demand rose; export rates on grain in January 1916, were quoted at 40 cents, a thousand percent advance over the January 1914 rate. Giving a decided impetus to manufacturing, an ever-increasing flood of orders for leather, cloth, munitions, and almost every article produced in the State poured into the Port from the European belligerents during the following 2 years and continued through the immediate post-war period. The *Boston Transcript,* December 14, 1918, noted that

there are sometimes hundreds of cars loaded with foreign freight at the Boston and Albany docks in East Boston and not vessels enough in Port to take half of their contents. Three men with large foreign orders, primarily for lumber, were in Boston last week looking for transportation and were unable to find vessels to carry their goods. There is a great demand for lumber abroad and one Gloucester fisherman has been chartered to carry a load of lumber to England. This is the first time a fisherman has been used for such a purpose; and that a sailing vessel is to be used is an indication of the lack of cargo space.

The World War brought unparalleled maritime activity to the Port of Boston. True, voyages to European waters were dangerous and marine insurance on freight cargoes in the North Atlantic had skyrocketed, but certain lanes were considered safe, and Boston sea captains and crews were willing to navigate them. Profits loomed large as a result of the suspension of European competition, and space in freighters was at a premium. Those who had commodities to export were so sorely pressed for carriers that every sort of vessel at all seaworthy appeared in Boston Harbor; even old long-unused square-riggers were replanked and hastily put into service. An item in the *Boston Sunday Herald* of March 19, 1916, indicated Boston's activity at the time.

Ten liners sailed from the Port of Boston last week, five of them carrying a total of more than a million bushels of grain. This was one of the largest shipments of grain made in a single week. The heaviest load was that of the *Essex Baron,* which sailed Tuesday for La Pallice, France, carrying 400,000 bushels of oats for the French Government. Of the total exports, 528,000 bushels were of wheat, 425,000 oats, and 83,000 barley.

Since Boston was 200 miles nearer Europe than any other large port in the United States, exports reached unprecedented figures, improving from $119,040,000 in 1915 to $334,387,000 in 1919. Imports correspondingly rose from $160,108,000 in 1914 to $391,830,000 in 1920. Shipments of meat, dairy products, and breadstuffs led the list of Boston's exports, which also included large amounts of leather, cotton, iron, and steel. Metal manufacturers throughout New England converted their mills and factories into munition plants, and their wartime freight moved through the Port in increasing quantities. Exports of iron and steel leaped from $4,770,000 in 1914 to $50,986,000 in 1917, while the value of miscellaneous metals sent abroad jumped from $16,388 to $40,984,000 during the same period. Great quantities of munitions were manufactured within a radius of 150 miles of Boston and shipped through the Port; arsenals and shipbuilding plants worked at top speed.

The World War brought disaster to many ships long familiar to the Boston docks. One of the armed British merchantmen sunk by a German submarine was the Leyland Line Steamship *Canadian,* which had operated regularly in the Boston-Liverpool run. The ship departed from Boston on March 24, 1917, with 101,000 bushels of wheat, corn, and oats, a large shipment of horses, shells, boats, provisions, and general cargo, but never reached her home port; torpedoed without warning on April 6, she sank 8 miles from the Skellings. Although her lifeboats were picked up within an hour, and the crew, including 56 Americans, was saved, the loss of the *Canadian* was costly to the Boston underwriters, who had invested heavily in her cargo. When the Cunarder *Ultonia* arrived in Boston a few months later, she had the unusual experience of carrying among her officers and crew more than 15 men who had been on ships sunk by German U-boats. Among these was Captain Turner, commodore of the Cunard Line, who was in command of the *Lusitania* when she went down. In November 1916, the sinking of British ships by the German submarine U-53 near Nantucket Light caused the suspension of many sailings from Boston. During the same month, Boston shippers learned with dismay that the American-Hawaiian steamship *Columbian,* bound for Genoa from Boston, had plunged to the bottom of the Bay of Biscay. Her crew had been compelled to abandon ship; Captain Curtis had been held a prisoner for 6 days and then placed on a Swedish vessel, which landed him in Spain.

But the crucial turn of events for American shippers did not come until 1917, when Germany announced that neutral merchant ships bound to and from ports of the Allies would be sunk without warning. All Boston sailings were held up, seriously delaying the forwarding of cargoes and mails and the conveyance of passengers. Massachusetts stood solidly behind the Administration when the President of the United States severed diplomatic relations with Germany and issued a declaration of war on April 5, 1917. Immediately the Federal Authorities seized at Boston six German steamers, including the *Krönprinzessin Cecilie* and the *Cincinnati*. Before surrendering the latter, however, her loyal crew had so badly damaged the engines that it was necessary to tow the *Cincinnati* to the Charlestown Navy Yard, where her broken cylinders were repaired by a special electric welding process. There the former German steamer was outfitted as an American troopship. Upon receipt of war orders at the Charlestown Navy Yard, Captain W. R. Rush, commandant of the First Naval District, hastily prepared naval defense measures. Boston Harbor was mined and netted as a precaution against German U-boats, and navigation instructions were issued to local skippers. The passage through the Narrows between Boston Light and Point Allerton was closed, and the South Channel and North Channel were kept open from sunset to sunrise each day, vessels being allowed to enter and leave under Federal pilotage.

Following the entrance of the United States into the World War, the first squadron of destroyers to start for Europe was fitted out at the Charlestown Navy Yard. Six destroyers were conditioned in short order, and they reached England on May 14, 1917. One of them, the *Conyngham,* took a prominent part in a skirmish with a German underseas craft on October 19, 1917. At that time the *Conyngham* was a part of a convoy which had gone out of formation temporarily to add to its fold a rescued American steamer and the destroyer which had saved it. Seizing advantage of the brief lapse in vigil, a German submarine rose to the surface and fired a torpedo which struck the British cruiser *Orama*. The *Conyngham* observed the submarine and dropped depth charges over the spot where it had submerged. The oil and debris which came to the surface was considered sufficient evidence to prove the destruction of the U-boat. A month later in another engagement the destroyers *Fanning* and *Nicholson* of the same convoy escort succeeded in capturing the crew of the U-58. Discovering a periscope heading toward several freighters, the *Fanning* promptly arrived on the spot and dropped a series of depth charges, and the *Nicholson* added to the barrage. The wrecked submarine managed to rise to the surface to permit the rescue of the crew. Operating from a base at Queenstown, the Boston destroyer flotilla successfully escorted large American fleets to and from Europe.

In the meantime a tragic disaster had occurred on this side of the Atlantic. When the Eastern Steamship Lines' *Northland* docked on the chilly evening of December 9, 1917, thousands of Bostonians besieged the weary passengers as they stepped off the gangplank for news of friends and relatives in Halifax. A munitions ship had collided with another vessel in Halifax Harbor on December 6, and the ensuing explosion had been so devastating that hundreds had been killed or maimed and a large section of the prosperous city had been reduced to shambles. When word of the Halifax disaster reached Boston, Governor McCall immediately offered as a relief ship the *Calvin Austin,* then temporarily on the Boston-Portland run. Wagons, trucks, and cars carrying food, clothing, surgical dressings, furniture, and building supplies crowded Fosters Wharf, where the ship was berthed. Quickly loaded until her holds were bursting, the *Calvin Austin* steamed out of the harbor under the command of Captain Eugene O'Donnell on December 9, 1917. Working day and night, Boston relief workers prepared more material for shipment, and the *Northland* followed the *Calvin Austin* with an $80,000 cargo for the relief of the victims.

Dramatic events were also taking place close to Boston Harbor. Rumors of a German submarine off the American coast were finally confirmed when the U-151 struck. While carrying coal from Norfolk to Boston, the schooner *Edward H. Cole* was sunk off the New Jersey coast by the U-boat, and a few hours afterward several freighters were torpedoed and sent to the bottom. When the crew of the *Cole* was landed in New York by a rescuing ship the next day, every press wire in the country hummed with Robert Lattugee's account of the sinking of the Boston schooner.

. . . I saw a submarine come to the surface half a mile away on the port bow. A Finn, who was steering, asked me why the submarine was moving around our ship at high speed. We both believed it was an American craft with some Naval Reserve cadets on board, who were trying to have fun with us sailors of the merchant marine. I thought it would be a good idea to have a little fun with our skipper . . . I yelled down the skylight, 'Tumble up deck lively, Cap. There's a big German submarine close astern, getting ready to attack us.' Then I took the marine glasses . . . For a moment or two I could not make out her nationality, and then a gust of wind . . . blew the ensign straight . . . I shouted in earnest to Captain Newcombe, 'It's no joke this time. By gosh, she is a German submarine.'

After making three circles to be certain that we did not carry a gun, the U-boat came up to the starboard quarter, and a tall, fair-haired officer on deck by the conning tower shouted in good English, 'What ship is that?' I replied that it was an American schooner . . . The next hail we got as Captain Newcombe joined me on deck was to heave to, and they would send an officer on board. This time the U-boat was fifty yards away, and we saw the tall officer get into a dinghey with three of his men . . . The officer, who wore gold shoulder straps and gilt buttons, and was the only one of the crew who was clean shaven, spoke courteously to Captain Newcombe, and after listening to the statements as to the name, tonnage, cargo, and ports of departure and destination, he made a brief inspection of the ship. Then he came to where we were standing and said, 'Well, Captain, get your crew together and tell them that they have ten minutes to leave the ship.' About 4:10 o'clock we pulled away from the *Edward H. Cole* and rowed hard to get away from the expected explosion. There was no water or food in the yawl, and no compass. The Captain brought his sextant and barometer with him. We saw the Germans, acting under orders from their officer, take four bombs . . . and light the fuses. Five minutes after we pulled away the bombs exploded . . . and in sixteen minutes the schooner had disappeared.

For the first time since the War of 1812, Massachusetts waters were actually invaded and her coast was bombarded by enemy craft. In the summer of 1918 the single German U-boat was followed by 4 more submarines. While German U-boats harried cargo ships, unguarded tankers, and coast-wise schooners from Newfoundland to North Carolina, sinking with shellfire and bombs a score of American and Canadian fishermen, including several Boston vessels, the U-156 attacked the Boston tug *Perth Amboy* and several barges 3 miles from Orleans off Cape Cod on July 21, 1918. Hundreds of bathers and cottagers summering on the Cape witnessed the shells bursting among the boats and saw the tug burn to the water's edge and 3 of the barges sink. After one of the shells flew inland and exploded in a pond about a mile from the shore, the German gunners secured a more accurate range on the next shot, which buried itself on the beach. Before the submarine disappeared, 4 shells were fired at the shore, but no one was injured. The heroism of the Orleans lifeguards saved the 11 men of the *Perth Amboy,* and the boats from the barges were given a rousing cheer when they safely pulled into Nauset Harbor.

During the war years, the United States Government played an important role in the maritime activities of the Port. Few of Boston's 16 coastwise steamship lines remained under private ownership, and the city's commerce was considerably influenced by the Federal Government's policy of shipping supplies and troops to the Army in France from only the larger North Atlantic ports. Boston ranked third in the United States as a port of embarkation, sending out 46,000 troops. In 1917 the Federal Government built the $26,000,000 Army Supply Base, with a frontage of 300 feet on the Reserve Channel in South Boston and 2 pier sheds each 3 stories high and 950 feet long containing a total floor area of 13 acres. Between the sheds was an 8-story reinforced concrete storehouse served directly by the New Haven Railroad and boasting a floor area of nearly 40 acres. The Boston Navy Yard Dry Dock No. 3 in South Boston was also a product of the world conflict. The largest in existence when completed, measuring 1,204 feet in length, with a bottom width of 115 feet and a sill depth at mean high water of 43 feet, it was constructed by the Commonwealth of Massachusetts and sold to the Federal Government in April of 1920 for $4,000,000.

The successful conclusion of the war was joyously greeted by Boston citizens, who welcomed the home-coming soldiers royally. The return movement of troops through the Port reached its peak in April 1919, when 6 transports docked with units of the Yankee Division. Escorted by a fleet of submarine chasers from below Boston Light, the vanguard of the division, 5,800 men and officers, arrived on the *Mount Vernon* on April 4. At quarantine the troopship was met by a fleet of harbor craft and excursion boats packed with welcoming officials, relatives, and friends. Two large hydroplanes circled overhead; sirens, whistles, and naval guns saluted the soldiers jammed against the rails and perched high in the rigging; and passing vessels of all kinds joined in the triumphal procession up the harbor. The cheers of 50,000 people gathered on Castle Island were answered by those on the *Mount Vernon*, as the ship moved toward her berth at Commonwealth Pier, where the men received their noisiest welcome. The arrival of the *Mount Vernon* was followed by the *America, Agamemnon, Mongolia, Patricia,* and *Winifredian.* Between April and July more than 50,000 troops disembarked at Boston, including the Rainbow Division and regiments from South Carolina and Texas. By summertime some of the spontaneous enthusiasm seemed to have lost its force, for a Boston newspaperman covering the arrival of a troopship told of a vessel docking "amid the customary joyful shrieks of steam whistles and sirens and the frantic cheers of 10,000 friends."

The end of the World War revealed great advances at the Port of Boston. The city had become the biggest wool center in any country, the largest exporter of boots and shoes, the leader in the importation of hides and skins, and the foremost fish market in the United States. Boston could proudly point to more than 141 miles of waterfront, over 40 miles of berthing space, and the largest pier in the world.

CHAPTER VIII

THROUGH PROSPERITY AND DEPRESSION

Into the Prosperous Twenties

THE YEAR 1920 found Boston slowly returning to normalcy. Thirteen months had elasped since the signing of the Armistice, and the feverish wartime atmosphere had cooled. The city's industrial plants had speedily reentered the peaceful channels of business enterprise; her financial institutions on State Street had joined with Wall Street in inaugurating a series of huge loans for the reconstruction of Europe; her population had reached the high figure of 748,000, of whom more than half were foreign-born or of foreign-born parentage; her trading area encompassed over 14,000 square miles, populated by three and one-half million potential customers; her factories employed 76,000 workers and manufactured 18 percent of the State's products. The city with a famous past was not without a mighty future.

On the waterfront the commercial life of Boston flowed fullest in the newer sections of South and East Boston, where the ocean liners made their brief visits amidst great excitement. Millions of dollars had been spent on improvements in these newly developed areas. The inner regions of the harbor, particularly Chelsea Creek, the Mystic River, and Weymouth Fore River, specialized in the receipt and shipment of oil, lumber, coal, and chemicals. On the Atlantic Avenue waterfront docked the coastwise ships, their cargo hoists and booms swinging wide above the pier sheds, their hawsers slack in the flood tide. A daily sight was the endless chain of stevedores carrying huge bunches of green bananas from the sleek white hulls of the United Fruiters into the wharf shed on one side of the ship and into freight cars, ranged on car floats, on the other side. On Atlantic Avenue the sailmakers, wharfingers, and chandlers were still a part of the commercial scene, and through flyspecked windows scores of little shops displayed diving helmets, model ships, sextants, hemp cable, bale hooks, officers' uniforms, Gloucester oilskins, compasses, and marine hardware of a thousand varieties. Here were preserved the memories and records of glorious seafaring days when tides and ships brought wealth and riches from the Northwest Coast and China Seas.

Even for its ordinary pursuits the changing waterfront area assumed a picturesque flavor borrowed from its maritime past. Off the South Boston shore a showboat, the four-master *Horace A. Stone,* once of the Buenos Aires trade, rode at anchor, a night club frequented by Boston's café society. At the end of T Wharf was the Waterfront Club, the city's most fashionable speakeasy, where a special guard was kept on Saturday nights to warn top-hatted inebriates of raiding Prohibition enforcement officers. T Wharf wafted its accustomed aroma of fish over a new set of habitués when a lady artist rented a studio in one of the lofts and was followed by 16 more "studio" dwellers. They pushed candles into the necks of bottles, hung fish-nets on the walls, and put on canvas trousers and berets, to the bewilderment and occasional annoyance of the Italian and Portuguese fishermen.

Shipbuilders

After the tense war years a comparative calm had settled over the Boston shipbuilding industry; the clank of chains, the chug-chug of hoisting machines and the hammering of riveters had died down in East Boston and along the Chelsea and Quincy shoreline.

Although the shipyards possessed abundant capital, skilled labor, and the equipment necessary for the construction of every type of ship, they did little new building, because of the existing "oversupply of unprofitable ships." Accidents, seasonal reconditioning, the daily wear and tear of the sea accounted for the largest share of the Boston shipyard activity. At this time the Bethlehem Shipbuilding Corporation acquired two of Boston's oldest shipyards, the Simpson Dry Dock Company and the Atlantic Works, both of which had been building whalers and clipper ships in East Boston as early as 1853. Engaged in repairing ships, building stationary engines and boilers, the Atlantic Works consisted of buildings, docks, and piers, with more than a 1,050 foot frontage on the main ship channel. The Simpson yard, which specialized in ship repair, contained three graving or sunken docks and one 10,000-ton floating drydock.

Scattered along the East Boston waterfront among docks devoted to the use of coal and lumber companies, fishing fleets, and trans-Atlantic liners were a number of small ship-building and ship-repair concerns. Here the repair plant of the Mystic Steamship Company was kept active reconditioning its own fleet. This company had been organized on January 18, 1924, to acquire the nine steamships of the Crowell & Thurlow Steamship Company and the fleet of colliers, barges, and towboats of the New England Fuel & Transportation Company. Bringing coal to Boston was their principal concern, although the company's ships were chartered to all ports of the world. Nearby stood the repair shop of the Boston Marine Works, Inc., and the small plant of Bertelsen & Petersen Engineering Company, which was succeeded by the General Ship & Engine Works in 1931. Out on Sumner Street the Marine Company, established in 1883, did fine interior woodwork and repaired and built cabins and other parts of boats. At Jeffries Point lay the small, picturesque yard of Carmelo Tringali & Sons, who specialized in building and repairing the boats of the Italian fishermen of Boston.

Across the harbor in Quincy the Bethlehem Shipbuilding Corporation had developed the Fore River Yard into one of the biggest American shipyards, yet here too the bulk of the business now consisted of repair work. In 1922 the *City of Miami* received extensive alterations, changing over her coal-burning furnaces to fuel oil burners, and adding 300 staterooms, parlors, and suites of rooms to the passenger accommodations. Under a 30-day contract the Quincy yard converted 3 mine sweepers, the *Austerlitz, Valmy,* and *Isly* into fishing trawlers; 17 ships underwent repairs in the years 1925-26. During this period the Fore River Yard built for the United States Navy several cruisers and the great airplane carrier *Lexington,* which was launched in the presence of 20,-000 spectators on October 3, 1925. The *Lexington* proved to be one of the world's fastest ships, out-speeding her escorts while carrying supplies to the survivors of the Nicaraguan earthquake disaster. The yard had additional contracts for seven 485-foot tankers, 2 scout cruisers, and 6 submarines for the United States Navy. By the close of the year 1925, a total of 400 ships of all types had been built at Fore River.

Expanding Imports—Declining Exports

Ships were built and ships were repaired, but few of those handled at Boston shipyards left the ways to take their place among locally owned vessels. For although at the end of the decade Boston ranked third among ports in the United States in the total volume of her ocean commerce, the city had abandoned her ship-owning tradition. The Port remained a convenient landing place for a large volume of merchandise, but few Boston ships carried the cargoes.

Boston in 1929 could not boast a single ship in foreign commerce, unless one counted the vessels trading with Canada, those of the New England Transatlantic Line, which flew the Norwegian flag, or those of the American Republics Line, which were chartered by C. H. Sprague & Son from the United States Shipping Board. In large part, the locally owned steamships were tankers belonging to the Beacon Oil Company and the collier fleet of the Mystic Steamship Company, while Boston sail was maintained by the big four-masters of Crowell & Thurlow.

Even more startling was the metamorphosis which the trade of the Port underwent between 1920 and 1929. Trade figures showed a steady and wholesome growth as they doubled in tonnage, four-fifths of which was in domestic commerce. Contrasting sharply was the small but extremely important foreign trade, which was especially weak in the export field. Imports were on the increase as New England industries demanded ever larger quantities of raw materials from the Port; the importation of rubber increased twelvefold; wood pulp jumped from 40,000 to 232,000 tons; cocoa imports were negligible in 1920 but reached 15,000 tons a decade later. The advantages of this growing import trade were, however, offset by a rapid decline in the export business of the Port, a decrease from 573,489 tons in 1920 to 303,120 tons in 1929. The loss of Boston's export trade has generally been attributed to adverse rail and ocean rates, which favored such shipping centers as New York, Philadelphia, and Baltimore. In 1882 Boston's share of the country's exports had amounted to 8.2 percent of the total, but by 1920 the percentage had fallen to 2.3, and in 1929 to less than one percent. Boston had remained second only to New York as an exporter until 1905, when Baltimore forged ahead, and Philadelphia followed suit 3 years later.

Besides adverse rates on inland grain and wheat and general merchandise, the changing nature of the country's export trade had a share in curbing the volume of the city's exports. A generation previously Boston had been the country's leading port in the European cattle trade. In 1897 exports of cattle

had totaled 162,620 head, but, owing to Great Britain's preference for Canadian and Argentine cattle, Boston shipments
had dropped to the vanishing point by 1929. It had become not
at all unusual for a Boston merchant to ship goods to New
York by rail to be loaded there for the Argentine, and an increasing number of ships entering the Port of Boston left
in ballast. However, the unfair freight differential was more
accountable for this inability to furnish return cargoes than
any failure in Boston enterprise.

Boston business men waged an unremitting fight against
the unfair freight rates which hampered the export trade of
the Port. Led by the eloquent Frank S. Davis, manager for
many years of the Maritime Association of the Boston Chamber of Commerce, local business leaders persistently and valiantly pleaded the cause of the Port at committee hearings
and before the Interstate Commerce Commission in Washington, D. C. The association petitioned for an equalization
of freight rates with other Atlantic and Gulf ports, and the
General Court appropriated money to fight for the removal
of this discriminatory differential. But in 1924, Boston lost
her case. On January 20, 1925, the United States Shipping
Board called a conference to end rate discriminations against
New England and Gulf ports. Achievement of parity would
have been a great victory for Boston, since all ports would
have been placed on a strictly competitive basis, but the conference failed because of the pressure of trunk-line railroads
whose interests lay in keeping the existing rates.

The wide-awake Maritime Association did secure improvements in harbor facilities and trade and boasted several notable accomplishments. Although the world's biggest drydock
was located near the Army Base, none of the larger ships could
dock there, since the North Broad Sound Channel was not
deep enough to accommodate them. At the request of the
association, the Federal Government remedied this anomalous
situation in 1925, when a contract was let out for the dredging
of the channel to a depth of 40 feet. This was sufficient to permit safe passage to any ship then in existence, as was amply
proven by the *Leviathan's* frequent trips to Boston for over-
hauling. The Maritime Association also established coopera-
tive relations between the South American coffee dealers and
exporters and the American steamship companies, which
resulted in the increased importation from that continent
not only of coffee, but also of hides and other products. As

the result of another of the association's activities, which this time proved that wood pulp could be distributed more cheaply to paper-manufacturing centers from Boston than from competing ports, the importation of this product increased 15 percent and reached a total of 110,000 tons between January and October 1924.

Coastal and Intercoastal Commerce

Throughout the 1920's Boston held second place in the coastwise trade of the Atlantic ports. As usual, New York took the lion's share, averaging three times as much as Boston, while Philadelphia and Baltimore, close runners-up in years past, had dropped to third and fifth places respectively. Between 1920 and 1927, Boston's coastwise commerce averaged 66.3 percent of the Port's entire business. In the order of their tonnage local receipts included coal, petroleum and petroleum products, sand and gravel, lumber and logs, fish and fish products, fertilizer, canned goods, hides and skins, sulphur, coal tar, and cotton. Boston's coastwise shipments were considerably below her receipts but involved such important commodities as petroleum, coal, coke, hides, poultry, fish, and miscellaneous articles. At this time the Port was characterized as "the terminus of an extensive coastwise and intercoastal trade which helps to feed the foreign shipments."

Boston was still the clearing-house for raw materials entering New England and for farming, fishing, and manufactured products shipped out. In 1928, coastwise services out of Boston were offered by eight steamship lines, each of them serving ports not reached by the others. Daily service was maintained to New York and four sailings a week was the usual schedule to the Middle Atlantic ports. Freight was carried to Gulf cities by the Mooremack Line and to Georgia and Florida by the Clyde and Savannah Lines, which returned with cargoes of sugar and thousands of bales of cotton. Scores of colliers and barges brought coal to Boston from Newport News, Norfolk, and the Chesapeake region, while empty American tramps could always stop for Boston-consigned coal on their return trip to the North. Coal had become the leading product received at the Port; its tonnage amounted to 68 percent of the entire coastwise receipts between 1920 and 1927. In return Boston continued to ship the staples of the Southern trade, as well as such manufactured commodities as plumbing fixtures, automobile parts, electrical apparatus, clothing, and many articles never before transported by water.

Boston services to the Pacific Coast showed a considerable gain during the 1920's, and by 1932 five lines offered 16 departures a month to California, Puget Sound, and Portland, Oregon. A thriving business via the Panama Canal was carried on by the American-Hawaiian and Luckenbach Lines, whose freighters brought back large quantities of wool from California. Tank steamers took on liquid cargoes of crude and fuel oil at Los Angeles, then the largest shipper of petroleum and petroleum products to Boston. San Francisco and Seattle sent canned and dried fruit, and canned fish and vegetables, while much of the lumber and logs imported at Boston originated in Tacoma, Bellingham, and Gray's Harbor. From further north, from Everett and Longview in Washington, came paper and paper stock. On their return voyages to the West, Boston ships carried iron, steel, manufactured articles, and a great many unclassified items.

Prominent in Boston's coastal and intercoastal trade were the Merchants & Miners Transportation Company and the Luckenbach Steamship Company, Inc. After the World War the Merchants & Miners had embarked on the most ambitious building program in its history, and by 1926 the company operated five of the largest passenger ships on the Atlantic Coast. The sister ships *Alleghany, Berkshire, Chatham, Dorchester,* and *Fairfax* measured 367 feet in length, had a displacement of about 7,000 tons, and provided the most modern passenger accommodations on their runs to Philadelphia, Norfolk, and points south. As a result of the heavy movement of freight between Boston and the West Coast, the Luckenbach Company established its intercoastal service out of Boston in 1923. At first the company maintained fortnightly sailings, but within a year the volume of freight moving out of Boston warranted the extension of the line's services to a weekly schedule. Westbound cargo consisted largely of New England manufactures, while Boston freight included general cargo, lumber, dried fruits, and wool.

Steamers did not yet have a monopoly on Boston's trade. Shipping notices in the Boston newspapers still announced the occasional arrival and departure of coastwise schooners. Generally these four-, five-, and six-masters plodded up and down the coast with lumber, stone, gravel, and other bulky material which could be moved slowly and cheaply. They plied between the North Atlantic cities and the southern and West

Indian ports with miscellaneous cargoes, and brought lumber and fish to Boston from Nova Scotia. Laden with $50,000-worth of mahogany logs, one Boston-bound four-masted schooner took more than a month in 1924 for the passage from Barbados. The white skipper and 17 Negro crew members faced, not only the perils of the sea, but starvation as well. When a bad storm severely damaged the vessel, the crew refused to abandon her. Twice the *Bluebird* was assisted by other vessels, twice her food supply was exhausted, and she had to beg stores; but each time the crew decided to stick rather than allow the expensive cargo to fall into the hands of salvagers. Not far off Boston, the lumber craft was completely disabled and unable to navigate under its own power. A call for help to a passing ship brought the Coast Guard, and the schooner was towed into port with her faithful crew still aboard.

Boston's coastwise trade was not greatly affected by the Cape Cod Canal until more than 10 years after it was purchased by the Federal Government in 1928. Built to enable local shipping to avoid dangerous shoals and stormy waters on the outside of Cape Cod, this waterway accommodated, between 1928 and 1938, only about 17 percent of the Port's domestic commerce. In part, this limitation was due to the Canal's narrow width and rapid currents. More important was the shallow depth, which prevented the passage of ships drawing more than 25 feet and thus sent most of the coastal tankers and freighters around the Cape. The Corps of Engineers, United States Army, pursued an energetic program of enlargement and deepening, which was begun in 1933 and completed in 1940, and now makes the Canal available to larger ships drawing up to 30 feet. A substantial increase in traffic was noted in 1939 when almost 5,000,000 tons of commerce, more than double the tonnage of 1929, passed through the Canal.

Strengthening Labor Bonds

On the Boston waterfront, labor organizations, especially the International Longshoremen's Association, made great strides. Since many of the "huskies" were of Irish descent, the visit of Eamon De Valera to the convention of the Massachusetts Branch of the American Federation of Labor, in September 1919, spurred them to increased nationalist activities, and their association in the nationalist movement gave impetus to waterfront organization.

By 1928, three unions of the International Longshoremen's Association controlled the cargo handling of all ships in the foreign and intercoastal trade. Their membership totaled 1,761, and the average wage for those employed fairly regularly throughout the year was about $27 per week. The membership was largely Irish or Irish-American of the second generation, with openings being filled by the sons of members. The 1,000 or more longshoremen in the coastwise trade received a lower hourly wage and averaged about $26 per week. Their work was more regular, since many of the coastal services operated on a daily or tri-weekly basis. Some shipping companies employed the same men on regular hours and occasionally paid them on a weekly or monthly basis.

The method of hiring longshoremen for work on deep-water ships, known as the "shaping up," remains much the same today as it was in the 1920's. Each morning that a ship docks in East Boston, Charlestown, or South Boston, groups of 100 or more men gather before a platform on which stands the stevedore foreman who picks the gangs. A gang is assigned to each hatch and consists of 21 or 22 men. They include a hatch tender, 2 winchmen, 6 hold men, who work on the ship, 2 "landers," who guide the loaded slings as they swing out of the hold, and 10 dockmen, who cart the freight to its proper place in the pier shed. A gang boss supervises the work. The gang which starts working a hold has full rights to all work, both unloading and loading in that hold. The equipment used in handling the freight is the property of the stevedore firm, which acts as an intermediary agent for the shipper and contracts for the labor in handling the cargo. After a ship has been worked, the men are paid off and must "shape up" again before they return to work. This system does not include any provision for an even distribution of work among the longshoremen.

The Boston waterfront throughout the 1930's was relatively free from the labor disputes which caused serious tie-ups in several of the leading United States ports. In 1931 a 2-months' strike of longshoremen and tally clerks resulted in a working agreement with the operators which established working conditions and wage rates satisfactory to both sides. Except for minor changes and slight increases in wages this agreement was renewed annually through 1935, at which time the Port

Authority said "there exists a real desire on the part of both operators and longshoremen to get together and work out problems with a minimum of friction." In 1936, West Coast labor troubles tied up intercoastal shipping, but Boston long-shoremen resisted efforts to call a sympathy strike. The organization of C. I. O. unions among seamen and some waterfront workers in 1937 resulted in a number of short strikes which did not seriously affect waterfront commerce. Although agreements have not been signed between operators and long-shoremen since 1935, a relatively smooth working relationship exists. Wage scales follow those negotiated at New York.

The Leading Fish Port

During the twenties and early thirties, Boston's fishing industry maintained a steady growth except in the years 1921 and 1922, when the post-war depression with its decreasing demand for fish, its falling prices, and labor troubles caused a temporary decline in the fisheries. In 1923, however, receipts of fish at Boston rose to almost 124,000,000 pounds and thereafter mounted annually, reaching 285,000,000 pounds in 1930. In the latter years, according to James B. Connolly in *Fifty Years of Boston,* "the dealers of the Fish Pier paid out more than $10,000,000 for fish purchased on the floor of the Exchange alone, an increase of 225 per cent in the last sixteen years." The Boston home fishing fleet of 208 vessels was the largest of any North Atlantic port in 1903, and was supplemented by hundreds of other vessels which landed their catches at Boston. The number of workers engaged in the Boston fisheries doubled and their wages trebled between 1914 and 1930. An idea of the importance of the industry may be gained from the fact that in the year 1922 the Boston fishing fleet accomplished 2,754 trips to and from the fishing grounds.

The position of Boston as the fish-marketing center of the Western Hemisphere remained fixed, despite the competition of Gloucester, New York, and Portland. The Boston fish market in 1922 sent 93 percent of its products to points in New England, New York State, and Pennsylvania; 56 percent of the total, however, did not go beyond Massachusetts. Sailing mainly from Nantucket and Hyannisport, the flounder fleet increasingly used the Cape Cod Canal to Boston, which succeeded in wresting a goodly portion of the flounder business from New York. Mackerel was brought to Boston from points farther south than ever before, and 583 fishing vessels with almost 10,000,000 pounds of mackerel passed through the Canal on their way to Boston in May and June of 1927. Although the halibut vessels landed their catches at all Atlantic ports, Boston held a predominant place in the halibut trade, 4,000,000 of the 6,000,000-pound catch being marketed here in 1922. Owing to the high cost of railroad transportation as well as attendant delays, trucks started transporting fish to Boston for processing and distribution as early as 1923. By 1930 several hundred trucks were bringing fish from such widespread points as Bangor, Maine, and Newport, Rhode Island, while others carried the packed fish products to Middle Atlantic and Midwestern States. The steamer, too, began to make a bid for the transcontinental transport of fish in 1923, after the first refrigerator vessel from the Pacific Coast to Boston—the steamer *Neponset*—arrived here in March 1922, via the Panama Canal. The *Neponset* brought a cargo of frozen halibut and of salmon frozen and salted, and took back a shipment of Boston fish presented by the Mayor of Boston to the Mayors of San Francisco, Seattle, and Los Angeles.

By the 1920's "big business," which by first taking over the operation of trawlers had commenced control of the Boston fisheries, was affecting directly the lives of thousands of local fishermen. Where once the deck of a little schooner had served as trading base, now the floor of the Boston Fish Exchange became the scene of daily trading. After mooring his vessel to the pier, the skipper went to the Fish Exchange to make a deal, and then returned to give the order of "break open." Soon the scales were ranged, and handlers stood by, ready to cart the fish away as quickly as it was weighed. Sometimes, if the fish were not as represented, there were arguments and haggling, followed by a reluctant compromise on a price lower than the one first agreed upon.

The fishermen were anxious about the price, since they still worked on a share system. This, however, was undergoing certain revisions designed to give the fishermen a fairer percentage. The introduction of trawlers increased costs and so changed the method of operation. Control passed from the hands of the fishing boat captain to that of the owners and some of the expense was thus transferred to the latter. When fishermen came to be regarded as employees, an unprofitable trip was no longer the responsibility of either the captain or the crew, and unpaid bills were collectible solely from the owner of the boat. With this change came the practice of guaranteeing the fisherman a minimum wage, which has grown from $10 to $15 in the 1920's to the present $25 per trip. The division of profits between owner and crew is still in use, however, and the minimum guarantee is applied only when the fishermen's share is below $25. The settlement method is known as "the 50/50 wage lay." After the costs of securing space at the dock for unloading, using the scales for weighing, and other docking expenses are taken from the gross receipts of a trip, the remainder is divided equally between the owners and the crew. The owners' half pays for company expenses and for operation of the boat. But the cost of fuel, ice, food, and a few other small items must be paid out of the crew's half. Captain, mate, cook, engineers, and fishermen share the remainder, though the captain is paid an additional bonus ranging from 7 to 10 percent of the owners' share. If the crew's half does not cover all bills usually paid by them, the owners meet any unpaid bills and the crew receives the guaranteed minimum agreed upon.

Powerful steam trawlers equipped with auxiliary engines, radios, and electric lights, had come into general use, and these big mechanized ships carried heavy dredges or drags, to which were attached long cone-shaped nets, open at the forward end and closed at the other. When the cone reached the sea floor, the trawlers moved ahead at a speed of about 3 knots until enough fish were caught to make it worth while to haul up, usually after a dragging period of 1 or 2 hours. Although steam trawlers accounted for the largest part of the Boston catch, they aroused serious objections, since small fish were not allowed to escape, and feeding and spawning grounds were destroyed, resulting in the dispersion of the fish. The latter objection was considered valid enough by several New England legislatures to justify laws prohibiting the use of beam and otter trawlers in waters close to the coast.

In 1921 a new processing method, the cutting of the meaty sides of a fish from the bone structure, had a revolutionary effect on the fishing industry. The boneless pieces of fish, called fillets, were wrapped in parchment paper, packed in tin boxes, and then shipped to dealers over the entire country. The waste material was utilized in the production of fish meal for poultry and stock raisers. From the beginning, Boston has been the leader in this new business, which grew from 50,000 pounds of fillets in 1921 to over 80,000,000 pounds in 1929.

Another important factor in the growth of the Boston fisheries was the development of fish inspection, which had been established by an Act of the General Court in 1919. Although the fish inspectors then had no authority to condemn spoiled fish, they accomplished much by persuading the wholesale dealers to cooperate, even to the extent of lending the services of their own employees to assist the officials in opening boxes for inspection, and by providing lists of retailers to whom imperfect fish had been sold. A similar cleanup of the fish peddlers' fleet also brought good results. The 1922 amendments to the Fish Inspection Act put the inspections on a thoroughly efficient basis; inspectors were empowered to enter any place where fish was sold and destroy such fish as was unfit for food. It became mandatory to grade fish, and "number three" could be sold only at wholesale and only as prepared fish products. Weekly inspection of the Boston Fish Pier and the 150 peddlers' carts, which obtained their fish at the pier on Thursdays, was put in practice.

While most Boston fishdealers were in sympathy with the aim of fish inspection—to supply the public with edible fish —it was 9 years before the fish inspector could say in his annual report for 1929 that "the idea of quality fish" was "well grounded in the minds of fish dealers." This result was achieved through the constant efforts of the inspectors to examine all fish brought into Boston by fishing vessel, truck, rail, or steamer, and to make certain that only the first two grades were sold as fresh or frozen fish. Although substantial amounts of fish were condemned each year, there was a drop from the high of 157,000 pounds in 1924 to 70,800 in 1928 and 59,300 in 1929.

The introduction of a course in fisheries engineering at the Massachusetts Institute of Technology climaxed the newly developed interest in the catching, preparing, and especially the refrigeration of fish, which permitted the storage of thousands of tons until the off season, when they could be marketed at a profit. As the result of a meeting, in Boston in 1921, of interested persons with Professor John N. Cobb, Director of Fisheries at the University of Washington, science had entered the fishing industry. The Technology course was approved by State and Federal authorities and fisheries interests, and the Federal Bureau of Fisheries offered experts as instructors. The Boston fishing industry aided in a financial way and the Massachusetts Division of Fisheries requested the General Court to appropriate $3,000 annually toward securing competent instructors.

Disaster on the High Seas

The Boston fishing fleet continued to suffer the mishaps and adventures inevitable on the sea. In 1920 the steam trawler *Loon* ran amuck at the end of T Wharf, ramming and sinking the harbor tug *Betsy Ross* and badly damaging the *Irving F. Ross*. While the *Loon* was making for the fishing grounds, her captain discovered that some one had stolen his bunker belt plates, and headed back to the pier for new ones; the ship's steering gear suddenly became deranged, and the crash followed. Luckily no lives were lost in this accident. A narrow escape from another disaster in Boston Harbor occurred soon after, when Captain King of the *Progress* sighted a stalled motor boat through the haze, just as his schooner was bearing down on her. Jamming his helm hard over, the captain cleared the little craft by bumping across the outer sand bar and landing plump on the inner bar near Bug Light.

Not all the Boston fleet returned safely to the Fish Pier. It took just a minute and a half for the schooner *Actor* and her cargo of fish to plunge to the bottom of Boston Harbor on September 26, 1924, after she was rammed by the Army quartermaster's boat *General Batchelder* in the Narrows between Fort Strong and Fort Standish. Fortunately Army privates and the crew of the *Batchelder* dived overboard and saved the members of the fishing schooner. Four years later, about 1:30 a.m. on December 15, 1928, the *Georgina M.*, a fishing schooner carrying 60,000 pounds of haddock to the Port of Boston, was cut across the starboard bow by a huge ship which suddenly loomed out of the darkness and disappeared in a wide swath of foam. After this clear case of hit-and-run, it took the *Georgina M.*'s crew of 10 men 5 hours of stiff rowing in the schooner's dories to reach Provincetown.

After an interval of several years, apparently without major shipwrecks in Massachusetts Bay, the year 1930 wrote the tragic story of a horrible sea disaster. An impenetrable fog hung over the waters of the bay on June 10, when the Merchants & Miners' *Fairfax* left Boston, bound for Norfolk, Virginia, with 71 passengers and a crew of 70. On the same day

the Mallory oil tanker *Pinthis* departed from Fall River with
12,000 barrels of gasoline, bound for Portland, Maine. While
the oil tanker nosed her way through the Cape Cod Canal
and then across the bay, the passenger ship crawled along at
half-speed, her whistle breaking through the fog with a lugu-
brious blast once every minute. About 23 miles from Boston
Harbor, off Scituate, the *Pinthis* suddenly appeared 150 or
200 feet off the bow of the *Fairfax*. One shrill scream came
from the whistle of the *Pinthis* and was followed by a quick
reversing of the *Fairfax* engines. But it was too late; collision
occurred, and a moment later the gasoline in the tanker
burst into a roaring geyser of flame. Burning gasoline shot
high over the masthead of the *Fairfax* and showered her with
a cloudburst of fire. Flames swept the port side of the *Fairfax,* and the surface of the ocean blazed up like an inferno.
The *Pinthis* had disappeared beneath the waves, but floating
fires, fed continually by oil which welled up from her shattered hull, marked the grave of the tanker and her crew of
19 men.

Meanwhile order was gradually achieved on the *Fairfax.*
The deluge of fire had ignited the clothing of some of the
crew and they and a few frenzied passengers rushed to the
rail and jumped into the burning sea. Heroic seamen fought
their way through smoke and flame to the lifeboat stations
and succeeded in getting the women and children into boats
on the side of the ship farthest from the fire. Another group
of crew members hastily repaired the burned antenna and an
SOS was radioed. As the ship pushed her way out of the
flaming oil, a lifeboat was lowered to search for survivors
among those who had jumped overboard, but none was found.
Three hours later, the *Gloucester,* another Merchants &
Miners' ship, arrived in response to the call from the *Fairfax*
and took off the remaining passengers.

Rum-Running Days

During the era of Prohibition, weird scenes were often enacted along the Massachusetts coast by rum-runners and ships
that came into contact with these smugglers. The Boston Coast
Guard unit patrolled with especial vigilance the strip of coastline reaching from Cape Ann to Provincetown, one of the
most vulnerable areas on the Atlantic seaboard. Every cove and
bay in this sector was a likely spot for rum-runners. Public
apathy and even open resentment against those charged with

enforcement recalled the attitude of the colonists toward smuggling before the American Revolution. The desolate islands of St. Pierre and Miquelon in the Gulf of St. Lawrence became the main source of supply for the smugglers, who dropped anchor on Rum Row, outside the 3-mile limit between Gloucester and Provincetown, and there traded with smaller, faster boats which operated between them and the shore. Rum Row soon became an institution, and it was not unusual to see as many as 12 or 15 vessels there at one time, rolling in heavy seas with decks awash and maintaining their position, in fair weather and foul, with the precision of a naval squadron carefully avoiding a territorial deadline.

Occasionally the Boston office of the United States Coast Guard received advance information of the departure of a smuggler from St. Pierre. In consequence of such a report, the Federal authorities were vigilantly patrolling the waters off Boston in December 1921. On the twenty-ninth, their close watch was rewarded by the capture of the British schooner *Golden West,* which was brought into Boston by the Coast Guard Cutter *Acushnet* with about 8,000 gallons of alcohol in her hold. The skipper of the British schooner claimed that he had been having trouble with his sails for several days and had been forced to anchor close to the shore. According to the Collector of the Port, however, the *Golden West,* formerly a Nova Scotian fishing schooner, was owned and operated by a former Boston bartender.

The Boston Coast Guard unit carried out one of their most carefully planned attacks on Rum Row in the fall of 1924. Accompanied by a squadron of 30-foot speedboats, the cutter *Tampa* moved into position for the raid on October twentieth, and for 5 days was out of contact with the shore. The coastguardsmen maintained a constant watch, cruising between Cape Ann and Cape Cod, eating and sleeping at irregular intervals. On Friday night more than a dozen runners were discovered at Stellwagen Bank, about 20 miles off the coast. The *Tampa's* squadron formed a blockade around the smugglers, and just before dawn the order to close in was given. Under a grey-streaked sky the smugglers caught sight of the *Tampa,* and within a few seconds their speedy crafts were scattering in all directions. Immediately the machine gunners on the patrol boats opened fire on the escaping rum-runners, while the *Tampa* turned its 3- and 5-inch guns on those who were out of range of the smaller boats. When the

Tampa's shells began to fall, most of the fugitives decided to surrender, although several of the fastest boats made good their escape. The hail of bullets had shattered every bit of glass in the cabin of one of the smugglers and had begun to rip out her partitions. Although hundreds of cases of liquor were thrown overboard, the total value of the liquor seized amounted to about $100,000 in terms of bootleg prices. The captured vessels included the British schooner *Marjorie E. Bachman*, which carried 850 cases of brandy, whisky, and champagne, and 7 power boats still loaded with 100 cases of liquor.

Despite a reorganized Coast Guard and the international recognition accorded to the 12-mile limit, smugglers continued to land liquor along the Massachusetts coast under cover of fog and on moonless nights. When "dry" enthusiasts gleefully reported that Rum Row had at last been deserted, a Boston reporter flew over Massachusetts Bay and discovered no less than 12 ocean-going ships riding at anchor on the Row. An even stronger shock to local "dry" morale was the presence in Massachusetts Bay of 5 or 6 runners, visible on a clear day from the piazza of the summer White House at Little's Point in Swampscott. In a clean-up that preceded President Coolidge's visit to the North Shore in the summer of 1925, the ships were driven to sea by destroyers. At the same time, Federal authorities confiscated $30,000 worth of whisky cached in a cottage next door to the summer White House, and a dispatch to the *New York Times* reported that Swampscott was "reasonably dry."

Speed had become an increasingly important factor in liquor smuggling, and within a few years smugglers had turned from ordinary fishing craft to the undisguised "rummies" which were powered by two or more airplane engines and were capable of showing their heels to the best boats on the Atlantic coast. The fastest rum chaser in the Federal service came to grief in the pursuit of one of these boats in 1932, when the Coast Guard chaser *Peg* was beached at Provincetown with 2 feet of water in her hold, after a 100-mile chase in which the "rummie" had all the best of it. The *Peg* had been powered by two 750-horsepower airplane engines, whose terrific pounding had opened her seams in the course of the chase. Whatever curiosity the Coast Guard had about the target they had chased across the width of Massachusetts Bay until it outstripped them was dispelled a week later when a trim grey craft slipped into Provincetown Harbor with her papers in good order. Carrying three airplane engines under her decks, the "rummie" had been especially designed and built for the illicit liquor trade. In Nova Scotia, noted naval architects were designing and building armored rum runners, which were low-masted, broad, set low in the water, and powered by the most modern engines. In its endeavor to cope with these rum ships, the Coast Guard was forced to enlist the services of the same architects, who drew plans for the construction of several 75-foot rum chasers driven by twin-screw propellers.

Meanwhile national indifference to Prohibition had changed rapidly into militant and organized opposition. The killing of 3 rum smugglers by coastguardsmen off the New England coast was denounced as "the Newport Massacre" at a mass meeting in Faneuil Hall in December 1929. At this meeting speakers, including a former mayor of Boston and two congressmen, delivered a fiery attack against the Government's Prohibition policy. According to official reports, at least 150 vessels were engaged in smuggling liquor along the New England coast at this time. So the fascinating, but illegal game went on until 1933, when the repeal of the Eighteenth Amendment went into effect and another phase of Boston's marine activity came to a close.

Foreign Trade

Normal commercial activities continued without the ballyhoo attached to the more exciting rum-running activities. Although foreign commerce remained an important factor in the Port's life, it gradually reacted from the artificial stimulation of the war years. The valuation had fallen by 1925 to the pre-war level, and even then the decline did not stop. Boston dropped to eighteenth place in the overseas export trade, from $192,330,000 in 1920 to $45,942,000 in 1929. The exportation of metals and metal manufactures had declined immediately after the signing of the Armistice, although some of the abnormal features of the Port's wartime trade persisted until the end of the decade. In 1920 more than 270,000 tons of meats, grains, and other food products were shipped abroad, and in 1929 food exports still accounted for 101,400 tons of the Port's business. By 1925 leather was again the leading export, followed by cottonwaste, wheat, footwear, and packinghouse products, two-thirds of which went to Great Britain and Germany.

In the import trade, Boston stood much higher, being second only to New York, and Boston's imports constituted the bulk of her overseas commerce, amounting to $255,944,000 in 1929. The importation of petroleum and petroleum products from Mexico ranked first in tonnage, while more than half of the Boston-bound hides came from the vicinity of the River Plate. It is interesting to note that many raw materials which originated in South America and British possessions were shipped to Boston by way of England, that Australia was the source of much of Boston's wool supply, and that shipments of tea, silk, and spices arrived from the Orient. Vegetable oils and pepper came to Boston from Sumatra, while thousands of tons of Egyptian cotton and fruits and wines entered the Port from the Mediterranean. Between 1920 and 1929 Boston's imports were larger than they had ever been before in the long course of her commercial history, and Boston's foreign trade was marked by the greater gains of her competitors rather than by her own losses.

Although receipts at every Atlantic port were greater than shipments, nowhere was this disparity more noticeable than at Boston, where the ratio between shipments and receipts was 1 to 4 in 1920 and 1 to 10 in 1929. The absence of western grain and the comparatively small amount of foreign shipments had unbalanced Boston's commerce. Her foreign trade suffered a further loss because New England commodities were increasingly exported through the Port of New York. On a basis of valuation, New York received 65 percent of all New England exports in 1928, and only 16.3 percent of the hardware and cutlery exported by New England firms passed through the Port of Boston that year; of the total wood manufactures exported from New England, only 10.8 percent was shipped from Boston.

Boston had regular steamship services to and from every important trade area in the world: European, African, Far Eastern, Australian, and South American. In 1928, monthly or semi-monthly schedules to European and Mediterranean ports were offered by 18 steamship lines; 3 lines maintained services to the Far East, and 3 carried freight to South America; there were occasional departures for Australia in steamships with a limited passenger service. The Barber Steamship Company listed a monthly freight service between Boston and West African ports, and the Isthmian Steamship Line operated on a similar schedule to Honolulu and the East

A coal schooner, the *Mertie B. Crowley*, in 1907. *Courtesy of the Society for the Preservation of New England Antiquities.*

The south side of T Wharf in 1907. *Courtesy of the Society for the Preservation of New England Antiquities.*

Indies. Due to her deficiency in export cargo, Boston was used
as a port-of-call by some lines which did not maintain regular
outbound schedules. Between the years 1928 and 1932 the
total number of steamship lines serving the Port of Boston
increased by 19, although sailings were numerically fewer.

After the World War, the Furness Withy Company resumed services to Liverpool under the name of Johnston
Warren Lines, Ltd., operating ships between Boston, Halifax,
St. Johns, and Liverpool. The singlescrew steamships *Digby*
and *Sachem* were used on this route until 1925-26, when they
were replaced by the *Newfoundland* and the *Nova Scotia,*
modern steamships of about 6,700 gross tons with accommodations for 193 passengers. Sailing every 3 weeks, the *Newfoundland* and the *Nova Scotia* made the trans-Atlantic crossing
from St. Johns to Liverpool in 6 days. In recent years the
Johnston Warren Line ships have carried from Boston many
of New England's manufactures, as well as coffee, sugar,
meats, and some wheat. From Liverpool they have brought
back widely diversified freight; liquors, cotton, wool, leather,
and hides had a prominent part on the manifests of the company's inbound cargoes.

Boston's overseas services were increased by the inauguration of the Dollar Line's bi-monthly sailings to 17 foreign
ports. Pioneers in the development of a round-the-world steamship service, the Dollar Line sailings began early in 1924.
Something of the spirit of the merchant adventurers of the
nineteenth century inspired this twentieth-century enterprise.
To start the service, the company purchased from the United
States Shipping Board 7 combination passenger and cargo
ships, with a capacity of more than 10,000 tons. Paper, wire,
and confectionery were carried from Boston to the West
Coast, where other cargoes were shipped to Honolulu, Japan,
and China. Although Boston provided the Dollar ships with a
lucrative freight business to the Pacific coast, a much larger
part of their traffic at the Port consisted of imports from the
Far East, India, and the Mediterranean. Boston imported
quantities of wool, skins, and rubber. Tea, bamboo, and hemp
came into the Port from the Far East while Bombay and
Ceylon furnished the Dollar Line with wool, rubber, and
skins consigned to Boston. Naples, Genoa, and Marseilles
sent Mediterranean fruits, nuts, cheese, and olive oil.

Arriving and departing on precise schedules, the Cunard
and White Star liners berthed in lordly splendor for a few

hours each week at East Boston and South Boston. Although the World War had witnessed the destruction of all the Cunarders which operated out of Boston, 19 new ocean liners were built for the company between 1921 and 1925. The tonnage of the new ships ranged from 13,000 to 21,000 tons, and included the *Carinthia, Samaria, Laconia,* and *Franconia.* Directors of the Cunard Line had shrewdly anticipated the development of tourist travel and the course of Congressional legislation affecting immigration and had planned the ships to meet these changes. The company's tourist service established a high standard of comfortable travel at low prices and greatly encouraged summer travel to Europe. These ships maintained a regular weekly service from Boston to Ireland and Liverpool between April 15 and November 15, with less frequent sailings during the remainder of the year. Freight moving in and out of Boston in this service consisted of clothes, furs, and other valuable merchandise.

A marked decline in trans-Atlantic passenger travel through the Port of Boston set in after the World War. Previously large profits had been made from passenger traffic, some lines realizing three-fourths of their net returns from this source. During the year 1914, 100,000 passengers either had entered or left Boston, but by 1920 passenger arrivals at the Port had dropped to only 19,096, and until 1929 they fell far short of their pre-war average. A drop in the number of immigrant travelers did not entirely account for this decline, since lack of export cargo and the consequent tendency of major trans-Atlantic lines to give up Boston as a base port undoubtedly diverted some of the Port's passenger traffic.

The disproportionate number of foreign flag services at the Port of Boston was typical of any United States port. It was the outgrowth of a national situation, and not due to any local peculiarities or problems. Directed by poor management, American flag lines had maintained unnecessary and unimportant route services and had failed to consolidate whenever practicable. Moreover, foreign flag lines often did not adhere to the rate structure, and thus gained an extra advantage. The public relations of the American flag lines had been very poor, American passengers and shippers did not understand and appreciate their services, and the failure to exchange information produced a reluctance on the part of American investors to put their money into the steamship business. In 1932, 26 non-American lines were offering services in foreign areas to Boston traders as compared with 14 American-owned and operated lines. In addition, a great many foreign-owned tramp steamers, of which a large number were Japanese, called at the Port. By the closing years of the decade, however, önly a few tramp steamers were carrying logs, lumber, and coal to Boston, for the established lines had taken over even the more variable commerce.

In the Boston-South American trade, the passing of sailing vessels and the withdrawal of foreign steamship lines had left a clear field for C. H. Sprague & Son to obtain whatever business there was. Already prominent as coal carriers, the Spragues put about 10 steamships in the carrying trade along the Atlantic Coast and to South America in 1924. In addition, the company leased from the United States Shipping Board the 8 steamships of the American Republics Lines and operated them to South America. The most important commodity shipped to South America by this line was lumber, followed by machinery, steel, coal, manufactured articles, and general cargo. On their return trip the Sprague ships brought back hides, wool, rubber, coffee, quebracho, and a little mahogany. Between 1920 and 1925 the Sprague Company also operated 6 steamships from Boston to Scandinavian ports, chiefly exporting corn and importing pulp. Carrying agricultural machinery and general manufactures, another of their lines maintained a service to the Black Sea, calling at Turkish, Georgian, and Danubian ports. There ore and grain were loaded for Scandinavia, where additional wood pulp was obtained for Boston.

New Life to the Port

Confronted with an adverse trade situation at the Port, the General Court established the Boston Port Authority on April 17, 1929. The work of this board has been defined to be the facilitation, regulation, and expansion of the commerce of the Port of Boston. This unpaid board was composed of five members, two appointed by the Governor of the Commonwealth and three by the Mayor of Boston. Subsequently, the membership of the board was increased to seven, with three appointed by the Governor and four by the Mayor. The expenses of the board were paid by the City of Boston for the first 10 years of its existence, but today they are shared equally by the Commonwealth and Boston. Outstanding businessmen were selected for the board: Guy W. Currier, Chairman; Richard Parkhurst, Vice Chairman and Secretary; Louis E. Kirstein, Joseph W. Powell, and Harris Livermore. Mr. Livermore was killed a few weeks later and Charles E. Ware, Jr., was appointed in his place. Securing offices at the Boston Custom House, the Port Authority began regular work on January 1, 1930, and 6 months later, on the death of Mr. Currier, the board elected Louis E. Kirstein as its chairman. Determined to attract more shipping and commerce, the board immediately turned its attention to the rate situation and to the Port's physical facilities.

Early in its career the Boston Port Authority announced its intention to participate in all rate proceedings involving the Port of Boston, as well as initiating them on its own account whenever necessary. Accordingly it contacted many city and State commercial organizations; conferences were held with New England railroad presidents, representatives of shipping agencies, department heads of State and city bureaus, and other groups interested in the advancement of the Port. It kept constantly in touch with the labor situation, maintaining cordial relations both with the committee representing the steamship operators and with the waterfront unions. Members and counsel of the board attended hearings before the Interstate Commerce Commission on terminal services provided for shippers by railroads. In 1931 the board devoted much of its attention to the "free lighterage" case at New York.

The Boston Port Authority also made a strong bid for passenger traffic. Yet even in this field the New York octopus had to be fought, for practically all the big steamship companies had located their main offices there since 1902, when independent local management of lines had been discontinued. Since the steamship companies tended to route their passenger traffic by way of the largest flow, branch offices and tourist agencies almost invariably sent their customers to New York. After a careful investigation, the Port Authority recommended extensive improvement along the waterfront with a view to safety, convenience, and attractiveness, and then requested the steamship companies to change their booking policies. With the consequent cooperation of the companies, the departure of passengers from Boston to foreign ports showed an increase during the first 11 months of 1931 of 11 percent over the previous year, and in 1932 there was another increase of 21 percent. Although Boston was unable to furnish outbound passenger traffic equal to the overwhelmingly large inbound traffic, the city continued to hold her place as the "second overseas passenger port of the United States."

However, the first 2 years of the Boston Port Authority's existence were wisely given over mainly to investigations, reports, and planning. The menace of old and rotting hulks in East Boston was investigated, and more than 100 were removed; recommendations were made for the dredging and filling-in of certain areas; reports were issued concerning conditions and practices at the Army Base; harbor regulations were put into force, bearing especially on the prevention of oil pollution by steamers' bilges; plans were drawn up for port renovation and reconstruction, including a scheme for various terminal, belt line, and warehousing projects. The Authority effected changes at Commonwealth Pier, where, with the cooperation of the State Department of Public Works which operates the property for the Commonwealth of Massachusetts, berthing facilities were improved by the removal of useless storage material. In 1930 the Port Authority instituted a program of port publicity, issuing annually 2 sailing lists, which covered inward and outward sailings. In 1931 the Port Authority also called attention to the following facts: Boston was nearer than Los Angeles to the Panama Canal and consequently nearer to all ports on the west coast of South America; Boston was nearer than New York to Rio de Janeiro and therefore to most cities on the east coast of South America; Boston was nearer than New York to all countries of Europe and Africa.

Encouraged by the aggressive policy of the Port Authority, the Port of Boston managed to retain her commanding commercial position. In 1932 Boston stood fourth among the North Atlantic and Gulf ports in the total volume of commerce, surpassed only by New York, Philadelphia, and Norfolk-Newport News. In foreign commerce Boston ranked fourth among the North Atlantic ports, led by New York, Philadelphia, and Baltimore. Forty-three steamship lines served the city in foreign commerce and 13 in domestic trade; the physical appearance of the Port had been improved; the Boston Army Base had been placed in the hands of a capable private operator; the Congressional Rivers and Harbors Committee had voted favorably on a $5,000,000-program for channels and anchorage bases in Boston Harbor and adjacent waters. Boston again was looking ahead.

CHAPTER IX

THE CONTEMPORARY PORT

Busy Wharves and Piers

BOSTON's oldest waterfront section, off Atlantic Avenue, is still used by ferryboats, excursion steamers, and coastwise ships, but it is no longer entirely occupied with shipping. Lincoln Wharf has been converted into a powerhouse for the Boston Elevated Railway Company; Constitution Wharf and Battery Wharf have become distributing centers for soap and grocery concerns. Between Commercial Wharf and T Wharf are ranged the stalls of wholesale and retail fishdealers who have not yet gone to the Fish Pier. Barrels and baskets of fresh-caught fish overflow onto the sidewalk, and in a sheltered cove behind the stores ride the many-colored boats of the Italian and Portuguese fishing fleet. Only six wharves have maintained a semblance of their former activity. Lewis Wharf is the home of the Clyde-Mallory Line and the Boston Towboat Company. Long Wharf receives weekly large loads of bananas, brought by ships of the "Great White Fleet" of the United Fruit Company. From India and Central Wharves, the passenger boats of the Eastern Steamship Lines depart for New York and the Maritime Provinces, and during the summer, thousands of people embark at Rowes Wharf and Fosters Wharf for a sail to Nantasket and Provincetown.

Contrasting sharply with Atlantic Avenue, the South Boston waterfront is almost entirely devoted to maritime activities. Busiest of all the piers in this section of the Port is the New York, New Haven & Hartford's No. 2, occupied by the Merchants & Miners Transportation Company which schedules five sailings a week. An adjacent pier, No. 4, is an unloading berth for West Coast lumber and the home of one of Boston's fishing companies. Commonwealth Pier No. 5, a fine example of modern terminal construction, attracts many deep-draft passenger ships and large freighters. This pier is usable on two levels, both of which are resounding grottos of activity. Freight cars nose in and out, and an entire unloading job is often accomplished in a few hours. At the adjacent Fish Pier there is never a dead stop of movement, since trawlers and fishermen know no regular hours. Nearby, "tramps" of all nations, loading scrap iron, crowd speedy modern freighters at the Army Base, one of the Port's chief facilities for handling exports and imports.

Variegated, colorful, and cluttered is the East Boston waterfront, which extends from the airport to Chelsea Creek. Several of the most active ocean terminals in Boston are concentrated in this relatively small area. The National Docks and the five piers of the Boston & Albany Railroad are visited by almost a score of lines operating to all parts of the world. The passenger ships of the Cunard Line until recently made regular trips to the Boston and Albany Pier No. 3. At No. 2 modern pumping equipment quickly drains cargoes of vegetable and palm oil directly from ships into tank cars. Flanking these docks are several ship-repair plants, centers of intense industry, as steel plates are hurriedly replaced, engines overhauled, or deck fittings installed on ships cradled in drydocks or tied snugly to the wharves. Activity along the inner harbor, largely occupied by lumberyards, proceeds at a more leisurely pace, adjusted, it would seem, to the mood of the Down-East lumber schooner which is usually in evidence.

Boston's most important inner harbor development, Chelsea Creek, has been taken over by special industries, which receive large shipments of bulk commodities. Today the Creek boasts a channel 30 feet deep and 150 feet wide, which accommodates an increasingly important movement of oil tankers. The adaptation of this area to the expeditious and economical handling of oil cargoes has resulted in the establishment of large oil depots, distribution points for most of northern New England. But the only time the sheltered creek reveals its activity to the casual observer is when the drawbridges swing out and ships steam through.

The Charlestown waterfront, although sorely in need of rebuilding, presents a variety of enterprises including naval and commercial shipping. The crowded Boston Navy Yard, dominated by the masts of "Old Ironsides", occupies a strategic position at the head of the harbor. Alongside are the Hoosac Tunnel Docks of the Boston & Maine Railroad, once the point of departure of Frederick Tudor's ice ships and now capable of accommodating seven ships simultaneously. These docks have become the lading and discharging point for freighters and small passenger ships from Southern, and Gulf ports, and the Boston terminal of the globe-encircling American President Lines. At the Mystic Piers, between the Mystic and Little Mystic Rivers, Swedish, British, and coastal steamers are most frequently seen. A lively center of specialized commerce has grown up along the Mystic River, where West Coast lumber steamers unload at Wiggin Terminal Dock, and the New England Coal & Coke Company, the Mystic Iron Works, the United States Gypsum Company, the Colonial Beacon Oil Company, and the Merrimac Chemical Company have established plants and installed up-to-date unloading equipment.

Harbor Agencies

Inside the harbor, the Boston Fire Department operates 3 fireboats, which have divided responsibilities for safeguarding the Port's 500 docks, 140 miles of waterfront, and property worth millions of dollars. These marine fire engines have a combined pumping capacity of 28,000 gallons of water per minute and are equipped with gas masks, inhalators, first-aid kits, a deep-sea diving outfit, and 2-way radio sets. Flagship of the fleet is the *Matthew J. Boyle,* built at Lawley's Yard in Neponset at a cost of $350,000. This boat, which can surround itself with a water curtain, is now licensed to operate anywhere in Massachusetts Bay, although she was restricted to Boston Harbor at the start of her career. On one occasion the *Matthew J. Boyle* did answer a call in Salem and, as a result, was assessed a fine of $500 for traveling outside her prescribed territory. When it was found that a minimum of 10 days would have been necessary to receive permission to answer the call, the fine was canceled. This fireboat is berthed at the Northern Avenue Bridge and responds to all first alarms from Long Wharf to South Bay and Reserve Channel. The *Angus H. McDonald* protects the Charles River, Mystic River, and Charlestown area, while the *John P. Dowd* covers the East Boston waterfront.

On a windy March day in 1937, the three fireboats sped to the upper harbor to answer a five-alarm fire in the Little Mystic River. The *Laila,* on her maiden voyage from Chilean ports with a load of nitrates and iodine, had caught fire while unloading at Mystic Pier No. 45. The three boats butted their bows against the stricken freighter and, from vantage points the land crews could not reach, strove desperately to prevent the fire spreading to the iodine in the afterhold. Severe explosions of burning gas sent orange flames 100 feet in the air and buckled the plates of the ship. Several times the fireboats caught fire, and the crew had to turn to save their own ship. The explosions shook the crews badly and injured every man on the *McDonald*. But the fireboats fought valiantly and prevented the spread of the fire. Although $200,000 damage was done the ship was saved and beached upstream to prevent her from sinking under the weight of the water poured on the fire. The fireboats here conclusively demonstrated their superiority over land equipment in fighting fires aboard vessels.

Boston's waterfront police, a companion protective agency, has succeeded in making the Port one of the most orderly in the world. The harbor police force started in 1853 as a rowboat unit manned by 2 officers. For years the water patrol was known as the softest beat on the force, since there were no boxes to ring and the officers could spend much of their time fishing. After the turn of the century, the waterfront division met changing conditions by acquiring steam launches, which saw lively service during the lawless prohibition days. Patrolling the harbor now are the 3 fast launches *Michael H. Crowley, William H. Pierce,* and *William H. McShane,* each equipped with a 2-way radio, tear gas, guns, searchlights, grappling irons, and other paraphernalia. In charge of the waterfront division is the harbor master, who holds the rank of captain in the Boston Police Department. He is appointed by the Mayor of Boston, upon the recommendation of the Boston Marine Society, and has direct charge of the anchoring of ships in the harbor. Strange as it may seem, there is a considerable "parking" problem in the harbor, and often ships anchor in forbidden waters. In such a case, the harbor police merely summon tugs and have the offending ship towed out of the way. No parking ticket is issued, but the offender must pay the towage charges. For violation of other harbor rules, offenders are taken by the harbor master to court, where judgment is passed and fines imposed. The police are always on the lookout for ships polluting the harbor with waste fuel oil, which spoils the bathing, destroys lobsters stored in the water, and endangers public health. The recovery of dead bodies, as many as 50 a year, is the most unpleasant task of the waterfront unit.

More directly concerned with the safety of every ship from foreign ports are two small schooners, which cruise night and day off the Graves, the large black figures on their sails and their blue and white pennants notifying arriving ships that they are ready for service. The pilot who leaves the schooner and climbs up the side of an arriving vessel takes charge of all that the ship carries in life and property and guarantees a safe conduct into Boston Harbor. Carrying a cook, engineer, and 20 boatmen, apprentices, and licensed pilots, the *Pilot* and the *Northern Light* alternate weekly out on the station. It is the ambition of the boatmen and apprentices to join the Boston Pilots Association and become full-fledged pilots. Usually a young man receives his pilot's license after a 5- to 7-year apprenticeship, during which he lives and studies aboard a pilot boat. The final requirement made of him is to spend 3 months, in company of an experienced pilot, taking ships in and out of the harbor. The Boston Pilots Association, offspring of the Boston Marine Society, America's oldest marine organization, has an unusual feature in the communal character of its finances. All pilotage fees are turned over to the association, which defrays the expenses of the boats and office staff, and distributes the balance to its members. Several present-day pilots can boast of fathers, grandfathers, and even great-grandfathers, who also spent their lives piloting ships in local waters.

Assisting the pilots in the work of docking or sailing a ship, the tugboat captains control their powerful and versatile craft with an extraordinary skill. Handling a large ship is the most delicate work that a tug does. Sometimes only one tugboat is needed, though usually there are two or three; when the U. S. Airplane Carrier *Lexington* left Fore River, six tugs were required to guide her down the river, and the old *Leviathan* had a large flock to push her into drydock at South Boston. The more usual duties of a tug are hauling strings of barges, loaded with bulk materials, to various parts of the harbor or to the harbor entrance where the barges are picked up by ocean-going tugs and towed up and down the coast from Eastport to Sandy Hook.

Most of Boston's tugs are owned by the Ross Towboat Company of T Wharf and the Boston Towboat Company of Lewis Wharf. Boats of the latter company have been operating in the harbor since 1857 and now number 19, of which 2 are rated among the most powerful on the Eastern Coast. The Ross Towboat Company is an outgrowth of a single towboat owned by Captain Joseph Ross, whose son is now president of the company. Occasionally the towboats engage in unusual operations. When the *City of Salisbury* was wrecked off the Graves in April 1938, they assisted in the work of salvage and spent several weeks pulling in barges loaded with an assortment of East Indian goods.

An account of a ship's departure from the Port of Boston dramatizes the roles of the tugboat and pilot. A freighter in the Central American trade, the *San Blas*, is lying at the foot of State Street, the winter shadow of the Custom House falling just short of her bow. Her blue peter has been flapping in the raw February breeze since early in the forenoon, and "Sailing Time, 4 p.m." is chalked up on the gangway board. The skipper has just returned from a flying trip home. The first mate and the deck crew are busy battening down the hatches. A meek little man in an old green mackinaw trundles up the gangway, a magazine in one hand and a wrinkled Boston bag in the other. Displaying the imperturbability of all pilots, he says nothing to anybody but makes undeviatingly for the bridge to join the skipper, who knows with melancholy certainty that he will find the tide and current running vigorously in the wrong direction at the end of the pier. The pilot at his side laconically remarks, "It ain't nothin' here, Cap'n, to what you're going to get outside."

Fore and aft, tugs are made fast and wait with slack lines for the *San Blas* to cast off. The ship is "singled up"; only towlines and spring wire are holding her. The tugboat skippers stand in their wheelhouses shrilling cryptic blasts on the whistles. "Let everything go forrard, Cap'n," the pilot barks, "but hold your stern line." "All right, mister," says the captain, and bellows the order toward the fo'c'sle head. The wind plays havoc with the words almost before they leave the megaphone, but the mate senses the maneuver and shortly bellows back, "All gone forrard!" The propellers of the tugs commence to churn the water, and the *San Blas* starts to slant imperceptibly toward the center of the slip. The after-tug bunts against the ship's stern, holding her steady until the bow gets clear of the dock. Fighting against the clashing wind and tide, the tugs edge the steamer into the main stream and help her to turn outward. Shortly afterward, the two tugs cast off and depart across the harbor like alert and self-satisfied terriers, and the *San Blas* begins to quiver with her own life. The ship is carrying very little cargo and a third of her propeller blade shows at every revolution. By the time *San Blas* has reached the lower harbor, the bos'n and the day men have performed miracles. They have stowed the lines below deck, out of reach of the seas which will be upon them within the hour, and they have lowered eight 55-foot booms safely and accurately into their cradles—a ticklish job even on a calm and sunny day.

The wind's howl rises to a roar as the pilot guides the ship eastward through President Roads and then swings northeast through North Channel and out into the white-capped waters of Massachusetts Bay. Off the port bow stands the pilot schooner, a small boat's crew already putting off to meet the oncoming ship. On the bridge of the steamer, the pilot gives the final course to the sailor at the wheel, and stuffs his magazine firmly into the top of his Boston bag. "Slow her down, Captain, I can see the tender coming up on the lee-side." The *San Blas* settles into a lethargic rolling, and a pathetically tiny rowboat inches its way toward the ship, as the pilot swings himself over the rail. Three apprentice pilots, wearing life preservers, turn damp and glistening faces upward, while the pilot looks toward the bridge. "Pleasant voyage, Captain," he shouts.

A pleasant voyage for a captain connotes smooth seas, fair winds, an efficient crew, and officers well-trained in the fundamentals of their job. In recognition of the need for training deck and engine-room officers to handle the complicated mechanisms of the modern ship, the Commonwealth established the Massachusetts Nautical School in 1891 and placed it under a board of commissioners in the Department of Education. Boston is the home port of this school, which is held aboard a ship loaned to the commissioners by the United States Navy, although maintenance and supervision of the school was placed in charge of the United States Maritime Commission in July 1940. The schoolship is tied up at the Navy Yard during winter months while the cadets receive theoretical and practical instruction in navigation, seamanship, ship construction, maritime law, marine engineering, and electricity. Each summer the cadets put theory to practice, as the ship makes a 10,000-mile cruise to such ports as Ponta Delgada, Plymouth, Antwerp, Havre, Lisbon, Funchal and Norfolk, New York, and Nantucket. The present schoolship is the *Nantucket,* formerly the U. S. S. *Ranger,* a bark-rigged iron ship, built in 1876 and equipped with wireless, submarine signal apparatus, a steam capstan, steam steering gear, and complete electrical equipment. The *Nantucket* is still a staunch and seaworthy vessel, but a more modern ship is desired and the Commissioners of the Massachusetts Nautical School and the United States Maritime Commission will probably soon arrange for a replacement.

The United States Government has become actively interested in the training of crew members and attempted in 1939 to establish on Gallups Island, in quarters loaned by the United States Public Health Service, a seamen's training school, open only to unemployed sailors. This was abandoned in a few weeks when the expected recruits failed to appear. In June 1940, the same buildings on the island were opened for the United States Maritime Service Training School, sponsored by the United States Maritime Commission and operated by the Coast Guard. The school gives a 6-months course in radio work and general seamanship to 500 young men, volunteers selected in part from the Civilian Conservation Corps. Upon completing the course, these men will be eligible for the Naval Reserve or for the able-bodied seaman's or radio man's examination.

A highly trained staff is in charge of the United States Customs for the District of Massachusetts, with offices in the towering Custom House on State Street. A force of nearly 600 workers, under the direction of the collector of the port, is responsible for the collection of tariffs, which sometimes exceed a million dollars in a single week, and the enforcement of United States Maritime Laws. To promote efficiency and speed in the handling of homecoming passengers, the pursers of incoming ships distribute declaration slips upon which are listed the number and cost of foreign purchases. These slips, turned over to the inspectors on the dock, assist them in making their examination. The inspectors have to be alert to intercept the smuggling of valuable jewels, furs, and drugs.

Another Federal agency closely watching incoming ships is the United States Public Health Service which operates the Quarantine Station. The story of quarantine in Boston goes back to the year 1677, when 1,000 Massachusetts Bay Colonists died in an epidemic. As a result, Gallups Island was chosen as a voluntary quarantine station. After the Civil War, the island was purchased by the Federal Government for a permanent station and has since been the temporary home of thousands of immigrants and sailors. Operating from their headquarters at the Army Base, Boston's quarantine officers inspect an average of a thousand ships a year. Their work is somewhat lighter since an arrangement was worked out with passenger liners on certain routes whereby the certification of the travelers by the ship's doctor is sufficient examination. Other ships are visited at an anchorage in the outer harbor. Five diseases are quarantinable: bubonic plague, yellow fever, smallpox, Old World typhus fever, and cholera. The ships are closely watched for rats, and the officers have become so skilled in their work that they can estimate almost to a rat how many there are aboard and can determine immediately whether a ship should be fumigated.

The United States Immigration Service provides neat and clean quarters at East Boston for immigrants and aliens awaiting deportation or held for further examination. The office of local commissioner of immigration was abolished in 1940 in accordance with an extensive Government reorganization plan, and its activities were taken over by a district director of naturalization. The number of immigrants awaiting decisions on their cases naturally varies, but the figure is never large. For the year ending June 30, 1938, the Boston station examined and admitted 997 immigrants and 4,700 non-immigrant aliens. During 1936 and 1937, inspectors from the Boston Immigration Station boarded almost 3,000 ships and barred 22 aliens from entering the country. Criminal records, communicable disease, and improperly attested credentials are the main reasons for prohibition of entry.

The improvement of the harbor and adjacent navigable channels is entrusted to the Corps of Engineers, United States Army, which has been doing work in Boston since 1825, when Congress passed an act providing for "the preservation of the islands in Boston Harbor necessary to the security of that place." Since that time more than $42,800,000 have been expended by Federal, State, and local governments for the improvement of the Port of Boston's ship channels and anchorages. In addition to this work the engineers supervise the building and operation of bridges and drawbridges to prevent obstructions to marine traffic. They also compile complete records of the movement of ships and cargo through the Port, supplementing those kept by the Bureau of Foreign and Domestic Commerce and the United States Customs Service.

From 1919 to 1939 the local branch of the Lighthouse Service reached a high degree of perfection and modernization under the supervision of Captain George E. Eaton, Superintendent of the Second Lighthouse District. Captain Eaton retired in 1939, soon after the 100-year old Lighthouse Service ceased its independent existence and came under the command of the United States Coast Guard, which now cares for the colored lights and painted buoys guarding the harbor channels. Deer Island Light consists of a brown conical tower supporting a beacon visible for 13 miles, and Long Island Head Light, an iron and brick structure 120 feet in height, may be seen 17 miles away. Lovell's Island Lights, front and rear, are visible for a distance of 12 miles, while the two lights on Spectacle Island have a visibility of 13 miles. The other islands of Boston Harbor are illuminated by smaller lights such as those on Great Brewster Spit and Gallups Island. Scores of buoys mark the ship channels, and clanging bells and whistles warn the skipper of lurking shoals. A radio buoy, designed to direct large ships into and out of the Port during fogs, has been installed recently in the main ship channel off Deer Island.

Guarding the outer approaches to the Port are three large and well-known lighthouses: Minot's, off Cohasset; Graves, at the entrance to the North Channel; and Boston, off the Brewsters at the South Channel. Directly in the path of coastal shipping is Minot's Light, built of interlocking granite blocks in 1860. Eighty-five feet high, it shows a 1-4-3 flash ("I love you" to the romantic landsman) visible for 15 miles. The tower is anchored to a jagged granite reef, where even on calm days the breakers crash thunderously and only a scant hundred yards of rock show at dead low tide. The beam of Graves Light is flashed from a height of 98 feet and in clear weather may be seen for 16 miles. There is a legend that Graves was so named because the menacing ledges surrounding the light were the graveyard of a large number of ships in the early days of the Port. More probable is the story that the reefs were named for Thomas Graves, who as early as 1634 had noted the danger to navigation they presented. Neighboring Boston Light was the first of all American beacons. From its 102-foot conical tower, flashes a 100,000-candlepower beam, which is also visible for 16 miles. Supplementing the clear-weather efficiency of these lights are powerful fog signals which sound at regular intervals, each on a different time schedule to assist the mariner in getting his location.

The activities of the United States Coast Guard are of vital interest to maritime Boston and her seafarers. Almost daily, references to the Coast Guard appear in the Boston newspapers. The news may be of a gala occasion, perhaps reporting the patrol of an international fisherman's race course; it is more likely to be the story of a race to save some fisherman's life by rushing him to a hospital, or the struggle of a small, powerful boat to tow a disabled freighter through dangerous seas. Seldom does the Coast Guard lose its race. Every method of modern transportation and communication is at its command; fast boats and airplanes, sea and shore patrols, radio and teletype assist in its service to seamen and shipowners. The main local unit of the Coast Guard is based at the Boston Navy Yard and Commercial Wharf. The work of the patrol stations, maintained at City Point and Point Allerton, is in the main with yachts and smaller boats. In addition to aiding ships in distress, the Coast Guard removes from the sea lanes derelicts and other dangers to navigation, breaks ice in inner harbor channels, and enforces miscellaneous Federal laws relative to the fisheries, game, seal and bird reservations, smuggling, quarantine, and immigration. Every spring, two cutters from Boston maintain the International Ice Patrol on the North Atlantic sea lanes, warning ships of the presence of icebergs. No loss of life has been caused by icebergs since the patrol assumed this responsibility.

Sailing in the Bay

One of the most frequent sights of the harbor's summer season is the excursion boat, its decks crowded with city folks out for a few hours' sea voyage. Proof of the popularity of a sail through the island-studded waters is the continuous service for 122 years of the Nantasket Steamboat Company, probably the longest record of any American steamboat line. The line's success in recent years has not been an easy matter. About a decade ago a fire destroyed four steamers tied up at the Nantasket winter quarters, and only the action of residents of Hull, who subscribed $50,000 for stock, saved the company. Four newly-acquired steamers—the *Town of Hull,* flagship of the line, the *Mayflower,* the *Allerton,* and the *Nantasket*—have carried on through the depression years, when evening prices were reduced to attract a paying passenger load.

The route of these picturesque steamers is from Rowes Wharf, Boston, to Pemberton and Nantasket. They follow the main ship channel between Castle and Governors Islands, both of which retain their old stone forts, guardians of an earlier day. Most of the islands are publicly owned and have Federal, county, or city institutions on them. On the right are Spectacle

Island, site of Boston's garbage disposal plant, Thompson Island, with its Farm and Trades School, and Long Island, home of a large unit of the Boston Hospital Department. Off the port bow is Deer Island, synonymous with Suffolk County's penal institution. At Nix's Mate, customary gibbeting spot of Colonial pirates and now visible only at low tide, the steamers swing to the right of Gallups Island, where hospital buildings and barracks were formerly crowded with immigrants, and near Georges Island, home of a harbor defense unit. Beyond them, the voyager gets a glimpse of Boston Light on Little Brewster. Many of the Federal islands were beautified in 1934 when 100,000 evergreens were planted by the Civilian Conservation Corps. Off Pemberton, at the entrance to Hingham Bay, is Peddocks Island. Here, some 20 years before the settlement of Boston, a French trading vessel was raided by Indians and the entire crew was slaughtered. The quiet winding Weir River, lined with summer cottages, brings the steamers to Nantasket Beach, a very popular South Shore resort.

Sole survivor of regular operations within Massachusetts Bay is the Cape Cod Steamship Company, which operates the *Steel Pier* on an 8-hour daily sail to Provincetown, art colony and historic fishing town of Cape Cod. Gone are the excursions to Nahant, Salem Willows, and Gloucester, on the North Shore, and to Plymouth, home of the Pilgrims on the South Shore. An occasional trip through the Cape Cod Canal by the Nantasket or the Provincetown boats meets with a favorable response. "Picture and Bike" trips to Provincetown have stimulated business, and the "moonlight sail" has provided an additional source of revenue. In recent years, two rival lines have tried to establish themselves on the Provincetown run. The Bay State Steamboat Company operated the *Romance* until, on a foggy day in September 1936, she was cut down by the *New York* and sank off the Brewsters without loss of life. The company operated the *Governor Cobb* the next year and then ceased to function. The *Yankee Clipper*, a converted yacht formerly owned by Henry Ford, was put in service by another company in 1939 but was taken off the route in August 1940.

For the sea-loving landsman, yachting has a great appeal. Dorchester, Quincy, and Hingham Bays are dotted with white sails, as friendly rivals pit their skill in small-class races. From Point Allerton to Point Shirley are scattered the stations of some 25 yacht clubs, headed by the dean of them all, the Boston Yacht Club, which has its headquarters on Rowes Wharf and a station at South Boston. Other prominent clubs are the Columbian and South Boston at City Point, the Wollaston and Squantum in Quincy Bay, the Hingham at Hingham and Winthrop, Cottage Park, and Pleasant Park at Winthrop. The outstanding local races of the year are those held during Quincy Bay Race Week in midsummer. Many of the yachtsmen join with Marblehead in celebrating its famous Race Week in the middle of August.

Fishdealer Supreme

Boston is still the leading fish port in the Western Hemisphere; her fish and fish products were valued at $13,000,000 in 1937 and $18,000,000 in 1939. In recent years, however, large holdings of frozen fish have created a problem of oversupply, and local labor troubles have harassed the industry. During the winter of 1936-37, disastrous floods in the Mississippi and Ohio River Valleys blocked the shipment of frozen fish, which usually ran to 600,000 pounds a week. To complicate the problem further, landings were unusually heavy because of the open winter and inventories in the warehouses soared to 21,000,000 pounds over the previous 5-year average. Some relief from this surplus of frozen fish was achieved through the Federal Government's purchase of millions of pounds of the frozen product for free distribution to the underprivileged. Some Boston fishdealers fear an aggravation to the problem of oversupply through the present trade treaty between the United States and Great Britain, which relaxes certain duties on fish imports. An additional complicating factor arose in 1939 when General Seafoods Corporation entered into an agreement with the Newfoundland Government whereby fish caught in the company's vessels could be processed in Newfoundland, by native workers at lower labor rates, and brought to Boston as American fish. A clarification of the term "American fisheries" by the 1940 Congress, however, defines them as operated, both in catching and processing, by United States companies, ships, and workers; fish otherwise caught or processed is dutiable.

Wages, working conditions, and limitation of the catch have long been points of dispute between the fishermen and owners of the Boston fishing fleet. In 1928, the Atlantic Fishermen's Union (A. F. of L.) threatened to call a strike involving about

100 Boston and Gloucester trawlers, but an agreement was reached in time to avert an open break. In May 1939, a strike did tie up 21 Boston trawlers for 3 weeks. The settlement gave the fishermen an increase in wages. Demands for limitation of the catch have not been met, since to do so would cause restraint of trade.

One of the longest labor disputes affecting the local trawler fishermen began on March 15, 1940 and lasted 14 weeks before the terms of a new contract could be agreed upon between the Atlantic Fishermen's Union and the Federated Fishing Boats of New England and New York, an association of shipowners and operators. Early discussions found both parties agreeable to wages and working conditions similar to those in the previous contract. The strike was called when no decision could be reached over methods of selling the fish. The fishermen demanded the right to refuse to sell the fish the day they landed, if they felt market conditions would be better the next day. This the owners and operators refused to concede and the strike finally ended in the signing of a contract virtually identical with that of the preceding year. Although 55 trawlers were tied up, the draggers and line-trawl schooners were able to supply the fresh-fish market. The fish-freezing industry was more seriously affected.

In the past decade, the tonnage of the Boston fishing fleet has remained substantially the same. In 1940 the fleet numbered some 400 vessels, including 51 large otter trawlers (over 150 gross tons), 200 smaller otter trawlers, and 125 trawl schooners. The fleet was considerably reduced in August and November 1940, when the United States Navy purchased 14 large otter trawlers for use as mine sweepers. These will probably be replaced by wooden vessels, for local shipyards equipped to build steel boats are busy on naval orders. In addition to serving the local fleet, Boston is the marketing center for about 30 swordfishermen and 35 mackerel seiners which hail from other ports. The larger companies operating these vessels include the General Seafoods Corporation, O'Hara Brothers Company, Inc., Booth Fisheries Company, Irving Usen-O'Donnell Company, F. J. O'Hara & Sons, Inc., R. O'Brien & Company, Haskins Fish Company, Captain William H. Westerbeke Company, Atlantic Coast Fisheries Corporation, the Massachusetts Trawling Company, and the Cape Cod Trawling Company. These companies, and all other fishing interests, are daily supplied by the local division of the

United States Bureau of Fisheries with a Market News Service giving current prices and vessels' landings. The fishermen at sea also derive much benefit from the daily radio broadcasts of station WHDH in Boston, which sends out market news, information on arrivals, and weather reports.

The larger coal-burning otter trawlers are fast being superseded by Diesel-driven oil-burning vessels, each costing between $125,000 and $300,000. The Boston fleet has been equipped with the most modern devices for navigation and fishing, including a fathometer, which registers the depth of the water, and radio telephone equipment, which keeps the owners constantly informed as to the amount and character of the catch. This information is posted on the blackboard in the auction room of the Fish Pier, where an agent of the ship mounts the platform to receive bids for the catch or any part of it. A whistle blown twice signals prospective buyers to gather at the auction room to bid for the incoming catch. Three whistles indicate a "sell-over" or resale of fish found not as good as represented. At the present time the Boston fleet brings in swordfish, tuna, and shrimp, as well as the staples of the fishing industry.

New Additions to the Merchant Marine

Ten ships, including the airplane carrier *Wasp*, aggregating over 76,300 tons and $55,000,000 of commercial and naval marine construction, were launched at the Fore River Yard of the Bethlehem Steel Company from September 1938 to June 1940. In December 1940, there were in various stages of construction, or contracted for, several tankers, 4 destroyers, 16 cruisers, 4 aircraft carriers, and the 35,000-ton battleship, *Massachusetts*. The naval contracts alone totaled more than $500,000,000. The yard has seen steadily increasing activity since the keel of the cruiser *Quincy* was laid in 1933. Its building program has almost entirely consisted of contracts let by the United States Navy Department and the United States Maritime Commission as part of their plans to increase naval units and the merchant marine. Fore River has expanded to keep pace with its orders and was employing more than 10,000 workers at the end of 1940.

Outstanding among the ships constructed recently for the merchant marine are 3 liners of the Panama Railroad Company, the *Panama,* the *Ancon,* and the *Cristobal,* all delivered in 1939. Each is a 10,000-ton combination passenger and cargo vessel capable of carrying 206 first-class passengers. The use of all-metal furniture and of non-combustible materials in walls, doors, and structural parts make the ships completely fire-proof. The specifications follow those laid down after the *Morro Castle* disaster by the United States Maritime Commission and the Bureau of Marine Inspection and Research. The ships are subdivided into compartments to prevent sinking in case of collision, and are the first American boats to have the Schat skates equipment, which permits the safe launching of lifeboats even when the vessel lists sharply. The 8 cargo steamers built for the United States Maritime Commission, to be operated by the American Export Lines, are ships of about 8,500 gross tons, have a speed of 16½ knots, and cost in the neighborhood of $2,400,000 each.

The tremendous building program of the United States Navy, which has placed more naval tonnage on the ways in Boston in the last 7 years than at any time since the close of the World War, has also resulted in increased activity at the Boston Navy Yard. Two 1400-ton, six 1500-ton, and eight 1600-ton destroyers, in addition to several auxiliary craft, were built in the shadow of the old *Constitution* between January 1933 and June 1940, and in that month four other destroyers were in the process of construction. The Navy is also expanding and modernizing the Boston Yard's machine shops and equipment. The efficiency of the South Boston drydock has been increased through the construction of machine shops, assembly buildings, and a floating crane, improvements which have cost over $3,500,000. Extensive additional construction is planned for 1941.

Not all of Boston's shipbuilding is in the heavy construction class. Fishing boats, Coast Guard cutters, and pleasure craft keep the smaller yards busy. The firm of George Lawley and Son Corporation in Neponset is still turning out first-class yachts. Established in Scituate 64 years ago, it became famous for such American cup defenders as the *Puritan* and the *Mayflower*. Willis J. Reid of Winthrop and the Kennedy Marine Basin, Inc., of Squantum specialize in marine repairing, while George F. Lawson & Son, of Dorchester, produce boats of the Lake Sunapee, Duxbury Pilgrim, and Mount Desert Island classes. Reminders of Medford's old-time shipping days are to be found on the banks of the Mystic in the yards of Toppans Boats, Inc., which builds the Twosome class, and the Baltzer-Jonesport Boat Yard, which builds 30- to 38-foot cruisers.

Wings Over the Harbor

Judged by the plans for its development, the Boston Municipal Airport seems certain to play an increasingly important role in the activity of the Port. Located close to the large steamship terminals in East Boston within a half-hour's automobile ride of other harbor docks, and fifteen minutes of the Boston hotel and business district, the airport is in a splendid position to furnish trans-Atlantic passengers with direct service to inland points in the United States and Canada. From the airport the American Airways provides frequent service to New York and Buffalo, with connections to all parts of the country. The Boston-Maine-Central Vermont Airways, now the Northeast Airlines, Inc., serves northern New England and Montreal. Two other major airways applied to the Civil Aeronautics Commission in 1940 for permission to operate direct services to the Midwest, and a third line applied for a through route to Florida.

The airport was opened in 1923. Three years later airmail service was inaugurated, and in 1929 passenger service was placed on a permanent schedule. The previous year the City of Boston leased the land and began a development that has resulted in a Class A airport, with an administration building and numerous hangars for commercial and military planes. The area of the airport has been enlarged by filling in along the waterfront and the runways are now long enough to handle the largest planes.

The development of trans-Atlantic air services in the 1930's, prior to the outbreak of the European War, aroused the hope that Boston might have a share of the business. The location of the airport on the harbor's edge makes it easily accessible to hydroplanes. A vitally needed improvement, however, is the dredging of a seaplane landing and take-off channel. Plans for such a channel, 1500 feet wide and 12 feet deep, extending from off Wood Island Park have been approved by the Corps of Engineers, United States Army, which has jurisdiction over all waterways. A $2,300,000 authorization for the construction of this seaplane base was included by the 1940 Congress in the Omnibus Rivers and Harbors Bill, which was vetoed by the President. A later attempt to put through a similar authorization was killed in the Senate Commerce Committee at the request of the President, who opposed any non-military activities being undertaken by the Army Engineers at a time when national defense was the major problem. The need of the seaplane channel was subsequently reemphasized from the point of view of national defense, so that the project is again under active consideration.

Domestic Trade

Although world-wide shipping once made Boston, in commerce as in other respects, "the Hub of the Universe," domestic trade during the 1930's accounted for approximately 80 percent of the Port's entire business and for more than 14,000,000 tons in 1939. In terms of tonnage, coal, crude and refined oil, sand and gravel, lumber and logs, and fish constituted the bulk of Boston's coastwise receipts, while general cargo and petroleum products led the list of coastwise shipments. Relatively large cargoes of grain, flour, petroleum products, and canned foods arrived from the Pacific Coast, while general cargo, pigments, and chemicals made up a large share of Boston's shipments to the West Coast. Gains were shown in Boston's receipts of grain, grain products and wool, as well as cotton from Gulf ports for transshipment to Canada.

Most of the products, both inbound and outbound, have their destination or origin in industrial New England, which is linked to Boston by a radiating network of railroad lines. The Boston & Maine Railroad operates in northern Massachusetts, Maine, New Hampshire, and Vermont, and connects Boston with many points in Canada. The New York, New Haven & Hartford tracks extend across southern Massachusetts, Rhode Island, and Connecticut, and link Boston with every city of importance in southern New England. The Boston & Albany Railroad owns about 400 miles of track between Boston and Worcester, Springfield, Pittsfield, and Albany, joining with the Boston & Maine both at Athol and at North Adams. For its western connections, however, Boston is dependent upon trunk-lines railroads, which exercise control over the local roads; and because the interests of those lines center about other ports, Boston gets very little business from the hinterland.

Coal comprises as much as 45 percent of Boston's inbound commerce, and a vast area of the upper harbor waterfront is enveloped in a never-settling cloud of coal dust. Grimy coal ships plow one after the other through the Boston drawbridges, their decks almost awash under the weight of cargo ranging from 3,000 to 12,000 tons. Nine hours later, completely empty, riding high upon the surface of the water, and showing 15 feet of red underbody, they slither back through the drawbridges. The modern collier is well-liked by many seamen and officers because of the short coastwise run and opportunity for frequent visits home. Modern stateroom accommodations are provided for the crews. Constant communication by teletype between the railhead and the discharging point, and by radio between headquarters and the ship, keeps the traffic at an even flow. Captains are encouraged to make fast and safe voyages by the possibility of earning annual bonuses.

Most of the coal brought to Boston is carried by the collier fleets of 3 local companies. Of these, the Pocahontas Fuel Company operates the lightest boats. The largest concern, the Mystic Steamship Company, which in 1911 owned the first steam colliers, maintains a crack fleet of 16 huge colliers. Fifteen are capable of carrying 8,000 tons each, and the *Lemuel Barrows* can hold 12,000. Averaging 5-9 days per voyage, these ships completed over 700 trips from Boston to Hampton Roads and Baltimore in 1937. More than half of the coal brought in by the company is consumed in the manufacture of coke and illuminating gas by the New England Coal and Coke Company in Everett. The Sprague Steamship Company, headed by Richard Bowditch, whose grandfather, Nathaniel Bowditch, won everlasting renown by his pioneer standard text, *The Practical Navigator,* has 9 coal ships in the Boston trade. The pride of its fleet is the *Eastern Crown,* a converted Japanese passenger ship capable of carrying more than 12,000 tons of coal. She is considered one of the fastest coal ships in the world and is greatly admired by local seamen for the fine quarters afforded her crew of 40. On the Sprague Company's *Black Point* travels a little black dog, formerly the mascot of the Navy collier *Cyclops.* During the World War the dog became so frantic, as the *Cyclops* prepared for a voyage, that he refused to go aboard. The ship sailed and was never heard from again.

Probably the most impressive Boston waterfront apparatus is the coalhandling machinery. The coal towers average 90 feet in height and are equipped with steam or electrically operated buckets. Dipped into the open hatches of the colliers, these buckets lift and dump the coal into the hopper compartment of the tower, whence it is carried by conveyor belts to storage fields or processing plants. Quite similar in structure to the towers are the coal bridges, which are also equipped with buckets. The bridges are mounted on wheels and run along a

track line, while the buckets pick up or deposit a load anywhere within the length of the bridge. A close-up view of the
coal-discharging system at the Eastern Gas and Fuel Associates
shows the most modern methods of handling coal. A steep
climb up many winding flights of dirty stairs swept by waterfront winds brings the visitor to the dizzy pinnacle of the first
coal tower, through whose windows he may look down a sheer
drop of 90 feet to the hold of a collier, where 12,000 tons of
coal are being removed from five open hatches by buckets
with wide-open jaws, which dive unceasingly into holds and
emerge dripping with 2-ton mouthfuls of coal. The load moves
swiftly skyward, then the bucket opens, and the coal roars
noisily down the hopper. In just 9 hours, all the coal is
unloaded from the collier.

Oil, the companion to coal in modern industrial uses, flows
into the Port at the rate of over 3,500,000 tons a year. It comes
to Boston in all types of craft, from the 6,000-barrel barge to
the modern tanker carrying 120,000 barrels. Crews vary in size
from 40 men to less than a dozen, and the ships travel from
as far away as Venezuela or as near as Fall River. The tanker
is "not a thing of beauty unless you see beauty in utility."
It is usually steam driven and is divided into individual tanks,
a row on the port side, another on the starboard, each cross
pair connected on the deck with a Y outlet. On most modern
tankers, there is a double wall forward and aft between pairs
of tanks to avoid mixture in case of leakage. The tankers also
have a package hold to carry lubricating oil, grease, and wax,
which are packaged at the refineries and seldom carried in
bulk. After a 9- or 10-day voyage from the Gulf, the tanker
ties up at a modern but bare-looking dock with oil tanks squat-
ting in the background. Here pipe lines are connected to the
ship's outlets, the vessel's own steam-driven pumps go to work,
and in 30 hours or less they have emptied the ship of her
cargo. It was rather fitting that in 1939 one of these modern
ships of the sea should be in a position to answer the SOS
of the most modern of passenger carriers, the flying boat. On
January 21, the tanker *Esso Baytown* was heading south from
Boston. Suddenly a distress call from the *Cavalier*, the Imperial
Airways flying boat on the New York-Bermuda run, came
through the air. Hurried calculations were made, the course
was shifted, and the world waited at the radio for progress of
the rescue. After 9 hours of skillful navigation the captain,
Frank H. Spurr, brought his ship to the spot where the 10

survivors of the crash of the *Cavalier* were floating in the water.

Although two oil companies functioned in Boston before the World War, it was from war demands that the business received an impetus that has since carried it on at an ever-expanding rate. The Jenney and Standard Oil Companies were the first to locate here. They were followed in war years by the Mexican Petroleum Corporation, now the American Oil Company, the Massachusetts Oil Refinery Company, which was taken over by Cities Service in 1923, and the Sinclair Refining Company. The Colonial Beacon Oil Company established its Everett Refinery in 1920 and was followed 9 years later by Shell and Texaco on Chelsea Creek. Tide Water Oil and Hartol, the latter dealing exclusively in fuel oil, came in 1934. The Sun Oil Company established an ocean terminal here in 1936, and the next year Gulf Oil built a depot to handle its Metropolitan Boston trade. More than half of these depots are located on the Chelsea Creek, which is known as the oil center of Boston, more than three-quarters of its tonnage being devoted to this trade. Colonial Beacon, Cities Service, American Oil, and Standard Oil bring in over 5,000,000 barrels a year and have storage capacity for over 500,000 barrels at a time. The area of oil distribution from the Boston terminals is much smaller than for the general run of incoming cargo. Because oil is shipped at less cost by water than over the road, the oil companies have established depots at the major New England ports, and Boston's outlet is limited largely to eastern and central Massachusetts.

With the exception of the Jenney Manufacturing Company, the local oil trade is handled by great, nation-wide corporations. This comparatively small company has weathered many vicissitudes and today enjoys a thriving business in eastern New England. Established in 1812, the Jenney Company has been managed by fathers and sons for three generations. Before concentrating upon gasoline, it dealt in West Indian goods, whale and sperm oil, and the manufacture of a burning fluid composed of alcohol, turpentine, and camphene. When petroleum was discovered in 1859, the Jenney factory in South Boston was converted into a refinery. Crude oil was shipped to Boston in large wooden tubs mounted on flat cars, and was lightered across the harbor to the factory. In its early years, the company prospered in the manufacture of kerosene, which sold for $2 a gallon. Twenty years ago, it became unprofitable to refine oil so far from the wells, and Jenney turned its refinery into a processing plant. In 1930, the Jenney Company found it necessary to expand its storage facilities and built on Chelsea Creek a deep-water terminal six times as large as its South Boston depot. The company owns no tankers; it buys in the open market the 2,000,000 barrels used annually and has them shipped by the seller.

Boston's domestic steamship services (*see Appendix II*) were greatly increased and strengthened during the 1930's and in 1940 ships were regularly scheduled to all the important ports of the Atlantic, Gulf, and Pacific coasts. Sailings were frequent, and both passenger lists and bills of lading showed excellent local patronage. Leaders in the West Coast services are the American President Lines, formerly the Dollar Line, which maintains only westbound sailings, and the American-Hawaiian and the Luckenbach Lines, both of which offer weekly services to California, Oregon, and Washington.

For seven decades, the Savannah Line has maintained an uninterrupted coastwise shipping service at the Port of Boston. At the present time, northbound cargo includes naval stores and general merchandise, while southbound freight consists largely of general merchandise. The route of the line is from Boston through the Cape Cod Canal and Long Island Sound to New York and thence to Savannah. The company occupies under long-term lease Pier No. 42, Hoosac Tunnel Docks in Charlestown, where passenger and freight sailings take place three times a week. In keeping with its progressive record, the management is considering a plan to operate several latest-design combination passenger and cargo ships, which would enable it to offer more attractive services. Equally progressive is the Merchants & Miners Line, which provides a tri-weekly freight and passenger service to Baltimore and Norfolk and a tri-weekly freight service between Boston and Philadelphia. Their steamships, sailing from Pier No. 2, South Boston, carry cargoes of canned goods, sugar, candy, boots and shoes, liquor and wines, potatoes, tobacco, coffee, wool, cotton, and soap.

A leader in the Boston-Gulf ports trade in the 1930's was the Mooremack Gulf Lines, Inc., owned and operated by Moore & McCormack, Inc. This line made Boston its home port and on the run to Texas ports had four freighters of the "Hog Island" type, so called after their place of construction. These ships had special refrigeration equipment and offered the only service of this kind to the Gulf region. On the outbound trip, they carried miscellaneous goods and frozen fish and, on the return voyage, brought cotton, canned goods, and citrus fruits. Moore & McCormack are agents for the Calmar Line, to West Coast ports, and have leased from the Maritime Commission the American Republics Line to South America and the American Scantic Line to Baltic ports. In the fall of 1940 insufficient revenue from freight rates caused Moore & McCormack to stop the operation of the Mooremack Gulf Lines. Still serving Gulf ports is the Pan-Atlantic Line, which added several vessels in 1940. The Lykes Coastwise Line, which sold its ships to British interests in November 1940, anticipates a resumption of service early in 1941.

Boston's position in the southern coastwise trade was strengthened in 1932 by the entrance of a new steamship line and improvements in the services of another line. The Morgan Line began to operate a weekly freight service between Boston and New Orleans and Boston, Galveston, and Houston, and offered a combined freight and passenger sailing to New Orleans every 3 weeks. Until December 1940, when revenue returns forced cancellation of the service, the Morgan Line's 5,000-ton freighters brought large shipments of wool, cotton, and hides to Boston from the Gulf ports, while the bulk of the freight moving south consisted of New England manufactures, paper, rubber products, boots and shoes. Occasionally in the early 1930's the Clyde Steamship Company listed bi-weekly sailings from Boston to Charleston and Jacksonville, although the company always returned to its weekly schedule. Shortly after the merger of the Clyde and Mallory Lines in 1932, the Boston service was extensively improved and modernized. The line's northbound movement of freight consisted of lumber, naval stores, citrus fruits, canned goods, potatoes, cotton, piece-goods, and wool, while south-bound cargo consisted largely of general freight, canned goods, and potatoes. It was not unusual for a Clyde-Mallory steamship to unload potatoes and cotton textiles at Boston and then reload other consignments of the same commodities for the Carolinas, Florida, or Texas. Finding freight rates too low for adequate profit, the line announced that after December 26, 1940, it would omit Boston as a port-of-call. A technicality requiring a 30-day notice for cancellation of services, which was pointed out by an examiner for the United States Maritime Commission, caused the company to extend its sailing schedule to January 9, 1941.

The abandonment of these several services—the Mooremack

Gulf Lines, the Morgan Line, and the Clyde-Mallory Line—was caused by revenue factors quite unconnected with local port conditions. It has brought forth emphatic protest from shippers and port organizations both in Boston and in southern ports. Under the leadership of the Boston Port Authority and the Maritime Association of the Boston Chamber of Commerce, appeals have been carried to the United States Maritime Commission and the Interstate Commerce Commission. The Maritime Commission, lacking authority to restore services, did indicate its willingness to lease to private operators several of its ships for operation on the abandoned routes. The Interstate Commerce Commission, also at present without authority to intervene, will in February 1941 assume jurisdiction over coastal shipping rates. It is hoped that it will then so increase the rates on the affected routes as to make operation profitable. The steamship companies operating coastwise services could, of course, make such governmental action unnecessary by themselves resorting to an increase in charges in preference to discontinuing useful and potentially profitable services.

Only seven of Boston's steamship companies are still locally controlled, a far cry indeed from pre-steamer days. One of these, the United Fruit Company, operates regular year-round freight and passenger service to its own plantations in the Caribbean region. The Eastern Steamship Lines, Inc., is the only other locally owned company offering year-round passenger and freight service. The Boston-New York Line, which is maintained on a daily schedule, is the sole survivor of the four domestic lines this company formerly operated out of Boston. The growth of automobile and truck traffic forced the discontinuance of the Down-East lines: the Boston-Portland, Boston-Kennebec, and the Bangor. The company has had excellent results with its coastal runs to the Maritime Provinces, on which it operates the modern *St. John, Acadia, Evangeline,* and *Yarmouth.* Three concerns, the Mystic Steamship Company, the Pocahontas Fuel Company, and the Sprague Steamship Company, own a large number of coal boats. The Boston-Nantasket Steamboat Company and the Cape Cod Steamship Company offer summer services to local ports.

Some of the pioneering spirit of the past was briefly revived when three enterprising young men organized the Seaboard Navigation Company in 1937. They ran two shallow-draft freighters, the *Penobscot* and the *Kennebec* from Boston to Bucksport, Maine. There they loaded potatoes for the Middle Atlantic ports and then brought back canned goods to Boston. In the summer months the ships sailed every fortnight to Eastport to bring back newly tinned sardines. Mounting deficits due to lack of sufficient freight revenue, coupled with the refusal of local unionized longshoremen to handle their cargo loaded at nonunion ports, caused the company to cancel operations in 1939.

Foreign Trade

The decline in Boston's foreign trade, still a matter of deep concern, had by 1915 apparently been arrested. The situation remained far from satisfactory, and worse with regard to exports than imports. Boston's exports dropped steadily since the World War to $36,000,000 in 1930 and dwindled to $16,000,000 when the full effect of the depression was felt in 1932. Since then, there has been a favorable trend, although the figure has yet to pass the $30,000,000 mark. The import trade is in a much stronger position, after having dropped in 1932 to less than half of the 1930 figure of $187,000,000. A rapid recovery has ensued, and the total was higher in 1939 than in 1930. The reasons for the discrepancy between imports and exports, which is revealed by both dollar and tonnage figures, are many and complex. Important among them is the fact that the importation of large quantities of raw materials is essential to the industries of Boston and the surrounding area. The manufactured articles wrought from these materials are comparatively small in bulk, and the rate situation under which the Port continues to labor makes it impossible under existing conditions to obtain adequate bulk export cargoes. The Port consequently lists heavily under unbalanced freight.

This situation was emphasized before the United States Maritime Commission when it made a visit to Boston in 1938. At the 2-day hearing at the Federal Building, leading maritime and shipping as well as civic and business interests joined with the Port Authority in setting forth the needs of the Port. Among the proponents were Richard Parkhurst, Vice Chairman, John F. Fitzgerald, member, and Captain George P. Lord, Marine Supervisor of the Port Authority, John B. Leonard, member of Governor Hurley's Commission-to-Study-the-Port-of-Boston, and Frank S. Davis, manager of the Maritime

Association of the Boston Chamber of Commerce. These Boston leaders were unanimous in urging the Maritime Commission to place the Port of Boston on a parity, or at least on a competitive basis, with other Atlantic ports. According to the local authorities, a joint revamping of rates could be accomplished by the Maritime Commission in conjunction with the Interstate Commerce Commission, and the results would go far toward putting Boston again on the map as a great exporting center.

Incoming products originate in 73 countries and political divisions scattered all over the world. Vast quantities of foodstuffs arrive from Columbia, Honduras, Cuba, Brazil, and the Argentine. Large amounts of Australian wool help to make Boston a leading wool center. The largest single shipment of this product ever received in Boston came in 1937, when 31,000 bales were unloaded at Commonwealth Pier No. 5. Imports of cotton arrive from Egypt, hides and skins from South America, and jute and hemp from the Philippines and India. In recent years, Boston's export tonnage has been greatly helped by the heavy movement of scrap iron to Italy, Japan, Great Britain, and Rumania. Although this particular type of export is of doubtful permanence, iron and steel and their manufactures made up more than half of Boston's export tonnage during 1938 and 1939, followed by paper and paper stock, sugar, footwear, and rubber products.

Present-day ships carry notably diverse products in and out of Boston. Not unusual was the voyage in May 1939, of the *Hokuroku Maru* of the Osaka Shoshen Kaisha Line, which left Japan, picked up cargo at the Philippines, discharged part of her cargo at Los Angeles, and then unloaded the remainder of her Japanese products at New York and Boston. Here the ship took on asbestos and machinery, and then returned to Japan by way of the Panama Canal. On the other side of the world, the *Kota Agoeng* departed from Rotterdam for Java, loaded cargoes at the principal Javanese and Sumatra cities, stopped at Singapore and Penang, and then headed for North Atlantic ports via the Cape of Good Hope. Her second port-of-call was Boston, where she discharged such varied items as tapioca, flour, rubber, latex, palm oil, coffee, and tea. Here she packed into her hold general cargo and hundreds of bales of old newspapers, which are of great value in the Far East, being used to protect the tender sprouts of tea plants and to

serve for wrapping-paper in Chinese stores. Many native huts
are papered with brilliantly hued pages from the Boston Sunday comics.

Boston's position as the gateway to an industrial area has
led to a heavy trade in certain raw materials. The paper, wall-
board, rayon, and box factories necessitate the importation of
wood pulp and other cellulose products, which average over
7 percent of the total imports of the Port. They come in trim
little steamers from Sweden or in a motley collection of schooners, rusty tramps, and modern steamers from Canada, Norway,
and Finland. Four steamers of the Gypsum Packet Company
bring gypsum, lumber, pulpwood, and wood pulp from Windsor, Nova Scotia. These ships, the *Gypsum Empress,* the
Gypsum Prince, the *Gypsum King,* and the *Gypsum Queen,*
make about 15 voyages annually, beginning in April when the
ice goes out of Windsor Bay.

The importation of wool, long considered a barometer of
the Port's business, has been considerably higher than a year
ago. During the last 3 weeks in December 1939, over 16,000,000
pounds of foreign wool entered the Port, and one of the largest
quantities ever brought in in a single week, 7,613,483 pounds,
was unloaded the week ending February 10, 1940. Between
July 1, 1939, and June 30, 1940, wool imports totaled over
134,591,000 pounds, more than twice the amount of the preceding year. Much of this wool came from South American
and South African ports. At the same time there has been an
increase in the export of manufactured woolen goods. This
activity in the wool trade can probably be attributed to the
domestic demand for woolen textiles brought about by the
lessening of woolen textile imports from England because of
war conditions.

Imports of vegetable oil and rubber are becoming increasingly important to the Port of Boston. Most of the palm oil
comes from Africa, while cocoanut oil is brought from the
East Indies by ships flying the flags of many nations. A further
extension of this trade is anticipated as a result of the opening
of a new soap manufacturing plant on Town River, Quincy,
in June 1940. A comparatively recent method of treating
rubber with ammonia, so that it can be transported in a liquid
state, has proved a definite boon to the Port in the importation of this product, which comes from Singapore, Calcutta,
and Malacca aboard American, Dutch, and British ships. At
the Army Base, eight tanks were installed in 1938, complete

with pumps and hose that can rapidly unload the liquid rubber.

The outbreak of war in Europe in September 1939, with the resultant blockades of sea lanes, had immediate effects upon the shipping services of all countries engaged in trade with the belligerents, England, France, and Germany. The United States took the drastic step of forbidding her ships to enter the war zone. Boston services to United Kingdom, North Sea, and Baltic ports (*see Appendix II*), which formed one of her strongest trade routes, were immediately disrupted. The United States Lines, which operated to English ports on fortnightly sailings, and other American flag lines could no longer traverse their routes. The German-operated Hamburg-American and North German Lloyd Lines, which connected this port with Hamburg and Bremen for about half a century, were stopped by orders of the German Government because of the British blockade. The French Line discontinued its summer passenger service, and the Cunard Line substituted for its frequent freight and passenger calls a carefully concealed movement of shipping maintained primarily for war purposes. For several months Scandinavian, Danish, and Belgian ships attempted to carry on trade, subject always to the imposition of strict British contraband control, but the invasion of their countries by Germany early in 1940 caused a further breakdown of their schedules.

At least a score of steamship lines bring freight to Boston from Far Eastern ports. The American & Indian, American-Manchurian, American President, Java-New York, Bank, Prince, and Silver Lines are among those frequently bringing rubber, peat, goatskins, pig iron, wool, jute, burlap, tea, tapioca, rattans, sisal, cocoanut oil, and coffee. Every month the Osaka Shoshen Kaisha Line sends two ships laden with tea, coffee, china, canned goods, toys, rubber, silk, and frozen fish. In 1931, the Kokusai Line inaugurated a service between Boston, Kobe, Osaka, and Yokohama. Boston is the last port-of-call on the American President Lines round-the-world schedule, and receives on its ships large consignments of wool, skins, rubber, tea, bamboo, and hemp from the Far East and Mediterranean ports.

Until Italy entered the war in June 1940, and the Mediterranean Sea was included in the belligerent zone, Boston had more direct connections with the Mediterranean areas than it had with Far Eastern ports. On this route, the American

Export Lines supplied frequent direct import services, although it operated only an indirect export service through New York. American Export also served the Levant and Black Sea ports. The expansion of the war area also stopped the passenger and freight services of the Italian Line and the import services offered by the American President Lines from Mediterranean ports.

Several local shipping agencies represent a large number of the steamship lines which make Boston a port-of-call. Peabody & Lane, Inc., are agents for such important services as the America-France Line, the Black Diamond Lines, and the Wilhelmsen Line. Patterson, Wylde & Company handle the freight of the Holland-America and Italian Lines and act as agent for the Bank Line, Barber-Wilhelmsen Line, Blue Funnel Line, Canadian National Steamship Line, the Italian Line, Java-New York Line, and the Nippon (N.Y.K.) Line to Far Eastern ports. Norton, Lilly and Company, established in 1840, represents, among others, the Isthmian Line, the Essco-Brodin Line, the American & Indian Line, the Ellerman & Bucknall Line, and the M.A.N.Z. Line. Another important agency, A. C. Lombard's Sons, was established in 1825, and handles the trade of the Scandinavian-American and Kokusai Lines

At the present time the Furness Withy & Company, Ltd., are agents for the Prince and Silver Lines' round-the-world service. Both lines bring cocoanut oil, hemp, and fiber from the Philippines, rattan and rubber from Singapore and the Straits Settlements, and cinnamon, tapioca, flour, tea, and crepe rubber from Ceylon. The company also acts as agent for the freight service of the French Line, and for the Trans-atlantic-Swedish-American-Mexico and Clay Lines. The latter line brings cargoes of China clay from Fowey, England, and sometimes discharges wood pulp, cellulose, paper, steel, wire, and granite.

The old Boston firm of John G. Hall, established in 1847, was incorporated in 1925. It acts as agent for the Hamburg-American and the North German Lloyd Lines, the Osaka Shoshen Kaisha Line, and the American West African and the Elder Dempster Lines, which bring cocoa beans, palm oil, rubber, and piassava from Africa.

Boston has maintained its position as second passenger port in the United States. In 1937, passenger business on trans-Atlantic, West Indian, and Canadian runs increased almost 7 percent over the year before, and 73,000 travelers passed through the Port. Boston has made a determined bid for passenger traffic and its efforts have been rewarded by having passenger services of the Italian and Cunard Lines increased during the summer tourist season. French and Dutch passenger ships also made regular summer calls. The lack of outbound services has had an effect on passenger traffic similar to that on freight. Passenger arrivals continue to be heavier than departures.

The world situation created by the war is still in too nebulous a stage to be treated fully and accurately, but the changes which have taken place up to December 1940, and the trends which those changes indicate are portentous. Ships of belligerent nations and ships bound for belligerent ports keep their movements secret. The trade is still strong, however, and along with expansion in other trade routes, especially South American, indicates an increase at Boston in 1939 of about 40 percent in imports over the figures of 1938. Exports also have increased about 10 percent. Weekly imports figures continue to show that Boston is holding its own as the second importing port of the United States.

CHAPTER X

THE PORT ATTACKS ITS PROBLEMS

A Resolute Port

THE PORT OF BOSTON, in the total value of the commerce passing through it, ranks seventh (1938) among the seaports of the United States. Its harbor of 30,000 acres and 30 miles of berthing space accommodates some 2,700 ships a year. On those ships travel the 220,000 passengers a year who make Boston the second passenger port in the country, and the $200,000,000 worth of incoming foreign goods which rank it as also the second United States port in value of imports.

Deep channels, capable of receiving the largest liners afloat, lead to the busy waterfront terminals. There, engines pull the loaded freight cars off the docks and send them over the rails to the South, West, and North. Long lines of heavy trucks haul away loads of merchandise coming from the corners of the earth. On the eastern edge of the harbor, a modern airport and seaplane base gives the trans-Atlantic passengers quick access to interior points. Numerous shipyards launch new vessels of all kinds, from fishing trawlers to airplane carriers. At the Boston Fish Pier, the largest fish pier in the Western Hemisphere, catches valued at from $7,000,000 to $8,000,000 are handled annually.

Boston is, of course, still the principal port of New England. It serves the greatest wool market in the United States and receives more than one-third of all the raw wool imported into this country. The territory tributary to the Port includes the leading shoe and leather center in the world, the second largest cotton-manufacturing area in the Western Hemisphere, the leading center for high-grade American coffee, one of the three great rubber-manufacturing centers, and the third-largest center in the United States for wholesale trade. Of goods manufactured in New England and exported through New England ports, 57 percent flows through the Port of Boston.

Since the building of the railroads and the passing of the sailing ship as an important freight carrier, Boston has had to fight incessantly to maintain its proper position as a port. It has had to combat unfavorable railroad differentials, it has seen New England's own railroads financially controlled by outside interests, it has struggled to offset in some way the free, or almost free, services at the Port of New York. For a number of years, various port officials, shippers, and steamship agents have been convinced that, if Boston is to remain a leading port, local trade must be increased. The awakening of the New England people to take a more active interest in the affairs of the Port, a revival of the proud spirit of the clipper-ship days, would be of the greatest importance in encouraging local manufacturers to use Boston as their import and export center.

Various organizations have been developed to attract business from foreign and inland points and to stimulate greater maritime activity. The Maritime Association of the Boston Chamber of Commerce has been instrumental since its establishment in 1920 in promoting the well-being of the Port. It seeks to increase commerce through advertising the facilities of the Port, and in general to advance the maritime interests of the city. This agency has aided in harbor development, the attraction of new industry, and the investigation of foreign trade possibilities. The association publishes annually a book on rates, rules, regulations, and practices at the Port.

Working constantly in the interests of the Port, the Foreign Commerce Club of Boston is performing a signal service to the community. The club was formed in the fall of 1928, when the Port of Boston Boosters banded themselves together, and took its present name in 1929. Today its membership of more than 250 individuals participate in activities beneficial to Boston's foreign commerce.

The Propeller Club of the United States Port of Boston, Inc., is another organization working for the furtherance and protection of local maritime interests. Organized in 1927, its 175 active members include pilots, ship officers, steamship agents, ship brokers, railroad agents, members of the Boston banks' foreign departments, as well as warehousemen, truckmen, and others whose business contributes to port activity. The objectives of the club are to promote a greater merchant marine, to aid in worthy and justifiable harbor improvements, and to develop fellowship among shipping men. The activities of the club center about its monthly dinner meetings. Each year the organization awards long voyages for the best essays written about our shipping industry by high school students; 17 steamship companies offered prize trips in 1939.

The most active and influential port organization is the Boston Port Authority, which has shown gratifying results for its labors. In its 1938 report the Authority says:

> There is no one thing that the Port Authority can do or that the State or City government can do, which in itself will throw off immediately the Port's rate burden imposed upon it over the years by various means and for various reasons. There are, on the other hand, a number of things which can be and are being done, all directed toward the goal of establishing a fair competitive rate basis for the Port. Many are complex and interrelated. Time to pursue them thoroughly is required, and continuity of policy in that pursuit is of even more importance. The Board has the satisfaction, perhaps rare in public organizations, that in its efforts for the past ten years to help the Port and the port constituency, it has deviated in no important particular from the policies it originally established, based on the needs of the Port as it has believed them to be.

With a small staff of efficient workers it has tackled the problem of putting Boston on an equal basis with other North Atlantic ports in the matter of rates and terminal charges. It has labored to remove such artificial handicaps as discriminatory railroad practices at New York and other ports. It is constantly at work to improve shipping services and to interest shippers in the use of the Port. The Authority "firmly believes that the Port will be built up by its being made increasingly attractive to private business, rather than by additional administrative control, management or operation by the Commonwealth or by the City."

Organizations like the Maritime Association and the Port Authority are working intelligently and effectively to advance the interests of the Port. Although Boston is obliged to recognize New York's position as ranking port of the United States, it affirms that the metropolis of New England is entitled to an important place in the country's maritime affairs. Through these active agencies Boston manifests her will to continue as a major port.

More Ships Wanted

One of Boston's chief problems is the lack of ships, especially of American flag lines, to carry her export and import cargoes. Because of the inability of American steamship companies to establish services to meet Boston's shipping needs, the Boston Port Authority has been obliged to make overtures to foreign flag lines. The use of foreign ships, aside from failing to satisfy the natural desire to use our own ships, has the grave disadvantage that in time of war most of the foreign vessels are withdrawn, leaving Boston without adequate shipping facilities. Of the 54 active steamship lines engaged in foreign trade in the summer of 1939, only 17 were American. The lines, which are listed in Appendix II, offered on various trade routes 77 import services and 54 export services, of which about a third were covered by American ships. While most of the important trade routes were served by several lines, a majority of them were indirect, that is, the ships called at other American ports before or after visiting Boston. The resultant delay in the delivery or pick up of cargo at Boston tended to divert cargoes, especially exports, from this port to New York where more speedy handling was assured.

Improvement of the Port of Boston's steamship services in the foreign trade has been a major objective of the Boston Port Authority. The Authority specifically recommended in 1938-39: (1) that several additional ships be allocated to the American Scantic Line for service in the Baltic region; (2) that more ships be used in the import service from Africa and that at least one monthly sailing from Boston to that continent be established; (3) that the American Hampton Roads Line, which now has fortnightly sailings for London, Hull, Leigh, and Dundee, be divided into two divisions, a northern to serve Portland, Boston, and New York by continuing the present fortnightly sailings; and a southern division to serve Philadelphia, Baltimore, and Norfolk. Under present arrangements, Boston cargo often is left on the docks, because the ships are filled to capacity before calling here.

The Port Authority recommended also: (4) that additional ships be allocated to the United States Lines for service on the route to Liverpool and Manchester, England, in order that an outbound call might be made at Boston, or else that the defunct Oriole Line, for service to the same ports, be revived; (5) that further curtailment of the sailings of the Black Diamond Lines to northern European ports, which were then available only every 21 days, should be prevented, and a faster and more frequent service be encouraged; (6) that Boston and other northern ports encourage American flag line service to certain Mediterranean ports; (7) that ship service be established between Boston and the west coast of South America, and faster and better ships be placed in the service to and from the east coast; (8) that an export service from Boston to Puerto Rico be established; and (9) that there be established an American line, in addition to that of the United Fruit Company, on import service from Colombian ports and from Trinidad.

Improvements in services to Europe were in progress when the outbreak of war between England and France and Germany, in September 1939, and the subsequent application of the Neutrality Act by the United States Congress disrupted all American trade to belligerent waters. The United States Lines had taken over the American Hampton Roads and the Oriole Lines, but the barring of American ships from the war zone prevents any judgment upon the results of this move. The Black Diamond Lines have maintained their services, through the use of foreign flag ships chartered to replace the Black Diamond steamers now scattered all over the world on other trade routes. South American commerce has been advanced by the addition of faster and better ships than were formerly operated on these routes. Moore-McCormack added to its American Republics Line early in 1940 several new ships of the C-2 class, built by the United States Maritime Commission. Two of these, the *Mormacpen* and the *Mormacyork*, displace 17,600 tons, are 492 feet long, and average 18 knots. Their speed enables them to cut down the running time from Buenos Aires to Boston from 30 to 18 days and, consequently, to provide a fortnightly service between these ports.

Additional steamship services of this type will attract more export cargo and improve Boston's standing as a shipping port. Where the element of time is important, shipments often are made on the basis of specially quick service. Undoubtedly the frequency and multiplicity of its steamship services is one of the largest factors in diverting shipments to New York, and probably explains in great part why something like 65 percent (valuation) of New England's manufactured goods intended for export move through New York and only about 14 percent (valuation) through Boston. It helps to explain also why Boston's export business as a whole declined from about 1,300,000 tons in 1905 to about 321,400 tons in 1938, or to approximately one percent of United States exports.

The diversion of a large amount of bulk goods from Boston to New York, with consequent inroads on ship services, has resulted from New York's connections with the New York State Barge Canal System. The Barge Canal, the rejuvenated Erie Canal, connects New York Harbor by way of the Hudson River with Lake Erie; an offshoot of the Barge Canal, the

Oswego Canal, connects with Lake Ontario. The Champlain Canal links the Hudson near Troy with Lake Champlain. Thus New York City achieves all-water routes to Lake Erie and Lake Ontario and to northern New York State and Canada. Over these inland waterways, in 1937, were carried no less than 5,000,000 tons of cargo. From the West came grain, chemicals, drugs, and mineral ores; from other parts of the country to New York City came petroleum and petroleum products, sulphur, sugar, scrap iron, fertilizers, and farm and forest products. Large quantities of those commodities were shipped abroad through the Port of New York. If Boston had enjoyed a more independent and aggressive railroad policy and better steamship services, much of that merchandise might have been shipped through the Port of Boston.

A majority of the men actively interested in the Port see in the proposed St. Lawrence Waterway a threat to increases in Boston's steamship services through development of other means of exporting Midwestern products. The waterway project involves the construction of a 30-foot channel from Montreal to Duluth and Chicago, at a cost variously estimated at from $600,000,000 to $8,00,000,000. The primary purpose of the American advocates of the project is to provide a direct, low-cost, water route from our Middle West to the St. Lawrence River and thence to Europe. Owing to the configuration of the North American Continent, the mouth of the St. Lawrence is nearer Europe than is any seaport in the United States. Whether the proposed waterway is to be thought of as a good thing for the United States as a whole depends in part on its efficacy as a national defense measure; it has also to be determined whether our Middle West, through the proposed waterway, can increase United States foreign commerce beyond the volume obtainable without the use of the waterway. From the point of view of the Port of Boston, the proposed waterway would divert traffic between the Middle West and Europe from Boston, as well as from other American Atlantic ports, to Canadian ports, or else provide a through route from the Middle West to Europe without stopping at any ports east of the Great Lakes. Construction of the proposed St. Lawrence Waterway probably would further impede Boston's prospects of increasing her shipments of the products of our Middle West and serving as a port of entry for that territory.

The trade agreements which the United States recently has

signed with foreign countries, particularly with Canada and the United Kingdom, may help the Port of Boston and lead to increased steamship services. The Canadian agreement of 1936, revised in 1939, made it possible to enter non-British Empire products through Boston to Canada under conditions as favorable as if they had been imported through a Canadian port. Increased shipments of Canadian wheat, practically the only grain exported through the Port in recent years, is anticipated because of treaty provisions allowing the grain to enter United Kingdom ports without being assessed a heavy duty. Concessions on New England manufactured products and certain British goods also indicate possibilities of increased freight movements at Boston. Trade agreements with other countries, especially with those of South America, should also stimulate Boston's exports and imports. Any benefits from this source would make Boston's demands for better American flag services much stronger.

The Ocean-Rail Rate Fight

Accounting in large part for the inadequacy of Boston's shipping services is the railroad and steamship freight rate situation, the principles of which were discussed in Chapter VII. The Port Authority has stated the problem in its *Annual Report* for 1937:

> The Port can never be fully utilized until we are in a position to offer competitive through rates, *i.e.*, rail and ocean, by which goods from and to other than New England points are regularly attracted to it. By every port with which we compete, these through rates to the interior of the country are lower than the ones we have.

Since 1920 the situation has remained much the same, with Boston unable to take advantage of its shorter ocean route to Europe. The Port Authority, in its struggle to obtain more favorable rates for Boston, has closely watched rate cases in other parts of the country and has attempted to derive from them certain principles which might be applied to Boston.

The United States Supreme Court in 1933, in the case of the *Texas & Pacific Railway Company v. United States,* in respect to identical ocean rates, made a ruling which in theory could apply also to all North Atlantic ports. The Court said:

> The choice of route is determined solely by the rail rates from and to the ports. If these are equalized, the shipper has an option; but if they are disparate, the route through the port taking the higher rate is necessarily excluded.

Along the same lines, the Interstate Commerce Commission said in 1935, in the case of *Export and Import Rates from and to Gulf Ports:*

As all disparities in the rail rates to and from the different ports are reflected in the through rates to and from points beyond the ports, it necessarily follows that the choice of route is influenced by the rail rates to and from the ports. If these are equalized, consideration other than the rate will determine the route, but if they are different, the route through the port taking the higher rate is necessarily at a disadvantage.

The Boston Port Authority repeatedly has declared that import-export through rates should be the same for all ports on a given range, "for instance in our own case the North Atlantic range, which covers ports from Montreal to Norfolk."

Today, Boston's position may be briefly stated as follows: (1) export rail rates from the great central area of the country, where large amounts of bulk cargo originate, are lower by way of Baltimore, Norfolk, Philadelphia, and Montreal, than by way of Boston; import rates to the same territory are lower by way of Baltimore, Norfolk, Philadelphia, Portland, Montreal, St. John, and Halifax than by way of Boston; (2) import-export rail rates to and from the Central Freight Association territory, which is that part of the United States west of the Buffalo-Pittsburgh line, north of the Ohio River, and east of the Mississippi River, and even to and from many points in New England, are theoretically the same by way of New York as by way of Boston, but this parity is destroyed through free lighterage and allowances of one kind or another made by rail carriers at New York but not at Boston.

The principal competitors of Boston as a port are New York, Philadelphia, and Baltimore. In the cases of Philadelphia and Baltimore, as stated previously, there exist in their favor railroad differential rates which make it difficult for Boston to get the share of the export-import business to which it is entitled by virtue of its location and facilities.

This situation is all the more irritating because rate parity does exist on traffic moving through South Atlantic, Gulf, and Pacific ports. The Interstate Commerce Commission alleges that it has no power to apply the same measures to North Atlantic ports. The railroads serving those ports can exercise their rights of managerial discretion and bring about such a change. Since the trunk line railroads are apparently satisfied with the present rate adjustment, there is little hope that Boston can achieve a remedy through the Commission.

Attempts have also been made to obtain relief through Congressional enactment. In 1925, the Butler Bill, providing in effect for equalized through rates on the entire Atlantic seaboard, was introduced into Congress. Subsequently, however, it was withdrawn, lest the opposition it aroused place Boston in an even worse predicament. Despite that withdrawal, many champions of the Port of Boston still believe that some such legislation is the only effective solution of Boston's rate problem.

On some domestic goods passing through the Port of Boston, rate equality has been fairly well established. In 1934, the Interstate Commerce Commission, in connection with certain water lines operating regularly from the Gulf of Mexico to Boston, prescribed joint water-rail rates on cotton destined for Canada. Those rates made possible actual competition between rival routes. Again, in 1938, rates on cotton from the Gulf through Boston to up-state New York mill points found a parity with rates via New York. The Coastal Steamship Conference made good adjustments on joint rail and water rates, for rice coming north and potatoes moving south through Boston. The volume of water-borne commerce moving through Boston was increased in another case, when a permit was granted to the Ocean Steamship Company of Savannah to carry certain imports from New York via Boston, on their way to western destinations, at a favorable differential under the all-rail rates from New York. This ruling resulted in increased business for the Port. Such rate revisions are encouraging to port authorities and shippers who are working for the application of these principles on a broader basis, to cover all import-export commerce as well as domestic freight.

The Struggle for Port Equality

If Boston is to receive its share of the North Atlantic export-import business, it must achieve port equality with other North Atlantic ports not only in railroad and steamship transportation rates but in other charges for accessorial services, such as lighterage, dockage and wharfage, insurance, trucking, and storage. The Port of New York has virtually nullified the effect of equal ocean and rail rates with Boston through offering to shippers a number of these services free or below cost.

Interference with equality of rates may take any one or more of the following forms: permission for more than 10 days' free time on import traffic at New York piers; less than cost warehouse service in the New York Harbor area; free lighterage, trucking in place of lighterage, and insurance at less than cost. These and other sharp practices have deprived Boston of much water-borne commerce to which rightfully her Port is entitled, including a large tonnage from New England itself. The Interstate Commerce Commission and the United States Maritime Commission have heard a series of formal rate cases in which charges of discrimination have been alleged by complainants.

The Port of New York has developed an elaborate system of lighterage, or transport of goods by lighter or barge between ship and harbor-front rail terminals. At New York, it includes a "choice of deliveries through steamship piers, through railroads and through so-called contract terminals." Free lighterage, though expensive to the railroads, is a strong asset from the point of view of competition. In July 1934, the Interstate Commerce Commission, by a seven to three decision, dismissed a complaint filed by Boston in connection with the New Jersey Lighterage Case. Boston alleged that the practice of the railroads in performing lighterage free at New York while no such service was necessary at Boston, where transfer is made directly at the dock between ship and railroad car, was unduly preferential to New York and unjustly discriminatory against Boston. Boston contended that the difference in such terminal costs should be reflected in lower freight rates to and from Boston. The verdict was a severe blow to the Port of Boston, which is intervening in another New Jersey case of the same general character.

Boston is placed in an unfavorable competitive position also through "services and allowances in lieu of lighterage," including allowances to stevedores for off-side loadings, and below-cost trucking, storage, and handling charges. For example, vegetable oil was coming through New York in great quantities partly because of the excessive allowance given by rail carriers for flotage in tank barges. This concession more than offset Boston's admittedly more efficient services in offering direct unloading of vegetable oil from steamer to tank cars. An investigation by the Interstate Commerce Commission in 1934 resulted in reduced allowances at New York, so that Boston's position became slightly more favorable. Subsequent inquiry, however, revealed that this Port in 1939 still was handling no more than a small percentage of such oil for other than local use.

Another cause for irritation between the ports of Boston and New York has been less-than-cost warehousing, in the practice of which railroads at New York have absorbed part of the warehousing costs usually charged to the owner or shipper of goods. China clay and crude rubber, cargoes on the North Atlantic import list which are both valuable and heavy, and also European and Canadian wood pulp were being excluded from Boston because of trunk line railroad non-compensatory warehousing at the Port of New York. In 1935, there was a readjustment in the storage rates and practices with respect to China clay and wood pulp at New York which enabled Boston to compete successfully, but nothing was done in regard to crude rubber until April 1939.

In 1933, the Interstate Commerce Commission, in the New York Harbor Warehouse Case, condemned the practice of granting shippers non-compensatory warehousing and storage by railroads serving the Port of New York. The Commission declared that such a practice was discriminatory against the Port of Boston. On January 3, 1939, the United States Supreme Court sustained the findings of the Interstate Commerce Commission. It is too soon yet to know how large the increase in shipments of crude rubber will be at Boston, but after 6 years of litigation, Boston's competitive position has been considerably improved.

Meanwhile the issue of non-compensatory storage at New York arose from another angle. In 1934, Boston, Norfolk, Baltimore, and Philadelphia filed a complaint with the United States Shipping Board alleging that steamship companies were granting to shippers at New York less-than-cost storage, which resulted in discrimination against the other North Atlantic ports. Out of this complaint grew the Pier Storage Case, an investigation instituted by the Shipping Board. At the hearings it was revealed that large shippers in particular were granted free storage at New York for excessive periods of time, while no such concessions were made by the steamship companies at other ports. Not until 1937 was an examiner's report released on the case, and shortly afterwards the United States Maritime Commission, which replaced the Shipping Board, rendered a final decision favorable to the complainants. Water carriers serving the Port of New York no longer could grant more than 10 days' free storage on import traffic. Exception was sought by certain carriers with respect to coffee, and the examiner's report proposed to grant such exception. Boston contended, however, that if one exception were permitted it would lead to a general breakdown of the ruling and that the requirements of the coffee trade did not call for a longer storage period than 10 days. The Commission finally decided against the exception, and that decision was sustained by the courts.

For the past 3 years, the Boston Port Authority has urged the New England Freight Association to grant to New England railroads the privilege of offering storage-in-transit on water-borne freight moving west by rail from the Port of Boston on a rate basis similar to that applicable on such traffic at New York. This meant that either the transit charge at Boston of $6.93 a car should be eliminated or that this charge should be assessed at New York, where there was no transit charge. Approval of the Traffic Executives Association, Eastern Territory, was finally obtained in July 1940, and the charge was abolished at Boston, thus placing the Port in a position favorable to competing ports for this class of traffic.

Most attempts to correct discriminatory rates and charges have bogged down in the face of the marked lack of railroad cooperation. All three principal railroads serving New England are under the domination of trunk lines whose interests are centered elsewhere than in Boston. The Pennsylvania Railroad and its affiliate, the Pennroad Corporation, own enough stock to control the New York, New Haven & Hartford Railroad. The latter road, in turn, owns a controlling interest in the Boston & Maine, thereby insuring the Pennsylvania's control over that line also. The lease of the Boston & Albany Railroad to the New York Central Railroad Company completes the control of outside trunk lines over Boston's railroad services. An illustration of how this "alien domination" works out in practice is afforded by the Boston & Albany Railroad. The lease of that road to the New York Central Railroad provides, in substance, that rail charges to Boston shall not be greater than to New York on export traffic and that rail charges from Boston shall not be greater than from New York on import traffic. The New York Central, as well as other New York rail carriers, however, has granted to shippers through the Port of New York such valuable inducements as low warehouse rates and free lighterage, absorbing all or part of the cost of such services in the freight rates.

A campaign now is being waged to break up the trunk line control of at least two of New England's railroads, the Boston

& Maine and the New York, New Haven & Hartford. The opportunity may be favorable, as the New Haven, which controls the Boston & Maine, is in process of reorganization. In direct opposition to the aims of local interests is the plan of the Pennroad Corporation, which would result in the merger of the Boston & Maine and the New Haven under the control, direct or indirect, of the Pennsylvania Railroad Company. This proposal conflicts with the ultimate goal, as expressed by the Boston Port Authority, of having each New England railroad "establish such relations of its own with lines west of the Hudson as to leave no question of Boston's having access to the interior of the country under terms and conditions satisfactory to all concerned."

If port equality is to be attained, each port must be able to count on the business to and from its own immediate territory, and also must have an opportunity to compete on equal terms with other ports for the cargo of the hinterland. In the case of Boston, this means a parity of rates and incidental charges on shipments through Boston, as compared with other routes, from points in New England and from the Central Freight Association territory. Heretofore Boston has been the only North Atlantic port deprived of truly equalized rates to and from the central territory.

The fight for port equality, independence of New England rail lines, and non-discriminatory terminal practices goes forward slowly but persistently. Much of the difficulty would be removed if the railroads serving the Port were able to dictate their own policies. Assuming the ultimate independence of the New England lines, they must still face the problem of establishing satisfactory relations with rail carriers west of the Hudson. From central territory, Boston must have its share of traffic to build up its export business. Nor must the increased use of the Port of Albany, right in New England's backyard, be forgotten—Albany which enjoys equal ocean rates with Boston and other North Atlantic ports, but whose rail rates from the West are more favorable than those of Boston.

The Port of Boston still has ahead of it a serious struggle. In law courts, before Government commissions, in steamship conferences, and in State legislatures, friends of the Port are arguing their cases. The problems to be solved are many and complicated. Steamship services require adjustment and amplification, railroad freight rates on most commodities are out of line and railroad services need expansion, port charges call for greater uniformity, and local port facilities should be improved. Boston has many natural advantages that should be utilized to the fullest extent possible. The removal of artificial obstacles is imperative.

Local Terminal Charges

Seriously impeding plans to improve Boston's position as a world port is the diversified ownership of harbor property. Unlike such ports as San Francisco, Montreal, and Newport News, the Port of Boston never has been under the dominating control of any one interest. Yet it has been obliged to compete with ports which were either publicly owned and controlled or subsidized. The Boston Port Authority, though lacking power to force changes in port management, has brought about many improvements; many more should be effected.

The diversified ownership of waterfront property is reflected in the utter confusion of wharfage and dockage rates, which has greatly handicapped movement of traffic through the Port. Although the Port Authority has since 1929 worked unceasingly to bring charges into some semblance of order, the situation among the 200 piers and docks at the Port is still unsatisfactory. In 1934, terminal charges at all Atlantic ports were in an unsettled condition, and the Federal Coordinator of Railroads undertook to bring about a parity of such charges. But the office of coordinator was abolished 2 years later, the work never was concluded, and the problem reverted to the individual ports and railroads. To add to the confusion, the Boston & Maine and the New Haven railroads inaugurated in 1937 dockage charges of 10 cents a ton on cargo handled at their Boston terminals; a similar charge was made at the Army Base. The Boston & Albany terminals were left as the only railroad piers at the Port not charging dockage fees, and consequently considerable diversion took place toward those docks. This confused situation, which is not only discriminatory against certain shippers but detrimental to the Port as a whole, may be cleared by the action of the State in December 1940 in changing wharfage rates at Commonwealth Pier No. 5 to 50 cents a ton. The 3 railroads serving the Port and a number of private interests owning other wharves have established the same charge. This flat rate per ton will take the place of the old Howard scale, customarily used, which assessed a different charge on almost every commodity.

In their effect on competition between the various North Atlantic ports, terminal charges are of much importance. The Boston Port Authority, in its *Annual Report* for 1933, summarized the situation then existing. Port charges, including pilotage, tug hire, tonnage tax, customs fees, customs brokerage, watching vessel, and health inspection at quarantine, for a 10,000-ton vessel entering port, were about equal at Boston, New York, and Philadelphia; charges at Boston and Philadelphia, as a matter of fact, were slightly under those at New York. Most of the port charges were fixed by law and tended to be alike. Cargo charges, comprising wharfage, dockage, watching cargo, tallying and stevedoring, for a 10,000-ton vessel discharging 5,500 tons of general cargo, were lower for the steamship company at Boston than at New York or Philadelphia. To the consignee, however, the total charges at Boston were not always lower. Boston has become, for most overseas vessels, more often a port-of-call than a terminal port; consequently there has been a considerable amount of overtime and Sunday work, which has raised the actual costs to many vessels at Boston. Whatever advantages in port charges or cargo charges Boston has had over New York or Philadelphia have been practically wiped out through free lighterage, less-than-cost storage, and other services at New York, and by the railroad differential in favor of Philadelphia.

The cost of bringing a ship into the Port varies considerably in individual cases. Such factors as the use of pilots, the number of tugs needed, the docking above or below drawbridges, the amount of overtime work by longshoremen, and the size of the cargo affect the final cost. A freighter bringing about 2,000 tons of general cargo to one of the Commonwealth piers and taking out 500 tons of such cargo with no pilotage charge, but requiring the assistance of two tugs, and having no overtime work for the longshoremen, would cost its owners about $7,000, exclusive of the running expenses of the ship itself. Almost two-thirds of this would be for various kinds of manual labor. Wharfage and dockage fees would take close to another thousand dollars, and the remainder would cover miscellaneous charges such as running lines, water supply, and wharf storage.

In 1935, certain carriers serving North Atlantic ports presented to the Trunk Line Association a plan for assessing charges for loading and unloading water-borne freight. The plan was designed partly to bring about greater uniformity of rates and partly to eliminate certain non-compensatory services. But many of the powerful railroads apparently had little inclination to see such changes established, and no agreement was reached. Handling charges on lumber at all North Atlantic ports have recently been investigated by the Maritime Commission and, while a decision has been rendered that provides for certain corrective practices, the charges on lumber at Boston terminals still remain higher than those of many competing ports.

There is, nevertheless, a bright side to the rather dark picture of charges at the Port of Boston. Local control has brought lower insurance rates on stevedoring. At one time, rates on both stevedoring insurance and terminal cargo insurance were chaotic in Boston. In connection with stevedoring insurance rates under the Federal Harbor Workers Acts and the State Workingmen's Compensation Act, the Boston Port Authority, with the cooperation of the Massachusetts Rating Bureau, began in 1931 to investigate the rates and the hazards of working in the occupation. As a result of this joint investigation, Boston rates for insurance against accidents in stevedoring have been reduced in 9 years from $17 to $9.99 per $100 of payroll, which is one of the lowest insurance costs among competing ports in the North Atlantic range. The decrease in the cost of insurance to the stevedore concern aids substantially in the general competitive situation, for Boston stevedores may now successfully compete with those at other ports on the cost per ton for handling cargoes. The reduction is due in great measure to the emphasis placed on safety by the contracting stevedores, who are incited to continued vigilance by the Boston Port Authority's practice of calling attention to various unsafe practices and suggesting safe ways of handling cargoes.

In the matter of terminal insurance based upon the value of the cargo, the Boston Port Authority in 1934 made an investigation with the cooperation of the Boston Board of Fire Underwriters. The board surveyed conditions on every pier in Boston Harbor, and the rates for each terminal were reconsidered. The survey resulted in a general reduction. In the course of the investigation of insurance rates, a practice of charging a minimum rate on terminal insurance to shippers in New York, with the railroad or terminal operators absorbing the balance, was found to be general. This New York practice has since been stopped by order of the Interstate Commerce Commission.

Rehabilitation of Waterfront Properties

Another problem of the Port of Boston is the modernizing of the waterfront. At the present time, the best piers in the harbor are owned by the railroads or by the State and Federal governments, and the greater part of the remaining waterfront either has become obsolete or has been diverted to non-maritime uses. Property along Boston's waterfront has been neglected for more than 40 years, and has lapsed into a condition which represents one of the major obstacles to the development of the Port. Of the total wharfing facilities at Boston, amounting to 50,200 linear feet, less than one-half provide berths adequate to the uses of a modern port. Some of the busiest cargo piers in the harbor, including the Mystic and Hoosac terminals in Charlestown, the Eastern Steamship wharves on Atlantic Avenue, and the New Haven Railroad's piers in South Boston, are badly in need of repair. Although it is generally recognized that these terminal facilities are rapidly approaching the stage where they must be reconstructed or replaced, private means for undertaking this work have not been made available.

In 1938, after a study by a recess committee of the legislature, known as the Special Commission Relative to the Boston Port Authority and the Production and Development of the Commerce of the Port of Boston, the urgent need for construction of a new State pier or for the reconstruction of existing terminal facilities was recognized. A bill was introduced into the legislature providing for a division of waterways within the State Department of Public Works. This bill provided also for the acquisition and construction of terminal facilities, which were to be leased to private shipping and railroad interests under 40-year contracts. Rentals from piers taken over by the State were to finance the bond issues necessary to cover cost of construction. When this legislation was proposed, railroad and shipping company officials indicated their willingness to turn over to the State for a nominal sum privately owned terminal facilities. The cost of such a program over a period of years would be negligible, since in effect the State would merely be extending credit to companies desiring new or remodeled piers and would be reimbursed within a reasonable period from rentals. Adoption of such a plan would not only modernize the terminal facilities of the Port but would put Boston in a position to compete to better advantage with North American ports publicly owned or subsidized. The first step in the program was completed in July 1940, when the approval of the United States War Department was obtained for the 200-foot extension into the harbor of the pierhead levies along the South Boston-Atlantic Avenue waterfront.

As an alternative to the proposed construction of a new State pier, the repair and reconstruction of Commonwealth Pier No. 1 has been suggested by the Boston Port Authority. This pier could be double-decked and extended to the harbor line at an estimated cost of $1,500,000 to $2,000,000. The pier is badly in need of repairs, and the many stanchions on the property will not permit it to be used efficiently. Its reconstruction would provide modern terminal facilities for steamship lines carrying lumber, vegetable fiber, latex, and non-mineral oil cargoes. Plans for the rehabilitation of this pier were indefinitely suspended in October 1940 when the United States Navy took it over on a 5-year lease for use as a mine sweeper base.

Perhaps the most important section of the Port with relation to coastwise commerce is the Atlantic Avenue thoroughfare, now one of the most dilapidated areas on the Boston waterfront. As late as 1870, great sailing ships laden with cargoes from every part of the world lined this street and discharged into it their commerce. Today, the encroachment of non-maritime business into the district has diverted some of the most valuable waterfront property in the Port to the uses of a variety of enterprises, from tearooms to distributing plants for soap and grocery concerns. The elevated railway structure on Atlantic Avenue has been a cause of much traffic congestion, and its removal or conversion into an elevated highway has been urged. Plans for the reclamation of this area include an amendment to the Boston zoning laws establishing a maritime zone on the harbor side of the Avenue.

The Port's most modern terminal facilities are located in the South Boston section. These have not always been operated for the best interests of the Port. For instance, the uncertain policy of the Federal Government in leasing property at the Army Base has not contributed to the most efficient use of that terminal. Within the past 15 years, six different operating concerns have handled freight at the Army Base, and with every change of management, importers and exporters have faced uncertainty. The present lessee of the Army Base, however, is operating under a 10-year lease and is thus provided with the opportunity to make suitable plans for the accommodation of clients over a lengthy term. A major addition to the facilities of the Army Base was completed in the summer of 1940 when two electro-magnet cranes were installed. These are capable of handling 2,400 tons of scrap iron in a 24-hour day and bring the total crane capacity of the Army Base to almost 4,000 tons a day. Three cranes equipped for similar work are located on Mystic Pier, Charlestown.

The ambitious program for Port rehabilitation cuts across many local interests, but, with certain exceptions, has received the cooperation of waterfront property owners. The burden of the work falls on the State division of waterways, which is enthusiastically making plans. Final success depends upon legislative action, which is slow in coming but seems assured. Both Port interests and the general public demand a rebuilt, modernly equipped port.

Ship Channels

Although at the present time Boston's ship channels and anchorages are in the best condition in the Port's history, the attention of both State and Federal Authorities still is occupied with regular dredging operations. These have been necessitated through soil erosion, the existence of ledges in the harbor's main ship channel, and the need for improving other approaches to deep water. The most recent Federal project provides for the deepening of the southerly side of the harbor's main ship channel to a depth of 40 feet at mean low water. When completed, this channel will have a width of 600 feet and will extend from President Roads to Commonwealth Pier No. 1 in East Boston.

A major improvement recently accomplished was the dredging of a 40-foot deep anchorage basin at President Roads, which was completed in March 1937, under the direction of the Corps of Engineers, United States Army. The area prepared for vessels was 5,500 feet in length and 2,000 feet in width. Further rock removal and the extension of the 40-foot channel to Commonwealth Pier No. 1 in East Boston was completed in 1940. The deepened channel increases greatly the commercial value of the Port, and provides the Navy access to bases for its largest battleships. The Port of Boston now has a main ship channel with a high-water depth of 49 feet, compared with New York Harbor's 45-foot gateway. Boston's channel is able to accommodate the largest liners afloat.

Still another important Federal dredging project, started in 1938, will create a channel about 30 feet deep, 200 feet wide, and 2 miles long from the mouth of Chelsea Creek to important tidewater oil terminals. This channel will save transportation costs and remove navigational hazards for the large number of oil tankers now using this part of the harbor. Other proposed measures include projects to deepen the Mystic and Town River channels and the Reserve Channel off the Army Base. It is proposed also to work out a deeper and straighter channel through Dorchester Bay from President Roads to the Neponset River. The plan calls for a channel 30 feet deep and 300 feet wide to supersede the existing 18-foot channel. This would open up one of the few sections of the harbor front still available for building and development.

The Maritime Association proposed that Congress make an appropriation for a dragwire survey of the harbor, and the work was authorized for 1940. Within the past 2 years, uncharted rocks and obstructions in the harbor have damaged several ships and caused the loss of one. The American freighter *Cold Harbor* struck a ledge 22 feet below the surface in the North Ship Channel, where a depth of 27 feet was recorded on the vessel's chart. In the spring of 1938, the British freighter *City of Salisbury* became stranded on an uncharted rock near Graves Light and incurred a loss of $2,500,000. Such incidents are rare and less likely to happen in the future. The completion of the present dredging program will make Boston one of the safest and most accessible harbors on the Atlantic coast.

Reforestation and Physical Improvement

The Boston Port Authority has not neglected considerations of beauty in relation to the Port. In 1933, it initiated a program for the reforestation of the islands in Boston Harbor, to serve the dual purpose of improving the appearance of the harbor and of preventing further soil erosion on some of the islands. In 1934, pine trees were set out on Federal-owned islands by the Civilian Conservation Corps, and a survey of this planting in 1937 showed that some 90 percent of the trees had survived. Following the completion of a topographical and soil survey of the islands undertaken by an Emergency Relief Administration project in 1935, the Port Authority devised its plans for reforestation; further studies have been made, and costs have been refigured; only funds are lacking to continue this useful and farsighted program.

Another problem which has confronted the Boston Port Authority since its inauguration has been the removal of hulls which have become a menace to health and navigation. Between 1931 and 1935, a clean-up campaign resulted in the removal of 120 of those derelicts. More than $125,000 was spent on the work. The ribs, decks, timbers, and keels of the vessels were broken up and piled on shore, where needy families hauled them away for firewood. Old square-riggers which had carried the house flags of New England merchants over the oceans were pried out of their last berths in the harbor mud and disposed of in that way. But 62 of these rotting vessels still lie along the waterfront. Their splintered rails and planking remind one of the days when Yankee clippers sailed out of Boston Harbor bound for San Francisco or the China Seas. The drowning of a boy swimmer in the hold of one of the partly sunken schooners in 1939 induced the General Court to appropriate funds to resume the work of removal, and several hulks were towed out and sunk off the Graves in the spring of 1940.

A Forward-Looking Port

The renewed interest and faith of Boston people in the destiny of their Port were demonstrated in the gala celebrations of National Maritime Day in June of 1938, 1939, and 1940. Crowds of more than 100,000 persons lined the Boston waterfront on each occasion, and gathered on the piers and other vantage points to witness the most elaborate marine pageants ever staged in New England. The onlookers thrilled to the kaleidoscope of motion and color. No less than 250 vessels, including patrol boats, tankers, sailing yachts, and motor cruisers passed in review up the inner harbor. There were races between lifeboats, fishermen's dories, and Coast Guard boats. Open house was the order of the day on several naval vessels and on ships operated by the Coast and Geodetic Survey and the Bureau of Fisheries.

Governor Saltonstall and Mayor Tobin in their addresses on Maritime Day, June 23, 1939, issued a stimulating appeal to the New England public to support their leading port.

Asserted Mayor Tobin, "We shall continue to fight until Boston has an equal chance to compete." Governor Saltonstall declared: "We must fight shoulder to shoulder with the men who are making valiant efforts to make Boston Harbor the key to better times. New England must still turn its eyes toward the sea."

In Colonial times, Boston's small sailing vessels touched every port of the Western World and established a tradition of skillful trading which was the basis of Boston's maritime success for 200 years. From this Port sailed some of the most resourceful privateers and the greatest ship of our wooden navy, "Old Ironsides," to prove to the world that Bostonians could fight as well as bargain. Her ever-expanding commerce touched all seas and pioneered in the Pacific and China trade in the early 1800's. To her everlasting glory, her shipbuilders produced some of the most perfect clipper ships to ride the waves. Under sail, she swept to unexcelled heights. Bostonians, however, failed to capitalize on the railroad and the steamer. With the increasing use of steamers on the high seas and the routing of trunk line railroads to other ports, Boston dropped lower and lower in maritime prestige. She became especially weak in exports and thus lost her hold on shipping services. Since the World War, Boston's position has remained fairly constant, with a favorable showing in imports, domestic commerce, and passenger service. The organization of port interests behind the leadership of the Port Authority and the gradual crystallization of the exact needs of the Port have put Boston in a strong position at the present time. She is now making a valiant and successful fight to improve her situation.

EPILOGUE

THE OPTIMISM of the F.W.P. writers proved to be ill founded, for in the nearly half-century that has passed Boston's problems have became severe enough to threaten her continued existence as a major port.

The return of peace in 1945 found Boston facing the same problems that had bedeviled her in the prewar years: lack of exports, labor unrest, a deteriorating waterfront, and railroad rate discrimination. The last was a problem inherited from the late nineteenth century when rate wars among America's railroads threatened to wreak economic havoc. For the sake of sense and stability, in 1882 the federal government established standard rates. Those rates discriminated against Boston and New York among the east coast ports; although the distances were not appreciably different, the rates for goods traveling to and from the midwest via New York and Boston were higher than the rates for those going to and from Baltimore, Norfolk, and Philadelphia. The differentials were justified by the two northern ports' lower transatlantic rates. At the time that was true. But when the ocean rates were equalized during World War I, no change was made in railroad rates; thus Boston was at a distinct disadvantage in any attempt to tap the burgeoning midwestern market.

Clearly the port's difficulties needed immediate and serious remedy. Riddled by politics and possessing insufficient resources, the old Port Authority was incapable of addressing these issues.

With renewed optimism the Massachusetts Legislature abolished the old Authority and created a new Port Authority in 1945, vesting it with increased powers and fifteen million dollars in bond money to renovate decaying piers and wharves. Unfortunately, the new Authority proved to be too much like the old. Turnover was alarmingly high, and each new appointment brought with it a ritual announcement of the great days ahead for the port. The reality was padded payrolls and a budget insufficient to maintain, let alone improve, harbor facilities.

While the port became mired in its problems, the figures for overall trade remained relatively constant. With only minor fluctuation, volume in Boston hovered at the eighteen-million-ton mark, about where it had been in 1937. On closer examination, however, the figures were distressing. Despite increases in grain exports, the total volume for most products in foreign trade was actually falling. Domestic traffic was also down. The only increases were in the import category and here petroleum products accounted for the additional tonnage.

Compounding the port's problems was its well-deserved reputation for labor unrest. Labor relations reached a low point in 1951 when an Isthmian Line ship, *Steel Flyer,* was forced to lie idle at the army base for more than a month while the longshoremen refused to cross a picket line set up by a rival union. Longshoremen in Boston were famous for being quick to "take a walk," leaving vessels at the pier. Such conditions convinced many shippers not to use Boston and forced others to divert Boston-bound ships to other ports. In part because of labor problems, the port of Boston gained a reputation for being not only unreliable but also expensive.

Boston's difficulties hampered the Port Authority's already meager attempts to attract shippers to Boston. That failure coupled with incessant political squabbling led to another reorganization in 1953. From this emerged a new creature to oversee the port—the Port of Boston Commission. One of the first actions of the new commission was to fire approximately ten percent of its bloated staff, including the director of public relations, who had the unhappy task of announcing his own demise.

While the new commission gave the appearance of being more efficient than its predecessor, its accomplishments were just as slender. As long as a parsimonious legislature controlled the finances, the commission could never get adequate funding to maintain and refit the port. (When the legislature took an interest in the commission, it was usually to find someone a job.) Meanwhile, the trucking and railroad industries were nipping at Boston's heels and, more importantly, ports such as New York, Baltimore, Philadelphia, and even some in New England were ever anxious to draw away trade.

Based on the experience of other American ports, New York in particular, the best solution seemed to lie in the creation of an independent government agency vested with sufficient power to finance its own operations. However, an agency administering the port alone could never, at least in the then-present circumstances, be self-supporting. The only hope was the creation of a larger, more powerful agency with a broader base that would allow it access to sufficient resources. In 1956 the legislature created just such an agency—the Massachusetts Port Authority (Massport). This new agency was charged with running Logan International Airport, Hanscom Field (a small airport in the town of Bedford to the northwest of Boston), the Tobin Bridge (a toll bridge just north of Boston), and the public piers and terminals in the port. To support itself, Massport was authorized to issue revenue bonds, use income from investments, and collect rents and fees.

It was an ambitious plan and delays prevented its implementation until 1959. In many ways the problems of the port presented Massport with its greatest challenge. It found itself heir to huge numbers of properties, none of which had been well maintained—and some of which not maintained at all. At Castle Island for example, the Boston Fire Department was demanding that repairs be made "lest apparatus be damaged responding to alarms in the area." Commonwealth Pier, the harbor's largest facility, was in deplorable condition and required several hundred thousand dollars in repairs. Elsewhere in the harbor, at the Hoosac, Mystic, and East Boston piers, the severe corrosion found in the pilings required immediate and extensive work.

To justify their plans for port rehabilitation Massport had to promote the port. None of its predecessors had ever undertaken any large-scale strategy to sell Boston as a port. The need to recruit business aggressively became all too apparent when in its first year of operation Massport was informed that Luckenbach Steamship Company was being forced to sell nine of its fourteen vessels. Luckenbach had been bringing 2500 tons of cargo per week into Boston (mostly canned fruit from the West Coast) and taking out 1500 tons. That service would now be curtailed (and eventually cancelled). At the same time Massport had to face the yet uncertain challenge of the newly completed St. Lawrence

Seaway, which threatened to harm, if not destroy, Boston's grain export trade.

While planning for the future, Massport had to overcome the past—railroad rates. In 1954 the Port of Boston Commission had petitioned the Interstate Commerce Commission for a rate change. The petition was denied; at that point the problem went into litigation, where it still remained when Massport took charge. After moving through various levels of appeal, on 20 May 1963 the Supreme Court declared the rate discrimination unconstitutional. Boston finally had parity with the southern ports.

Using their newly won parity Massport launched a promotional campaign hoping to attract new business. It did not work. Decades of neglect, discrimination, and poor leadership had left Boston far behind; rate equality notwithstanding, faster and more regular service was offered by other ports, making them more attractive to shippers. Adding to Boston's woes was the rising volume of traffic using the St. Lawrence Seaway rather than funneling through Boston. This led to a staggering blow in 1965: the last grain cargo left Boston.

For three-quarters of a century grain had been the mainstay of Boston's export market. Although grain exports fluctuated from year to year, after World War II they accounted for approximately twenty percent of the total tonnage leaving the port. Since 1954 grain had been second in tonnage to scrap metal, a low-value commodity. With the elimination of grain exports, scrap would account for approximately eighty percent of Boston's export tonnage.

Boston's imports reflected the same unhealthy concentration in low-value goods. More than seventy percent of Boston's imports were petroleum products, and that had a direct effect on the waterfront. Unlike general cargo, low-value bulk commodities are handled mechanically and therefore do not produce much in the way of employment or expenditures. In addition, since bulk commodities require special facilities, they cannot use the conventional piers along the waterfront. At Boston the scrap business was centered along the Mystic River and the principal oil depots were located along the banks of the Chelsea Creek. The result was a downtown waterfront increasingly characterized by abandoned and decaying piers. Massport found itself with a considerable amount of surplus waterfront real estate. Not surprisingly, in its 1959 *Annual Report* the Authority alluded to "a need for a new and intensive use of waterfront land."

While struggling to overcome "years of uncoordinated small-scale efforts [that had] done little except to focus on superficial aspects of major problems," Massport also had to adjust to a revolutionary change in the world of maritime transport—containerization. By prepackaging cargo in standard-sized metal boxes that could be fitted into specially equipped ships, hauled on the highways as trailers, or loaded onto railroad flatcars, shippers could reduce handling costs to a minimum. Introduced first on an experimental basis in the late 1950s, the system proved so efficient that soon specially designed vessels—container ships—were being built, and a massive move to use the "box" was on.

The container revolution presented problems for the ports. Loading and unloading containers had to be done with special cranes positioned along the edges of wharves with large open spaces behind them to accommodate the containers in transit as well as to provide sheds for stuffing (loading) and stripping (unloading). Finger piers of the type that dominated Boston's waterfront were noticeably unsuited for this new business. In addition, Boston's downtown waterfront is virtually inaccessible to the large numbers of trailer trucks that would transport the containers to and from the piers. Longshoremen were less than enthusiastic about the new technology once it became evident that far fewer longshoremen would be required to move containers than were needed to handle the assortment of boxes, bales, and rolls in the old break-bulk style of vessel. Nevertheless, whatever the problems, containerization was clearly the path to the future and the survival of Boston as a major port depended upon Massport's response to the challenge.

After several delays, in June 1965 Massport signed an agreement with Sea Land Services and Wiggins Terminals to create Boston's first container facility at Castle Island. Massport agreed to finance the cost of the installation of a container crane and Sea Land in turn leased Berth 17 and ten acres of adjacent land for the container operation. In 1966 the new facility was ready to operate and hopes were high that Boston would be able to garner a sizeable share of container traffic. Unfortunately, before a single container came

A view of the Moran Container Terminal. *Courtesy of Massport.*

Aerial view of Boston Harbor today. *Courtesy of Boston Shipping Association and General Ship Corporation.*

across the deck labor problems intervened. Because of a dispute over work assignments, the longshoremen refused to work the new facility. The crane stood idle and Sea Land decided to bypass Boston and open operations elsewhere. Even after the labor dispute was settled, Sea Land refused to come to Boston; not until 1970 did they alter that decision and finally put into operation the facility that had stood idle for nearly four years. Boston seemed to be falling ever further behind.

Sea Land's terminal was not intended to accommodate other container lines and in 1968 Massport bought forty-five acres of land at the Mystic docks to create a second, but this time public, container facility. The Moran Terminal at the Mystic docks went into operation in the fall of 1971. With two modern container terminals, the number of containers passing through Boston mushroomed. In 1980 nearly 91,000 containers passed through the port—a total tonnage of 805,224 tons. Three-quarters of this traffic was handled at the Moran Terminal, which by this time was operating thirty to forty percent beyond its designed capacity. To accommodate future growth and alleviate present congestion Massport planned for two new container terminals. The first is the Conley Terminal located at Castle Island. The second facility will be built on land currently being filled in at the South Boston Navy Annex. The new land, some fifty-six acres in all, will be available toward the end of the 1980s.

In a scene reminiscent of the Sea Land fiasco the Conley Terminal was completed in 1982 but could not be opened. Its two cranes stood idle while management and labor debated work issues. Then in December 1983 the Steamship Clerks' Union began a labor slowdown at the Moran Terminal to protest layoffs. The slowdown, coupled with the ongoing problem at the Conley Terminal, persuaded Trans Freight Lines, the largest shipper in Boston, to shift its operations, temporarily, to Providence. A few days after that a second large shipper, United States Lines, also announced its intention to leave, not because of any particular labor problem but simply because it was no longer economical for them to do business in Boston.

The winter of 1983–1984 was a dark moment for the port. Negotiations with the International Longshoreman's Association over a new contract dragged on for weeks, with the threat of a strike looming near. The principal point of contention was the Guaranteed Annual Income (G.A.I.), first agreed to in 1966, by which longshoremen who work a fixed number of hours in a given year are guaranteed a minimum number of hours of pay for the same year. After some hard bargaining both sides agreed that the G.A.I. for Boston would be 1500 hours in the first year, 1600 in the second year, and 1650 in the third. With that the impasse was broken and a new three-year contract was signed in February 1984. The new contract also settled the issues at the Conley Terminal, allowing that facility to begin operation. The improved atmosphere convinced Trans Freight Lines to return their operation to Boston.

In the first half of 1984, with a good labor settlement in hand and a healthy national economy more than matched by the New England economy, the port of Boston seemed to be doing well.

Still the future remains uncertain. Ports after all are services. They manufacture nothing; their well-being is dependent mainly upon the efforts of others. In this regard Boston is highly susceptible to fluctuations in the national and international economies; to political decisions made in Washington, London, Tokyo, or any one of dozens of foreign capitals; and to business decisions made in boardrooms throughout the world.

What, for example, will be the effect of the federal government's encouragement of American exports? At the present moment the United States imports considerably more than it exports. For Boston and other ports, that translates to empty containers being carried by outgoing ships—hardly the way for carriers to make a profit.

Recently, President Reagan signed into law the Shipping Act of 1984. Consonant with administration policy, the new act is intended to strengthen the ability of U.S. flag operators to compete more flexibly in international commerce. As the Federal Maritime Commission moves to implement the new law, how smaller ports like Boston will fare is still an open question.

In 1940 the authors of *Boston Looks Seaward* could write that despite its difficulties the port of Boston was "in a strong position" and "making a valiant and successful fight to improve her situation." In the four decades since, the diffi-

culties have grown greater. The shift of New England manufacturing, so pronounced since World War II, away from
the traditional industries and towards high-technology industries, will continue to affect the port. The relatively high value
and low volume of goods being produced in New England
make them ideal candidates for containerization and air
freight. By their very nature containers are highly mobile
and can be easily transported by truck or rail to any port.
Economies of scale demand large container ships, which to
reduce unit costs and maximize efficiency can only call at
ports where they are likely to find full cargoes. Boston is not
such a port.

All this is not to say that the port is dying. Waterfront
Cassandras have been crying that lament for generations. In
fact the New England economy is growing and is likely to
continue to grow. With growth comes increased imports and
exports. However, more than half that trade now moves
through ports outside New England, with one-third going
through New York. If Boston is to prosper it must find a way
to attract more traffic from its own hinterland.

Boston has always been a sea-minded town, yet the sea has
never yielded its bounty willingly. Securing that bounty has
meant struggle, work, disappointment, and triumph. A his-
torian ought never to make predictions, but in the case of
the port of Boston it seems safe to say that the past is
prologue.

WILLIAM M. FOWLER, JR.

APPENDIX

TABLE 1

TRADE AT THE PORT OF BOSTON, 1920-1939[1]

(Tonnage expressed in short tons = 2000 lbs.)

Year	Tonnage				Value
	Import	Export	Domestic[2]	Total	
1920	1,673,899	573,489	7,023,605	9,270,993	$ 973,187,863
1921	2,149,392	512,967	7,090,482	9,752,841	616,096,284
1922	4,608,732	588,449	8,796,465	13,993,696	674,603,665
1923	3,031,479	481,961	11,704,223	15,217,663	862,346,185
1924	2,355,094	339,215	10,491,575	13,185,884	641,407,499
1925	2,586,065	338,779	12,284,776	15,209,620	1,053,222,686
1926	2,904,579	314,990	12,564,533	15,784,102	993,839,848
1927	2,662,184	292,452	13,644,467	16,599,103	1,056,891,407
1928	2,964,876	403,486	13,897,800	17,266,162	974,208,574
1929	3,261,301	303,120	15,500,629	19,065,050	999,683,062
1930	2,915,152	263,461	12,510,749	15,689,362	781,012,315
1931	2,460,148	230,539	13,869,090	16,559,777	604,215,215
1932	2,009,881	209,096	11,793,195	14,012,172	437,499,622
1933	1,822,960	166,090	13,389,083	15,378,133	548,550,364
1934	1,836,389	254,169	13,211,500	15,302,058	576,671,339
1935	2,693,223	330,090	13,361,645	16,384,958	581,362,571
1936	2,734,507	312,410	14,167,223	17,214,140	812,241,952
1937	2,678,094	473,073	15,239,223	18,390,390	955,281,523
1938	1,798,064	321,445	13,761,258	15,880,767	628,395,969
1939	2,169,610	428,999	15,243,603	17,842,212	(not available)[3]

[1] Compiled from *Annual Reports*, Chief of Engineers, U. S. Army, Part II, 1920-1940.
[2] Includes Intraport Tonnage.
[3] Valuation not computed by Corps of Engineers for 1939.

TABLE 2

PASSENGER TRAFFIC AT BOSTON, 1927-1939[1]

Year	Coastal	Foreign	Excursion	Ferry	Total
1927	421,105	109,627	1,170,878	3,792,251	5,493,861
1928	423,909	105,044	1,102,010	3,586,508	5,217,471
1929	439,917	116,669	1,064,266	3,457,655	5,078,507
1930	298,512	104,401	889,309	2,935,324	4,227,546
1931	336,613	90,310	1,092,357	2,778,678	4,297,958
1932	215,827	97,489	896,129	2,618,578	3,828,023
1933	223,668	83,556	718,383	2,393,785	3,419,392
1934	236,795	90,741	57,844	2,007,793	2,392,173
1935	282,758	95,977	870,000	8,472,216	9,720,951
1936	304,927	109,484	1,068,461	7,097,729	8,580,601
1937	244,414	110,411	1,220,582	6,605,045	8,180,452
1938	117,703	102,271	848,257	6,065,578	7,133,809
1939	216,418	72,240	921,895	5,985,611	7,196,164

[1] Compiled from *Annual Reports*, Chief of Engineers, U. S. Army, Part II, 1928-1940

APPENDIX II

FOREIGN STEAMSHIP SERVICES, SUMMER, 1939

(The services listed here were in effect prior to the outbreak of hostilities in Europe.)

Trade Route	Service[1]	Inward[2]	Outward[2]
Africa—North Coast	American Export Lines (A)	Fortnightly (D)	3-Monthly (I)
	Fern Line (F)	Monthly (D)	Monthly (D)
Africa—South and East Coast	American South African Line (A)	Monthly (I)	
	Robin Line (A)	Occasional (I)	
	Union Castle Mail S. S. Line (F)	Monthly (I)	
Africa—West Coast	American and African Line (A)	Occasional (I)	
	American West African Line (A)	Every 3 wks. (I)	
	Elder Dempster Line (F)	Monthly (I)	
Australia and New Zealand	American Pioneer Line (A)	Monthly (D)	
	M.A.N.Z. (Port) Line (F)	Fortnightly (I)	Occasional (I)
	North German Lloyd Line (F)	Occasional (I)	
Baltic	American Scantic Line (A)	Occasional (D)	Occasional (I)
	Scandinavian-American Line (F)	Monthly (D)	Occasional (I)
	Thorden Line (F)	Occasional (D)	
	Transatlantic-Swedish-American-Mexico Line (F)	Fortnightly (D)	
	Wilhelmsen Line (F)	Fortnightly (D)	Monthly (I)
Europe (United Kingdom and Continental Ports)	America-France Line (A)	Monthly (D)	Monthly (I)
	American-Hampton Roads Line (A)	Fortnightly (D)	Fortnightly (D)
	Anchor Line (F)	Fortnightly (D)	Fortnightly (D)
	Black Diamond Lines (A)	Fortnightly (D)	Fortnightly (I)
	Brocklebank's Cunard Line (F)	Fortnightly (D)	Fortnightly (D)
	Clay Line (F)	Monthly (D)	Monthly (D)
	Cunard-White Star Line (F)	Fortnightly (D)	Fortnightly (D)
	Hapag-Lloyd Line (F)	Fortnightly (D)	Fortnightly (D)

Appendix

FOREIGN STEAMSHIP SERVICES, SUMMER, 1939

(The services listed here were in effect prior to the outbreak of hostilities in Europe.)

Trade Route	Service[1]	Inward[2]	Outward[2]
	Holland-America Line (F)	Fortnightly (D)	Fortnightly (D)
	Johnston-Warren Lines (F)	Every 3 wks. (D)	Every 3 wks. (D)
	Osaka Shoshen Kaisha Line (F)	Fortnightly (D)	Fortnightly (D)
	United States Lines (A)	Fortnightly (D)	Fortnightly (D)
	Yankee Line (A)	Every 3 wks. (D)	Fortnightly (D)
Far East (China, East Indies, Japan, Philippines, and Hawaiian Islands)	American & Oriental Line (F)	Monthly (I)	Monthly (I)
	American-Manchurian Line (F)	Monthly (I)	Monthly (I)
	American Pioneer Line (A)	Monthly (I)	Monthly (I)
	American President Lines (A)	Every 2 wks. (I)	Every 2 wks. (I)
	Bank Line (F)	Monthly (I)	Monthly (I)
	Barber-Wilhelmsen Line (F)	Monthly (I)	Monthly (I)
	Blue Funnel Line (F)	Monthly (I)	Monthly (I)
	De La Roma Line (A)	Monthly (I)	Monthly (I)
	Dodwell-Castle Line (F)	Monthly (I)	Monthly (I)
	Isthmian Line (A)	Monthly (I)	Monthly (I)
	Java-New York Line (F)	Fortnightly (I)	Fortnightly (I)
	Kokusai (K) Line (F)	Occasional (I)	Occasional (I)
	Maersk Line (F)	Fortnightly (I)	Fortnightly (I)
	Mitsin Line (F)	Occasional (I)	Occasional (I)
	Nippon Yusen Kaisha (N.Y.K.) Line (F)	Fortnightly (I)	Fortnightly (I)
	Osaka Shoshen Kaisha (F)	Fortnightly (I)	Fortnightly (I)
	Prince Line (F)	Monthly (I)	Monthly (I)
	Silver Line (F)	Monthly (I)	Monthly (I)
India	American & Indian Line (F)	Three or four a month (D)	Occasional (I)
	American Pioneer Line (A)	Monthly (D)	Monthly (I)
	American President Lines (A)	3-Monthly (I)	3-Monthly (I)
	Brocklebank's Cunard Line (F)	Fortnightly (D)	Monthly (I)

FOREIGN STEAMSHIP SERVICES, SUMMER, 1939

(The services listed here were in effect prior to the outbreak of hostilities in Europe.)

Trade Route	Service[1]	Inward[2]	Outward[2]
Mediterranean, Black Sea and Levant Ports	Isthmian Line (A)	Monthly (I)	Monthly (I)
	Kerr Line (F)	Occasional (I)	
	American Export Lines (A)	Fortnightly (D)	Fortnightly (I)
	American President Lines (A)	Every 2 wks. (I)	
	Italian Line (F)	Fortnightly (I)	Fortnightly (I)
	Kerr Line (F)	Occasional (I)	
South America, East Coast	American Republics Line (A)	Fortnightly (D)	Fortnightly (I)
	Essco-Brodin (F)	Occasional (I)	Occasional (I)
	Lloyd Brazileire (F)	Occasional (I)	
	Northern Pan-America Line (F)	Occasional (I)	
	North German Lloyd Line (F)	Occasional (I)	
	Sprague Steamship Line (A)	Fortnightly (I)	Fortnightly (D)
West Indies and Central America	American President Lines (A)		3-Monthly (I)
	Canadian National Steamship Line (F)	Fortnightly (D)	Fortnightly (D)
	United Fruit Company (A-F)	2-Weekly (D)	2-Weekly (D)
Canada	Boston-Yarmouth Line (A)	2-5 Weekly (D)	2-5 Weekly (D)
	Canadian National Steamship Line (F)	Fortnightly (D)	Fortnightly (D)
	Gypsum Packet Co. (F)	Seasonal (D)	Seasonal (D)
	International Line (A)	1-2 Weekly (D)	1-2 Weekly (D)
	Johnston-Warren Lines (F)	Every 3 wks. (D)	Every 3 wks. (D)

[1] A — American flag ship
F — Foreign flag ship
[2] D — Direct service, Boston first American port-of-call
I — Indirect service, Boston not the first American port-of-call

DOMESTIC STEAMSHIP SERVICES, SUMMER, 1939

(The services listed here were in effect prior to the outbreak of hostilities in Europe.)

Trade Route	Service	Outward and Inward
Atlantic Coast and Gulf Ports	Cape Cod Steamship Co.	Daily (summer only)
	Clyde-Mallory Lines	Weekly
	Boston-New York Line	Daily
	Lykes Coastwise Line	Weekly
	Merchants & Miners Transportation Company	5-Weekly
	Mooremack Gulf Lines	Fortnightly
	Pan-Atlantic Line	Weekly
	Savannah Line	3-Weekly
	Southern Pacific (Morgan) Lines	Weekly
Pacific Coast (Via Panama Canal)	American-Hawaiian Steamship Company	2-Weekly
	American President Lines	2-Monthly
	Calmar Line	Monthly
	Isthmian Line	Fortnightly
	Luckenbach Steamship Company	Weekly
	Pacific Coast Direct Line	Monthly
	Shepard Steamship Company	Every 3 weeks

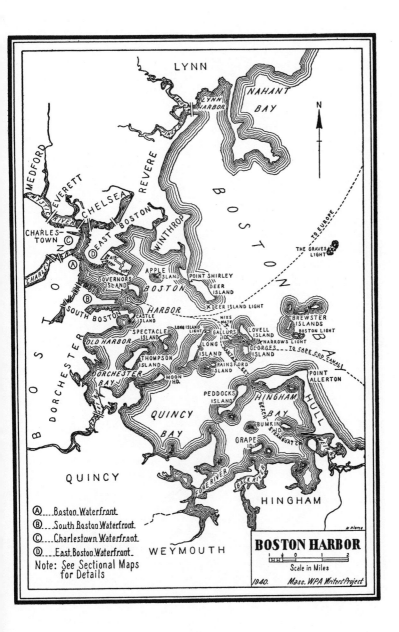

LYNN

NAHANT BAY

LYNN HARBOR

MEDFORD

EVERETT

MYSTIC RIVER

CHELSEA

REVERE

CHARLES-TOWN Ⓒ

CHARLES RIVER

Ⓐ

EAST BOSTON Ⓓ

WINTHROP

BOSTON BAY

N

TO EUROPE

THE GRAVES LIGHT

APPLE ISLAND

POINT SHIRLEY

DEER ISLAND

Ⓑ

SOUTH BOSTON

BOSTON HARBOR

DEER ISLAND LIGHT

CASTLE ISLAND

NIXS MATE

SPECTACLE ISLAND

OLD HARBOR

LONG ISLAND LIGHT

GALLUPS ISLAND

LOVELL ISLAND

BREWSTER ISLANDS

BOSTON LIGHT

NARROWS LIGHT

GEORGES ISLAND

TO CAPE COD CANAL

THOMPSON ISLAND

LONG ISLAND

RAINSFORD ISLAND

DORCHESTER BAY

MOON HD.

POINT ALLERTON

PEDDOCKS ISLAND

HINGHAM BAY

HULL

QUINCY BAY

BEACH

BUMKIN ID.

STEAMBOAT CH.

GRAPE ID.

QUINCY

WEIR RIVER

BACK RIVER

HINGHAM

Ⓐ ... Boston Waterfront.
Ⓑ ... South Boston Waterfront.
Ⓒ ... Charlestown Waterfront.
Ⓓ ... East Boston Waterfront.

Note: See Sectional Maps for Details

WEYMOUTH

H Pierce

BOSTON HARBOR

1 0 1 2
Scale in Miles

1940. Mass. WPA Writers' Project

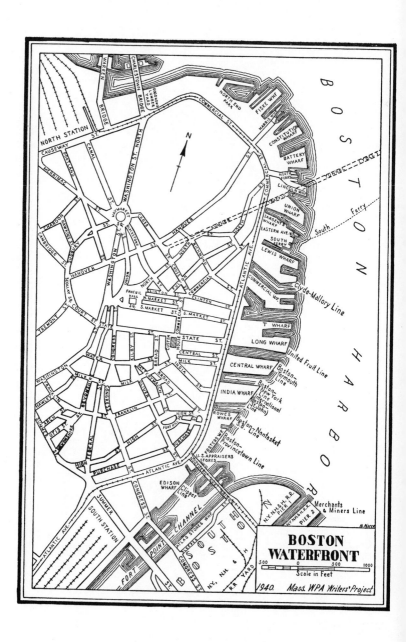

BOSTON
WATERFRONT

500   0   500   1000
Scale in Feet

1940.   Mass. WPA Writers' Project

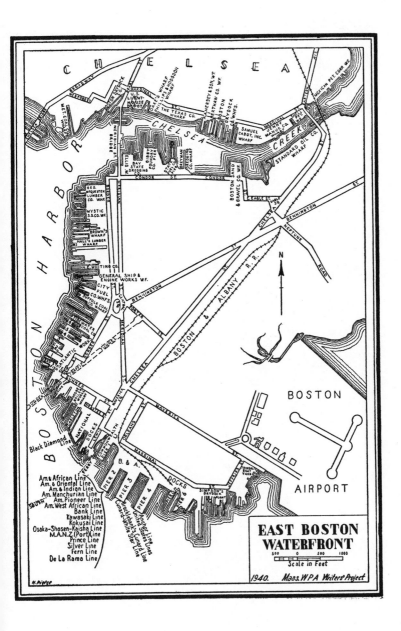

CHELSEA

BOSTON HARBOR

EAST BOSTON
WATERFRONT

500   0   500   1000
Scale in Feet

1940.   Mass. WPA Writers Project

BOSTON

AIRPORT

Am. & African Line
Am. & Oriental Line
Am. & Indian Line
Am. Manchurian Line
Am. Pioneer Line
Am. West African Line
Bank Line
Kawasaki Line
Kokusai Line
Osaka-Shosen-Kaisha Line
M.A.N.Z. (Port) Line
Prince Line
Silver Line
Fern Line
De La Rama Line

Black Diamond Line

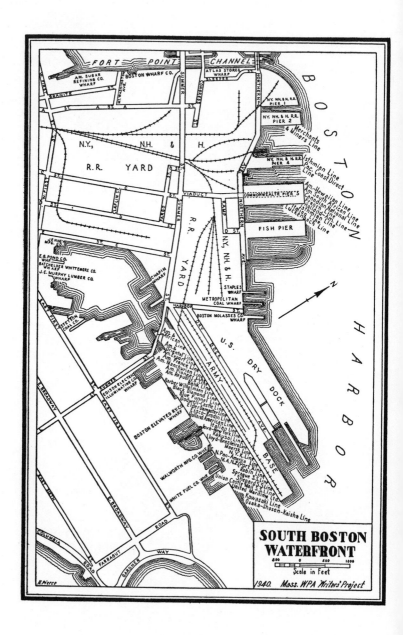

FORT POINT CHANNEL

AM. SUGAR
REFINING CO.
WHARF
BOSTON WHARF CO.
ATLAS STORES
WHARF

N.Y., N.H. & H.
R.R. YARD

N.Y. NH & H. R.R.
PIER 1
N.Y. NH. & H. R.R.
PIER 2
Merchants
& Miners Line

N.Y. NH & H. R.R.
PIER 4
Isthmian Line
Pac. Coast Direct
Line

VIADUCT

COMMONWEALTH PIER 5
Am. Hawaiian Line
Canadian National Line
South African Line
Roosevelt S.S. Line
Clyde-Mallory Line
Luckenbach Line

R.R.
YARD

FISH PIER

E.S. POND CO.
WHARF
BATCHELDER WHITTEMORE CO.
WHARF
J.C. MURPHY LUMBER CO.

CHAPIN
WHARF

STAPLES
WHARF
METROPOLITAN
COAL WHARF
BOSTON MOLASSES CO.
WHARF

N

BOSTON ELEVATED RY CO.
WHARF

WALWORTH MFG CO. WHF.

WHITE FUEL CO. WHF.

U.S. ARMY DRY DOCK BASE

SOUTH BOSTON
WATERFRONT

500   0   500   1000
Scale in Feet

R. Pierce

1940.   Mass. WPA Writers' Project

BOSTON HARBOR

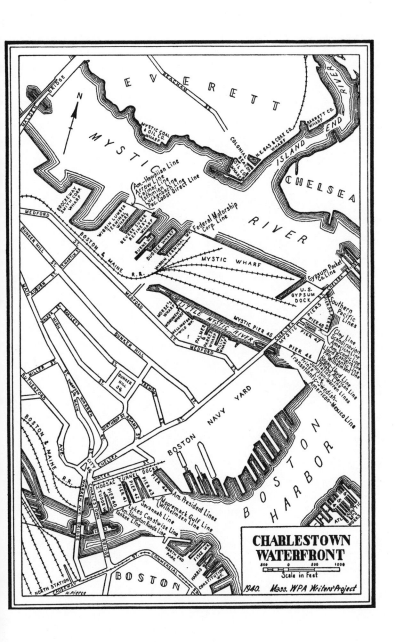

CHARLESTOWN
WATERFRONT

Scale in Feet

1940.   Mass. WPA Writers' Project

INDEX

INDEX

311